Beginning Responsive Web Design with HTML5 and CSS3

Jonathan Fielding

Apress®

Beginning Responsive Web Design with HTML5 and CSS3

Copyright © 2014 by Jonathan Fielding

ISBN-13 (pbk): 978-1-4302-6694-5

ISBN-13 (electronic): 978-1-4302-6695-2

Publisher: Heinz Weinheimer
Lead Editor: Louise Corrigan
Technical Reviewer: Daniel Grant
Editorial Board: Steve Anglin, Mark Beckner, Ewan Buckingham, Gary Cornell, Louise Corrigan, Jim DeWolf, Jonathan Gennick, Jonathan Hassell, Robert Hutchinson, Michelle Lowman, James Markham, Matthew Moodie, Jeff Olson, Jeffrey Pepper, Douglas Pundick, Ben Renow-Clarke, Dominic Shakeshaft, Gwenan Spearing, Matt Wade, Steve Weiss
Coordinating Editor: Christine Ricketts
Copy Editor: Mary Bearden
Compositor: SPi Global
Indexer: SPi Global
Artist: SPi Global
Cover Designer: Anna Ishchenko

Distributed to the book trade worldwide by Springer Science+Business Media New York, 233 Spring Street, 6th Floor, New York, NY 10013. Phone 1-800-SPRINGER, fax (201) 348-4505, e-mail orders-ny@springer-sbm.com, or visit www.springeronline.com. Apress Media, LLC is a California LLC and the sole member (owner) is Springer Science + Business Media Finance Inc (SSBM Finance Inc). SSBM Finance Inc is a Delaware corporation.

For information on translations, please e-mail rights@apress.com, or visit www.apress.com.

Apress and friends of ED books may be purchased in bulk for academic, corporate, or promotional use. eBook versions and licenses are also available for most titles. For more information, reference our Special Bulk Sales–eBook Licensing web page at www.apress.com/bulk-sales.

Any source code or other supplementary material referenced by the author in this text is available to readers at www.apress.com. For detailed information about how to locate your book's source code, go to www.apress.com/source-code/.

This book is dedicated to my wife, Charlene, because without her support and patience,
this book wouldn't have been written

Contents at a Glance

Contents

About the Author

Jonathan Fielding is a web developer working with a wide variety of clients across London building responsive web sites. In his experience working at agencies, and more recent through his own web consulting business, he has worked with many high-profile clients such as Sony, British Gas, BT, and most recently Beamly, the social network for television. He started developing responsive web sites in the early days of responsive design, so he has spent a lot of time exploring the intricacies of building sites that offer a great experience, regardless of the device being used. He is very active in the web development community, not only through giving talks at a wide variety of events but also through his contributions to open source code. As a contributor to open source, he has launched several of his own open source projects including several jQuery plug-ins and several JavaScript Libraries, the most notable of which is SimpleStateManager. In addition to this, he regularly publishes tutorials on his blog with the aim of sharing knowledge.

About the Technical Reviewer

Daniel Grant is a designer and front-end web developer. He began his career in print design working with organizations including the UNDP and AusAID. Excited by the internet, he transitioned into web development and now works primarily with startups experiencing rapid growth.

Daniel specializes in responsive web design and user interface development. He led the redesign of the accounting application KashFlow, which became one of the first large-scale responsive web applications. More recently, and shortly after its inception, he joined the kids' publishing studio, Lostmy.name, to build an e-commerce platform for creating and buying personalized books.

Daniel enjoys contributing to the development community, whether that is by writing articles, speaking at tech events or working on open source projects. He is the author of the responsive CSS framework, Chameleon.

Acknowledgments

There are a number of people I want to thank for all their help in putting this book together. First and foremost I need to thank my wife for being so supportive while I was writing this book. Not only has she put up with me during this time, but she has also read through every page time and time again checking that everything made sense.

The web development community as a whole has been really supportive of me writing this book. Although I can't possibly mention everyone individually, in particular there are a few developers who have helped so much they deserve a special thanks. First, I thank my technical reviewer Daniel Grant, who has been really good at providing solid feedback. He went above and beyond what I would expect, taking time to read the relevant specifications to ensure the accuracy of the book, and his knowledge of the subject area really helped add value to the book.

Second, I thank Patrick Hamann whose talks on web performance were really helpful in ensuring nothing was missed when it came to me writing the chapter on performance. In addition, he was really helpful in answering any additional queries I had. Third, I thank Natasha Rooney, whose talk on how the mobile phone networks affect web performance really helped me understand how these networks can influence the performance of a web site. I also thank her for the feedback she gave me on the explanation I wrote about mobile phone network performance.

Finally, I thank the team at Apress who have been really patient with me as I have made change after change to the book. In particular I want to thank both Christine Ricketts and Louise Corrigan who have worked closely with me with the aim of making this book the best it can be.

Introduction

Responsive web design (RWD) is the technique used when designing and building a web site to optimize a web site to work well across a wide variety of different devices. Through this optimization, developers are able to provide a much better experience for the users of their web sites.

The aim of this book is to take you from knowing how to build a web site with HTML to CSS right through to building great responsive experiences that work across a variety of devices. In particular I will focus on these areas:

- An introduction to responsive design

- Testing responsive sites

- The power of media queries

- Using fluid layouts

- Frameworks in responsive design

- Adapt an existing site

- Tools and workflow

- Making the user's journey responsive

- JavaScript across responsive states

- Optimizing your responsive site

There are many ways you can build a responsive site, and in each of these chapters I will explain different techniques that can be used to help you build your web site more efficiently.

CHAPTER 1

∎ ∎ ∎

Introduction to Responsive Design

The way in which web sites are built has evolved over the past 20 years. The 1990s were dominated by web sites being built in tables, and although the cascading style sheet (CSS) specification was released in 1996, CSS didn't really take center stage until mid-2003. This brought the launch of CSS Zen Garden, which demonstrated the power of CSS and how it could be used to completely restyle a site without even touching the HTML. With the subsequent rise in popularity of CSS, the development community standardized on targeting screens with a resolution of 1024 by 800, with larger screens being left with white space around the edges and smaller screens requiring scrolling. This was rolled out so that sites could be designed and built in a way that worked for the largest possible audience, as the majority of users were accessing them from the 1024 by 800 resolution.

With the launch of the iPhone in 2007, the full experience of the Internet was available anywhere. Gone were the simplistic, difficult to use mobile browsers of before, and suddenly we had a full, desktop-grade browser in our pockets. The first reaction from companies was to make a separate, mobile-optimized site, following the theory that offering a targeted user experience would increase sales. More often than not, these sites were scaled-back versions of the full web site and would often fail to offer the visitor the content they were after, meaning ultimately they would either leave the site or switch to the full web site anyway.

In 2010, CSS3 (cascading style sheets 3) media queries were implemented in mobile browsers, starting with Android 2.1 and followed by iOS 3.2. The arrival of media queries brought with it the ability to target specific styles at different screen resolutions.

Aside from the size of the screens changing, there has also been a huge drive to improve the quality of the screens that are in use, with high pixel density screens becoming more commonplace. The term *retina display* was conceived by Apple in June 2010 to describe their own high dpi (dots per CSS inch) screens found on their phones, and they are credited with bringing the high-dpi screens to the mainstream. As they are not the only company deploying the technology, it is becoming increasingly important to consider high-dpi displays during your build to ensure your web site looks fantastic on these devices. The optimum way of ensuring and achieving this is through use of responsive design methodologies.

Responsive design has rapidly become the current trend in web development, and this book aims to take you through the different approaches you can take to achieve responsive design.

This chapter will introduce you to responsive design. The sections contained in this chapter are:

1. What is responsive design?

2. Why is mobile so important?

3. Responsive design vs. device-specific experiences

4. Responsive web design is not limited just to mobile

5. When would you not use responsive web design?

6. Examples of responsive web design

7. Looking at HTML5 technologies

8. What's new in CSS3

What Is Responsive Design?

The term *responsive design* is derived from the way in which the browser responds to its environment. Responsive design is an approach to how a web site is developed that aims to provide users of a web site with a good experience regardless of the browser, device, or screen size used. Web sites designed with a responsive design approach adapt their layout by using fluid grids, fluid content (e.g., images, videos, and text), and CSS3 media queries.

Responsive design moves away from using fixed units like pixels and more toward relative units like percentages. This means that the widths of the different sections of a site are designed to be a percentage of the viewport.

It was Ethan Marcotte who first coined the term responsive web design in his article for A List Apart, in which he compares the web to architecture. He made a key point about how we should treat the increasing number of web devices as facets of the same experience.

> *Rather than tailoring disconnected designs to each of an ever-increasing number of web devices, we can treat them as facets of the same experience. We can design for an optimal viewing experience, but embed standards-based technologies into our designs to make them not only more flexible, but more adaptive to the media that renders them. In short, we need to practice responsive web design.*[1]

—Ethan Marcotte, A List Apart

What Ethan is suggesting here is that all displays should receive the same content. However, it needs to be built to be flexible in order to fit correctly to the display. The site should adapt in a way that optimizes the experience for the device.

Why Is Mobile So Important?

With the advance of the smartphone, people have access to the Internet at any given moment with a simple pluck from their pocket or bag. From checking out the reviews for the television you are interested in at your local electrical goods outlet to finding the closest place to get a pizza, the Internet no longer requires you to be tied down to a computer with a plethora of cables, but it can be with you everywhere. With this in mind, the very idea of developing a web site that is not optimized to work well on a mobile device is absurd.

The smartphone market is no longer a niche part of the mobile phone industry but instead is booming with popularity, with smartphones accounting for 57.6% of mobile phone sales in 2013 globally.[2] Although you would expect a portion of these sales to simply be the result of a smartphone being the device given as part of a mobile phone plan, this is still a phenomenal figure.

One of the most interesting things about the growth of the smartphone market is that the percentage of web traffic deriving from mobile devices is rapidly increasing, with WalkerSands Digital estimating a 67 percent increase of mobile traffic in 2013 alone (see Figure 1-1). When we look at these statistics in more detail, we can clearly see that the growth of mobile cannot be ignored.

---

[1] Ethan Marcotte, A List Apart. http://alistapart.com/article/responsive-web-design
[2] Natasha Lomas, Tech Crunch. http://techcrunch.com/2014/02/13/smartphones-outsell-dumb-phones-globally/

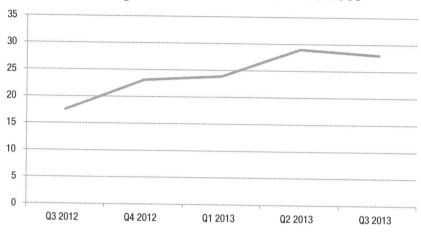

Figure 1-1. *Percentage of web traffic coming from mobile devices in 2012-2013*

One thing to bear in mind is that these data do not separate out business and consumer traffic. If data were specific to consumer traffic, we may find that the percentage of traffic coming from mobile is much higher. The reason that we might expect this is because during business hours it would be expected that most users were using desktop computers to access the Internet.

Joe McCann discussed the expected online impact of mobile on large retailers during his talk at Full Frontal in Brighton in November 2013. As part of his talk on the importance of mobile he mentioned a discussion he had had with someone from Target.com about the impact mobile is having on their business, and his claim supports our expectation that consumer traffic for mobile would be higher than the combined business and consumer traffic. He said:

"This year, more than half of all traffic to Target.com is expected to come from mobile devices on cyber Monday for the first time ever."[3]

—Joe McCann, Director of Creative Technology at Mother NY, 08/11/2013

This would be an incredible figure, which is only expected to continue to rise as use of mobile devices becomes more widespread. Mobile has the potential to achieve true ubiquitousness, which may never have been possible with desktop computers and notebooks. The reason for this is twofold: first, the cost to entry is much lower, a tablet can now be purchased for less than $50 and a smartphone for less than $30. Second, touch interfaces are more intuitive than their desktop counterparts, meaning people who may have previously had problems using computers are more likely to be able to engage a mobile platform. While there are now touch interface desktops and notebooks, these have been cited to cause arm strain, particularly in the shoulder region, making the mobile platform much more appealing.[4]

Another indicator of an upturn in the mobile market are the sales data for mobile phones. They reveal that the market for smartphones has not yet been saturated, with only 1.5 billion of the 5 billion mobile phone user base being smartphones. Additionally, in Q4 2012 tablet sales surpassed the combined total sales of desktop PCs and notebooks.[5]

---

[3] Joe McCann, Director of Creative Technology at Mother, New York, August 11, 2013.
[4] http://www.theguardian.com/technology/2013/apr/09/windows-8-touchscreen-laptops-pain
[5] http://www.pcpro.co.uk/news/384172/tablet-sales-to-overtake-pcs-this-quarter

Responsive Design vs. Device-Specific Experiences

As just discussed, mobile is a huge growth area and you might be wondering why we don't just build device-specific experiences tailored to the platform we are targeting.

Well, when comparing responsive vs. separate sites, it is very easy to assert that a separate site would allow you to offer a better experience. This is the view that Jakob Nielsen has taken and a summary of a post he has written reads:

"It's cheap but degrading to reuse content and design across diverging media forms like print vs. online or desktop vs. mobile. Superior UX requires tight platform integration."[6]

—Jakob Nielsen

In reality I believe this is a misguided view. Responsive development allows you to define the user experience that mobile devices receive, and as such, content can be adapted through hiding and showing content that is not specific to the platform.

One of the key benefits of responsive web design is simplicity. There is no need for a separate mobile presence, as responsive allows use of the same URL and the same code base. With one code base, testing becomes simpler, especially useful if you work in a workplace that uses test-driven development, as two code bases could potentially lead to many more unit tests being needed.

Part of this simplicity is that with responsive design you only have to manage one lot of content instead of essentially managing the same content on multiple sites. This is especially important in organizations where content of the site needs to be approved by several people or a legal team. This will, of course, speed things up, resulting in both saved time and money.

For the majority of web sites it is important to rank well on search engines, and Google offers guidance on how they would prefer you to build your sites. As part of their guidance, Google recommends responsive development with the following notes:

1. A single URL for content makes it easier for your users to interact with and share the content.

2. A single URL for content helps Google's algorithms index your site.

3. No redirection or server side device detection is needed for users to get to the device-optimized view, which reduces loading time.

4. Googlebot user agents have to crawl your pages once, as opposed to crawling multiple times with different user agents, to retrieve your content.

With these recommendations, it makes even more sense to go the responsive route, especially if your business relies on being found through Google.

When weighing up the pros and cons of using responsive web design or separate sites, it is also important to consider how you will continue to support the sites with updates, modifications, and additional new features. Two code bases are twice as much work, time, and effort to update and support.

If you already have a web site you are happy with, you could potentially look at converting your current site rather than embarking on a full rebuild. Although this approach is not mobile first (so by definition you would be taking a graceful degradation approach instead of a progressive enhancement approach), it could potentially allow you to make your site responsive and quicker. Converting an existing site consists partly of refactoring existing code and of adding media queries to the CSS.

This comparison may seem to lean heavily on the side of responsive development; however, there are some benefits of a separate site build. First, it is a lot easier to optimize the performance of a mobile site, because you don't have the overhead of the media queries, JavaScript, and JavaScript libraries required for the desktop site to worry about. Additionally, having a separate site build means you do not need to touch your existing desktop site, which in turn means no rebuilding and retesting required.

---

[6]Jakob Nielsen - http://www.nngroup.com/articles/repurposing-vs-optimized-design/

Responsive Web Design Is Not Limited Just to Mobile

So far a lot of the discussion about responsive web design has been focused on how responsive development allows you to build sites that work well on mobile devices. However, it is not only mobile devices that can benefit from responsive web design techniques.

Despite the huge growth of web-based television services like BBC's iPlayer, Netflix, and Amazon's Lovefilm, which are all available on mobile devices, television is still the center of family entertainment. The most common use for the television is to consume media: watching television shows, playing on a video games console, or simply using it for background music or listening to the radio.

In April 2013, Deloitte's Media & Entertainment Practice ran a survey that found that video games consoles can now be found in 50 percent of homes; they also found that 26 percent of televisions are connected to the Internet either directly or through a set top box (examples of set top boxes include games consoles, media PCs). When looking at future growth in this area, we also need to bear in mind that since October 2012, all major games consoles include a web browser, meaning there is the potential for further growth as additional users connect these to the Internet.

Aside from televisions, desktop or notebook computers with higher resolution and bigger displays are becoming more commonplace. As previously mentioned, historically web site widths have been built with the aim toward screens with a 1024 by 800 resolution, however, as of March 2012 1366 by 768 screens have become the most common resolution. With responsive techniques, you can take advantage of this extra space rather than simply have large margins on either side of your web site. Images can be bigger, content can be more spaced out, and more content can be visible to the user before they have even started scrolling.

If we look at just a small cross-section of devices, it is very easy to see that there are a wide variety of screen resolutions. Figure 1-2 shows the different screen resolutions of the mobile devices from just one manufacturer (in this case, Apple) along with the most common screen resolution and a common television resolution.

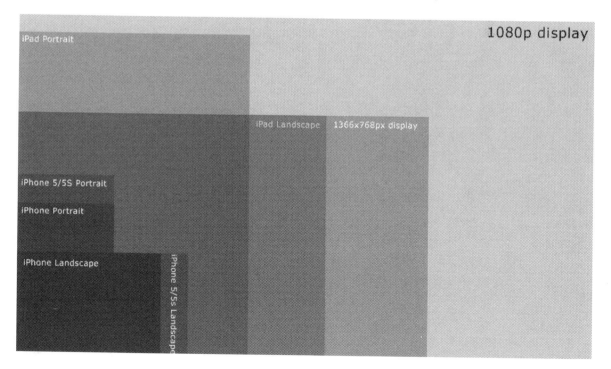

Figure 1-2. *Screen resolutions of Apple devices*

As this simple example demonstrates, from only one device manufacturer there are a variety of resolutions that will need to be supported, and when you then take into consideration the vast amount of other manufacturers' devices, the sheer level of different resolutions that are now commonplace is staggering. We also have to remember that new devices, with new screen resolutions, are regularly being developed and released, so you need to ensure your site is flexible enough to work with these new devices, no matter what they may be.

There is more to responsive design than simply mobile vs. desktop; therefore, when you think about responsive design, it is important to not simply think in these terms but instead think about how you can make your designs work on as many devices as possible, regardless of screen sizes and their capabilities. A good example of this is rather than make the assumption that all mobile browsers support the geolocation API (application programming interface), you can use feature detection to allow you to identify the features supported by the users' browsers and progressively enhance the site.

When Would You Not Use Responsive Web Design?

Sometimes it is not always appropriate to use responsive design techniques, but instead it would be better for the user experience to build device-specific experiences.

A prime example of when responsive design is not appropriate would be for web applications offering a desktop-like experience in the browser. Google Docs is one such web application where on the desktop browser you get a full-featured word processor, but because this experience cannot be achieved in a mobile browser, you instead have a heavily simplified mobile version. The reason for this is that for a feature-rich web application like Google Docs, the small screen size offers a major challenge. On a larger viewport, it is easy to put all the features into a toolbar, however, on a mobile device, this is just not possible. Therefore, to provide a better user experience it makes sense to strip the interface back to only what typical users will actually use. This striped back interface would be very different from the desktop interface to allow the code base to be lean, and it then makes sense for the mobile and desktop experiences to be built separately.

Aside from large web applications, if you are looking to convert an existing site rather than rebuild it, it is important to look at your existing code base to ensure it is not bloated. Converting an existing code base to a responsive build should only be done if the existing code base is reasonably lean. If you find that your existing site is bloated, you could choose to spend time slimming it down prior to converting the site; however, if this is not possible or the budget won't allow a rebuild, you could choose to build the mobile site separately.

Understanding the Viewport

One of the important concepts in responsive design is the viewport. The *viewport*, as the name suggests, is the view through which you see your web site.

Prior to HTML5 and CSS3, we typically thought about a web site in relation to the size of the browser window. Typically our users would be using a minimum display size of 1024 by 800 with the window full screen, we therefore would build our web sites to a fixed width, typically around 960px to 980px wide. When developing the early smaller devices, however, manufacturers faced a problem. The majority of sites at the time were built to be this fixed width, which was much wider than the width of the screens their new devices had. If they loaded the site at the native resolution of the device, the user would then need to scroll both horizontally and vertically to view the site.

The solution to this was to set the viewport width to be larger than the device width, which would mean the site would be scaled to fit the screen. iOS for example set the viewport width to 980px wide by default so the full width of the typical site would fit to the screen without horizontal scrolling. The site would therefore be scaled down, so to read the content of the site, the user would then zoom into the content they were interested in. This provided the best compromise for older sites to ensure they were usable on smaller devices.

To give the developers control over the viewport width, a *meta tag* was introduced, which allows the viewport width and initial scale to be set; I cover how to use this meta tag later in this chapter. What this means is that you can tell the mobile browser to render the site at a different viewport width. Where responsive design techniques are being used, you can choose to tell the browser to set the viewport width to be equal to the width of the browser window (or in the case of a single window device to be the width of that device).

Figure 1-3 shows where the viewport width and viewport height are measured in relation to the browser window.

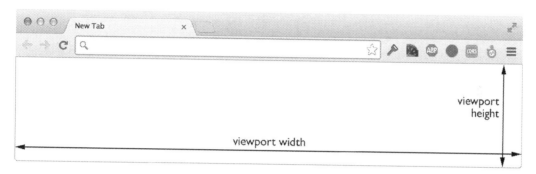

Figure 1-3. *A diagram illustrating the viewport width and viewport height*

The wide variety of devices means that you need to ensure you are testing at a wide variety of different viewport sizes. To easily look up the viewport size of a large variety of popular devices you can check out `http://viewportsizes.com`, which allows you to search through a list of devices, with information on the device viewport size.

Understanding Breakpoints

Along with understanding the viewport, you need to have a good understanding of what a breakpoint is. A *breakpoint* in responsive design is the width at which the web site changes layout based on the media query declaration. Typically a responsive site will be built to work with at least two but normally three distinct breakpoints aimed at specific types of devices. The most commonly used breakpoints are:

1. Extra small devices, for example, Phones (<768px)

2. Small devices, for example, tablets (≥768px and <992px)

3. Medium devices, for example, desktop computers (≥992px and <1200px)

4. Large devices, for example, desktops computers (≥1200px)

Aside from breakpoints, another piece of important terminology you need to understand is the *state*, which is the version of the site in between each breakpoint. So mobile, tablet, and desktop are your states and in between you have two breakpoints.

It is important to remember that media queries respond to the width of the viewport rather than the width of your screen. This is why you can simply resize your browser to test your breakpoints.

Examples of Responsive Web Design

Prior to writing responsive web pages, let's look at some of the best examples of responsive web sites. It's best to visit these online to see the features being described. They are described here as of the time of writing.

August

Our first example is August (`http://www.agst.co/`), which is a place to discover the world's most talented artists. The web page is a single-page site with a form to register your interest at the end of the page.

When you resize the site, you'll notice that the changes appear to be very subtle. When you look at the changes that happen between each breakpoint, you notice the differences discussed in the following sections.

Large and Medium Devices

For both large device and medium device states, August use an HTML5 video playing on a loop. The background's stretched full width, while the content is centered in a container. As you scroll down the page, you'll see that the site is very image heavy, with images wrapping carefully around the text (see Figures 1-4 and 1-5).

Figure 1-4. The initial view of the "august" site, with the video playing in the background

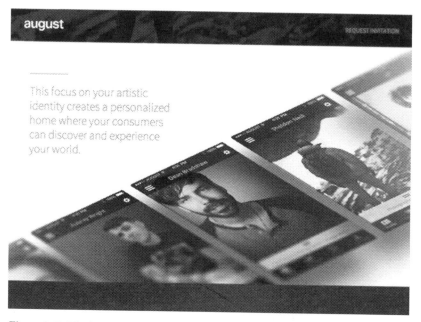

Figure 1-5. *The imagery on the "august" site wraps around the copy on large and medium devices*

Small Devices

With the smaller devices (e.g., tablets), August disables the video playing in the background, opting instead to replace it with an image (see Figure 1-6).

Figure 1-6. *On small devices, the "august" site replaces the background video with a static image*

The way in which the text wraps the images is adapted so the text sits farther up the images so as to not cover the main imagery (see Figure 1-7).

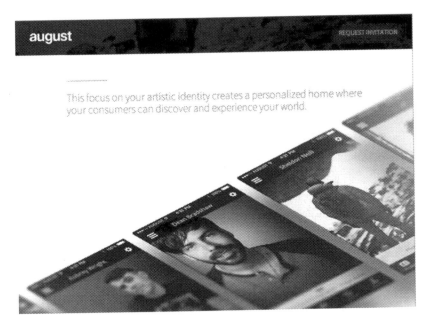

Figure 1-7. The wrapping of the copy is adapted to better fit the screen of smaller devices and not cover the image

Extra Small Devices

On the smallest view, aimed at mobile devices, the site adapts to the smaller device by replacing images that are not suitable for mobile. Media queries that target the height of the viewport are used to adjust font sizes further to ensure the text sits properly on the page (see Figure 1-8).

Figure 1-8. On our extra small devices, the text is resized and the imagery is sized to be fit the smaller display better

When you look at how the imagery has changed, you can see that it is now cropped by the width of the viewport and the text is again moved farther up the image to prevent it from overlapping the imagery (see Figure 1-9).

Figure 1-9. In the content sections, the copy is moved up above the imagery to prevent it overlapping

Nyetimber

The Nyetimber (http://nyetimber.com/our-story/) web site is very different from the August site in that it is a multipage responsive site. The site features a section titled "Our Story," which uses a parallax scroll effect to tell you the story about the business; this page will be the focus for the examples that follows.

Large and Medium Devices

The story of the company is told using a parallax effect on desktop, as you scroll the site the different elements are brought into view at different time intervals (see Figure 1-10).

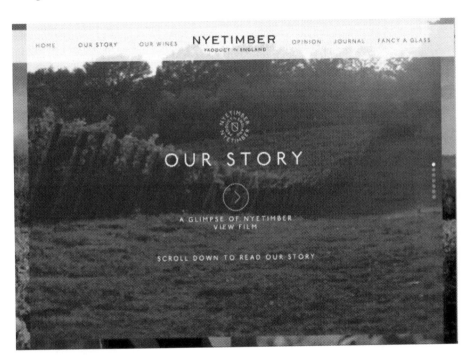

Figure 1-10. *The Nyetimber site starts wth an introduction to the story*

If you click any of the view film buttons, you are taken to a video that fills the viewport (see Figure 1-11).

Figure 1-11. *When opened, the videos fill the viewport*

As you scroll the page, you encounter a section where you can hover over panels to find out more information about the company (see Figure 1-12).

Figure 1-12. *Tiled panels allow the user to hover over them*

Small Devices

On a tablet, the navigation has dropped below the logo and the parallax functionality has been removed (see Figure 1-13).

Figure 1-13. *Instead of*

Rather than opening full screen, the videos are now inline (see Figure 1-14).

Figure 1-14. *The videos are shown inline on small devices, uses the Vimeo HTML5 player for playing the videos*

As the user cannot hover on a touch device, the panels no longer feature a hover action but instead are shown as a list of information about Nyetimber (see Figure 1-15).

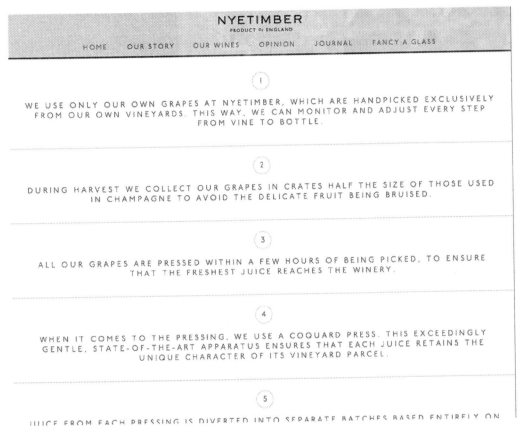

Figure 1-15. *The information panels are visible by default on small devices*

Extra Small Devices

On mobile, the header has been reduced further to remove the navigation and show the logo on a strip across the top (see Figure 1-16).

Figure 1-16. *The menu be default is collapsed on extra small devices, with a menu icon now available to toggle it*

Upon tapping the Navigation button on the header, the navigation now opens up (see Figure 1-17).

Figure 1-17. *Taping the menu icon expands the menu*

The rest of the content is resized to be narrower, and font sizes are smaller throughout (see Figure 1-18)

The Nyetimber estate counts three major landmarks in its history. Its earliest beginnings saw it first recorded in the Domesday Book in 1086. Then there was the planting of the first vines, almost exactly 900 years later. Most recently, there was the decision in 2006 that Nyetimber wines deserved an audience on the world stage.

Figure 1-18. *The content is narrower, blocks are all stacked and the text size optimized for the device*

Other Examples

There are a lot more examples available at the AWWWards site, where they have a whole section dedicated to responsive design.[7]

Getting Started with HTML5

Responsive design is built on top of the new technologies brought along with HTML5 and CSS3. Let's look at the changes brought about by HTML5 so we can better understand the code we are writing.

HTML5 is the draft specification for the newest version of the HTML language specification, which is agreed upon by the World Wide Web Consortium (W3C). The HTML5 specification is part of a larger set of technologies that the W3C terms the "open web platform," which in a nutshell means it allows us to build web sites and web applications that work anywhere. When people refer to the term HTML5, they are normally talking about the "open web platform."

There are lots of benefits of using HTML5 with your projects, which I'll discuss now.

---

[7]https://www.awwwards.com/websites/responsive-design/

Accessibility

HTML5 makes it a lot simpler to make your site accessible. The new HTML5 semantic tags allow screen readers to more easily identify types of content, and this allows them to provide a better experience for the user. Additionally, HTML5 has support for ARIA (accessible rich Internet application) data roles, which allow you to assign roles to sections of content. This can be especially useful where you are updating the content of the page using JavaScript, as you can define ARIA roles that watch parts of the page for changes and notifies the user.

Video and Audio Support

HTML5 has native support for both video and audio codes. One of the key benefits of HTML5 video and HTML5 audio is that they deliver strong mobile device support as they work in the browser without any plug-ins like Adobe Flash. One area that is currently being discussed is whether HTML5 should support digital rights management (DRM) for content, and it is likely that DRM in some form will be added to the specification with the purpose of preventing piracy of digital media like movies and music.

Smarter Storage

Prior to HTML5, the main way to store data on the client side was to use cookies; the disadvantage of this is that they are sent to the server along with the HTTP request, even if they are not used by the server. HTML5 introduced DOM (document object model) Storage, which includes localStorage (which is persistent) and sessionStorage (which is only available for the duration of the session). The benefits of DOM Storage are the data remain client-side only, so they do not affect the size of the HTTP request and it allows you to store a lot more data; currently DOM Storage allows you to store 5MB of data per domain.

New Interactions

HTML5's new JavaScript APIs enable you to add new and improved interactions. An example of this is new APIs such as drag and drop, geolocation, and history. The aim of these new interactions is to enable you to build richer and easier to use interfaces.

Canvas

HTML5 introduces the canvas element, which is the new HTML5 tag that can be used for drawing. It allows you to build rich Internet applications similarly to how Adobe Flash had been used in the past.

Mobile

HTML5 introduces a lot of improvements for mobile, new APIs such as geolocation allow the site to determine the location of the user and offer location-specific data. HTML5 features a viewport tag, which allows you to define viewport widths and zoom settings. There are also device-specific tags that enable developers to interact with browser-specific features, an example of which is, when using a meta tag, the developer can tell iOS that if bookmarked on the home page, it should be opened as a full screen web application.

Looking at HTML5 Technologies

Now that you are aware of the benefits brought with HTML5, let's look at some of the individual core changes.

The doctype

The doctype tells the browser how it should parse your document; as such, it is an important part of the document and it should be included in the first line of your HTML document. The previous doctype not only defined the document as HTML4, it also provided a URL to the specification document, as shown in this example:

```
<!DOCTYPE HTML PUBLIC "-//W3C//DTD HTML 4.01 Transitional//EN" "http://www.w3.org/TR/html4/loose.dtd">
```

The new HTML5 doctype is a lot simpler, and you no longer specify the version of HTML or the URL of the specification document, as shown in this example:

```
<!DOCTYPE html>
```

The reason for the change is that HTML is a living specification where browsers will continue new parts of the specifications as they pass through the standardization process. The idea is that in the future new features can be added without further changes to the doctype.

New Semantic HTML Tags

When you first open an HTML5 document, the first thing you will notice is that there are many more semantic tags used throughout the document. The most notable ones are:

1. `<article>`: Defines an article.

2. `<aside>`: Defines content alongside the main content.

3. `<figure>`: Defines related content, an example of use is photos or code listings.

4. `<figcaption>`: Defines the caption for your `<figure>` element.

5. `<header>`: Defines a header for the document or section.

6. `<footer>`: Defines a footer for the document or section.

7. `<nav>`: Defines a series of links used for navigation around the site.

8. `<section>`: Defines a section of content.

A simple example of how an HTML5 document may be laid out follows:

```
<!DOCTYPE html>
<html>
    <head>
    <title>Title</title>
    </head>
    <body>
            <header>
                    <h1>Hello World</h1>
            </header>
            <div class="content">
            </div>
            <footer>
            </footer>
    </body>
</html>
```

New Meta Tags

In addition to the new semantic tags that were introduced with HTML5, there has also been the introduction of some new meta tags.

Viewport Meta Tag

The most important of the new meta tags is the viewport meta tag. This meta tag was initially introduced by Mobile Safari and is used as a way to allow developers to define the width and the scaling of the viewport. When used incorrectly, the viewport meta tag can cause a terrible experience for users.

The viewport meta tag content consists of a comma-separated list of key value pairs, the values that can be used are:

1. `width`:– The width of the viewport.

2. `initial-scale`: The scale of the site when it initially loads.

3. `user-scalable`: By default, the user can zoom the site, setting "user-scalable" to "no" disables this. This is bad for the accessibility of the site so it is discouraged.

4. `maximum-scale`: Allows you to define a maximum level that the user can zoom the site. Although not as bad as user-scalable, this can still be harmful to accessibility.

If you were to add this meta tag to a nonresponsive site, you would set the viewport meta tag to have a sensible width to display the site comfortably. If you take an example of a 980px site, which is centrally aligned, you would want to include a bit of spacing around the edges, so you might set the viewport width to 1024px, as shown in this example:

```
<meta name="viewport" content="width=1024, initial-scale=1">
```

For responsive design, you want the width of the viewport to be equal to the width of the device you are using. This is for two key reasons: first, you will be building your CSS to target the width of the viewport so you want the viewport width to match the device width. Second, it tells the device that the site is mobile optimized and that it therefore does not need to load the page with a large default viewport zoomed out.

To make the viewport equal to the width of the device you are using, you set the value for the viewport width to `device-width` instead of specifying a specific size. You also want your site to start with a default zoom level, so you have `initial-scale` set to 1, as shown in the following example:

```
<meta name="viewport" content="width=device-width, initial-scale=1">
```

Apple Touch Icons

Another new meta tag that has been introduced is the Apple touch icon meta tag, which allows you to define icons that will be used on iOS when the user saves a web page to the home screen, as shown in the following example:

```
<link rel="apple-apple-icon" href="apple-icon-iphone.png">
<link rel="apple-apple-icon" sizes="76x76" href="apple-icon-ipad.png">
<link rel="apple-apple-icon" sizes="120x120" href="apple-icon-iphone-retina.png">
<link rel="apple-apple-icon" sizes="152x152" href="apple-icon-ipad-retina.png">
```

Although not part of the HTML5 specs, these icons are necessary to allow iOS users to have a nice icon if they save the web site or web application to their home screen.

Web Forms

Input form fields have been upgraded with the HTML5 specification. Previously, we have been limited to radio, check box, and text fields, however, we now have a much larger range of input types:

1. search

2. email

3. url

4. tel

5. number

6. range

7. date

8. month

9. week

10. time

11. datetime

12. datetime-local

13. color

One of the benefits of using the new input types is that it allows the browser to render relevant controls. For example, on mobile devices if the input type is set to email, a keyboard specific for inserting e-mail addresses is shown. Alternatively if the input type is set to date, a native date selector is shown instead of the keyboard. This provides a really good user experience as it makes form entry much quicker. A simple example is provided of the custom controls that are shown for the date field:

```
<input type="date"  id="field" name="field" />
```

When you access this on a mobile phone, in this case an Apple iPhone running iOS7, it shows up in the browser with the native date picker barrel (see Figure 1-19).

Figure 1-19. *<input type="date" id="field" name="field" />as shown on an iPhone running iOS7*

When you load the same control in a desktop browser, you then get native controls for the desktop (see Figure 1-20).

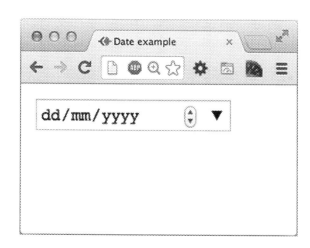

Figure 1-20. *The date input control shown on a desktop in Chrome*

HTML5 allows you to add placeholders to input fields; what this means is that you can provide the user with an example of what sort of data they should be inputting to an input field. An example of adding a placeholder attribute to an input field is:

```
<input type="input" placeholder="Sample placeholder" id="field" name="field" />
```

When loaded into the browser, you see a grayed out text box for the placeholder (see Figure 1-21).

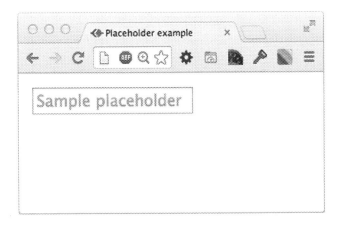

Figure 1-21. *Input element with a placeholder*

In HTML5, you can also easily add validation to the form. To demonstrate how this works, let's look at a couple of simple examples.

The simplest form of validation is to make the field required, you would do this by adding the attribute required to the input field, as shown in this example:

```
<input type="text" placeholder="e.g example@example.com" required />
```

When you click the Submit button in the browser, the user is then shown an error message to remind them to fill in the field (see Figure 1-22).

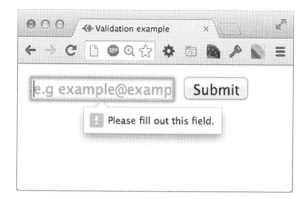

Figure 1-22. *The browsers error message shown when user tries to submit the form without filling in a required value*

If you want to validate an e-mail address, you would simply need to set the input type to `email`, as shown in this example:

```
<input type="email" placeholder="e.g example@example.com" required id="email" name="email" />
```

When you click the Submit button in the browser, the user is then shown an error to tell them the e-mail address they entered was invalid (see Figure 1-23).

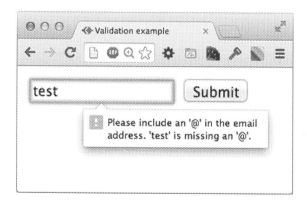

Figure 1-23. *The browsers error message shown when user tries to submit the form with an invalid email address*

Polyfilling

With all these fantastic new features in HTML5, it can be disappointing to find not all of them play nice with the legacy browsers we are required to support. Thankfully, this is where polyfills come in. The term *polyfill* was first coined by Remy Sharp in 2009 when he was writing "Introducing HTML."

Remy stated "Shim, to me, meant a piece of code that you could add that would fix some functionality, but it would most often have its own API. I wanted something you could drop in and it would silently work." `http://remysharp.com/2010/10/08/what-is-a-polyfill/`.

So as per Remy's definition, a polyfill is a bit of code that simply adds the missing functionality to the browser, which is normally achieved using JavaScript. The term is not meant to implicate older browsers as often newer browsers also need to be polyfilled with the latest features.

There are already a significant number of polyfills available for HTML5 technologies, some of the popular ones are:

1. Respond.js: `https://github.com/scottjehl/Respond` Respond.js adds support for min/max-width CSS3 Media Queries to older versions of Internet Explorer (IE6-8). If you are planning on making mobile first responsive sites and need to support older IE, this is required.

2. HTML5 Shiv: `https://github.com/aFarkas/html5shiv` HTML5 Shiv enables support for styling HTML5 semantic elements in older versions of Internet Explorer.

3. CupCake.js: `http://www.rivindu.com/p/cupcakejs.html` CupCake.js adds support to both localStorage and sessionStorage with a generic API.

4. FlashCanvas: `http://flashcanvas.net/` HTML5 Canvas Polyfill based on using Adobe Flash.

Validating the HTML5 Page

You may have previously used the W3C validator to validate your HTML; however, you may not be aware that it has been updated to have experimental support for the draft specification of HTML5.

To validate your HTML, visit the W3C validator (`validator.w3.org`) and either validate by entering the direct URL of your site or paste the HTML of your site into the text area provided.

Validation of HTML can be used:

1. *As a debugging tool*: The simplest bug to fix in HTML are those caused by writing invalid code. A simple validation should highlight problems with your HTML, which you can promptly fix.

2. *To maintain quality of code*: By ensuring code always passes the W3C validation, it maintains a level of quality in the code.

3. *Ensuring ease of maintenance*: Although invalid code may not break your site in the short term, unexpected bugs can crop up when you later amend that code, and validating helps minimize this.

What's New in CSS3

Along with the changes that have been brought about by HTML5, we also have the new CSS3 specification. CSS3 is the third incarnation of CSS, which expands CSS to allow us to build deeper and richer user interfaces. Before you can jump into using responsive design, it is very important that you have an understanding of what you can achieve using CSS3 as it will form the foundation of a lot of the work you will do inside media queries.

Browser Vendor Prefixes

Before you start looking at examples of CSS3, you need to understand a bit about CSS browser prefixes.

As the CSS3 spec is still a working draft, browser vendors often implement the new features behind vendor-specific prefixes. This means that they are able to implement features where the specification has not been completely agreed upon by all browsers. Each of the vendors has its own prefix, and the prefixes for the most popular vendors are:

1. `-moz-` Firefox and browsers using Mozilla's Gecko engine

2. `-webkit-` Safari, Chrome, and WebKit

3. `-o-` Opera

4. `-ms-` Internet Explorer

As you will see in some of the examples, not all browsers require a prefixed version of CSS3 properties as the property has already been developed for long enough to not need browser prefixes and some browser vendors never implemented a prefixed version.

Where a prefixed version of a CSS property has been implemented, often the implementations are very similar. However, there are some properties where prefixed CSS properties differ from one another. An example of this is the linear-gradient property, which has different implementations for each of the browser prefixes.

It is important to note that with Google migrating to the new Blink engine they have forked from WebKit, they are moving away from adding new features under browser prefixes. To quote them for the reason behind this:

"Historically, browsers have relied on vendor prefixes (e.g., -webkit-feature) to ship experimental features to web developers. This approach can be harmful to compatibility because web content comes to rely upon these vendor-prefixed names."[8] – Blink Information page.

What this means to developers is that we won't be able to immediately use some of the new experimental CSS3 features when they make it into the browser as they won't be enabled to our sites' users. This does not prevent us from enabling the experimental features in our own browsers and trying them out as they can be enabled in Chrome's about: flags.

A comprehensive list of vendor prefixed CSS properties can be found at:
http://peter.sh/experiments/vendor-prefixed-css-property-overview/.

CSS3 Examples

To really explore what you can do with CSS3, let's look at some common elements and discuss how we would have previously styled them and how CSS3 enables us to make styling easier.

Buttons

Web sites use buttons for a variety of purposes, with common examples being call to actions, form submit buttons, and action buttons. Historically, styling buttons could be quite tricky as you would need to use images for things like gradients, none web safe fonts, and shadows. When we had different sized buttons, we would then need a different set of images. With CSS3, you are able to achieve all this simply by writing code. Not only is this simpler, it also means you can scale your buttons to different sizes without redefining the general button styles. Listing 1-1 defines a single button size with a gradient.

Listing 1-1. A Single Button with a Gradient

```
<!DOCTYPE html>
<html>
    <head>
        <title>Button example</title>
        <style>
            .button {
                display: inline-block;
                border: 1px solid #1f84ef;
                padding: 0px 50px;
                line-height: 50px;
                -webkit-border-radius: 5px;
                -moz-border-radius: 5px;
                border-radius: 5px;
```

---

[8]Blink Information page http://www.chromium.org/blink#vendor-prefixes

```
                    background: #6db3f2; /* Old browsers */
                    background: -moz-linear-gradient(top, #6db3f2 0%, #54a3ee 50%, #3690f0 51%, #1e69de 100%);
                    /* FF3.6+ */
                    background: -webkit-gradient(linear, left top, left bottom, color-stop(0%,#6db3f2),
                    color-stop(50%,#54a3ee), color-stop(51%,#3690f0), color-stop(100%,#1e69de)); /*
                    Chrome,Safari4+ */
                    background: -webkit-linear-gradient(top, #6db3f2 0%,#54a3ee 50%,#3690f0 51%,#1e69de 100%);
                    /* Chrome10+,Safari5.1+ */
                    background: -o-linear-gradient(top, #6db3f2 0%,#54a3ee 50%,#3690f0 51%,#1e69de 100%);
                    /* Opera 11.10+ */
                    background: -ms-linear-gradient(top, #6db3f2 0%,#54a3ee 50%,#3690f0 51%,#1e69de 100%);
                    /* IE10+ */
                    background: linear-gradient(to bottom, #6db3f2 0%,#54a3ee 50%,#3690f0 51%,#1e69de 100%);
                    /* W3C */
                    text-transform: uppercase;
                    font-family: Impact, "Arial Black", sans serif;
                    color: #fffffe !important;
                    font-size: 20px;
                    font-size: 1.42857rem;
                    text-decoration: none;
                    -webkit-font-smoothing: antialiased;
                    text-shadow: 1px 0px 2px #1f84ef;
                    filter: dropshadow(color=#1f84ef, offx=1, offy=0);
                }

            .button:hover, .button:active, .button:focus {
                    text-decoration: none;
                    background: #54a7f0; /* Old browsers */
                    background: -moz-linear-gradient(top, #54a7f0 0%, #3c97ec 50%, #1f84ef 51%, #1c5fcc 100%);
                    /* FF3.6+ */
                    background: -webkit-gradient(linear, left top, left bottom, color-stop(0%,#54a7f0),
                    color-stop(50%,#3c97ec), color-stop(51%,#1f84ef), color-stop(100%,#1c5fcc)); /*
                    Chrome,Safari4+ */
                    background: -webkit-linear-gradient(top, #54a7f0 0%,#3c97ec 50%,#1f84ef 51%,#1c5fcc 100%);
                    /* Chrome10+,Safari5.1+ */
                    background: -o-linear-gradient(top, #54a7f0 0%,#3c97ec 50%,#1f84ef 51%,#1c5fcc 100%);
                    /* Opera 11.10+ */
                    background: -ms-linear-gradient(top, #54a7f0 0%,#3c97ec 50%,#1f84ef 51%,#1c5fcc 100%);
                    /* IE10+ */
                    background: linear-gradient(to bottom, #54a7f0 0%,#3c97ec 50%,#1f84ef 51%,#1c5fcc 100%);
                    /* W3C */
                }
        </style>
    </head>
    <body>
        <a href="#" class="button">Call to action</a>
    </body>
</html>
```

This code will create a button in the browser, as shown in Figure 1-24.

Figure 1-24. *The finished CSS button*

RGBA

In CSS, colors have generally been defined as hexadecimal or RGB (red, green blue). If we had wanted a translucent background, it would have required using a 1×1px 24-bit .png; however, with CSS3, we can now do this with RGBA colors. A RGBA color is an RGB color with alpha transparency applied to it. The benefit of this is that you no longer need to include an image. To demonstrate RGBA, let's place some text over a random image with a translucent background (see Listing 1-2).

Listing 1-2. Demonstrating RGBA

```
<!DOCTYPE html>
<html>
    <head>
        <title>RGBA example</title>
        <style>
            .rgba-container, .rgba{
            width: 220px;
                height: 220px;
                position: relative;
            }
            .rgba{
                background: rgba(255,255,255,0.5);
                position: absolute;
                top: 0px;
                left: 0px;
                margin: 0px;
                line-height: 220px;
                text-align: center;
            }
        </style>
    </head>
```

```
    <body>
        <div class="rgba-container">
                <img src="http://lorempixel.com/220/220/" alt="random image" />
                <p class="rgba">Hello World</p>
        </div>
    </body>
</html>
```

As you can see in this listing, you have set the background to rgba(255,255,255,0.5), which is white at 50 percent opacity. As per RGB values, the first three values you define are red, green, and blue, the fourth value is the opacity of the color as a decimal number. This is visualized in the screenshot shown in Figure 1-25.

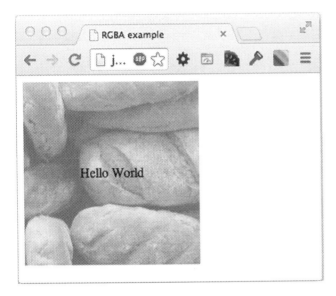

Figure 1-25. *The finished text over a translucent image*

Multiple Columns

In the past, if you wanted to achieve multiple columns of text, it was very difficult. You either had the option of calculating in the backend how many words should appear in each column or using JavaScript to set up the columns. CSS3 allows the addition of multiple columns, meaning you are able to define the columns in your style sheet rather than programmatically. In Listing 1-3 you'll separate the content in the paragraph tag into two columns with a 10px column gap.

Listing 1-3. Creating Two Columns

```
<!DOCTYPE html>
<html>
    <head>
        <title>Multiple col example</title>
        <style>
            p{
```

```
                -moz-column-count: 2;
                -moz-column-gap: 10px;
                -webkit-column-count: 2;
                -webkit-column-gap: 10px;
                column-count: 2;
                column-gap: 10px;
            }
        </style>
    </head>
    <body>
        <p>Sed posuere consectetur est at lobortis. Fusce dapibus, tellus ac cursus commodo, tortor
mauris condimentum nibh, ut fermentum massa justo sit amet risus. Donec id elit non mi porta gravida
at eget metus. Integer posuere erat a ante venenatis dapibus posuere velit aliquet.</p>
    </body>
</html>
```

In this listing you have set `column-count` to 2 so that the content will show up as two columns. You then defined the `column-gap` as 10px to space out the columns. As you will notice, you also included prefixed versions of these CSS3 properties for browsers that require the prefixed versions. You can see the outcome in Figure 1-26.

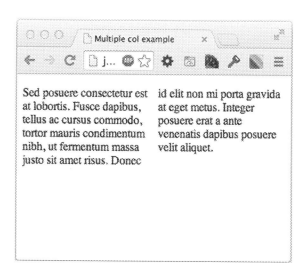

Figure 1-26. *The finished two columns*

Gradient Panels

As part of a design you may want to have a radial gradient, so rather than using images, you can use CSS3 to achieve this. The benefit of this for a responsive site is that it will scale with the width of the block. See the example in Listing 1-4.

Listing 1-4. Creating a Radial Gradient

```
<!DOCTYPE html>
<html>
    <head>
        <title>Gradient panel example</title>
        <style>
            .panel{
                width: 220px;
                height: 180px;
                padding: 20px;
                background: #77b7ef; /* Old browsers */
                background: -moz-radial-gradient(center, ellipse cover,  #77b7ef 0%, #000000 100%);
                /* FF3.6+ */
                background: -webkit-gradient(radial, center center, 0px, center center, 100%, color-
                stop(0%,#77b7ef), color-stop(100%,#000000)); /* Chrome,Safari4+ */
                background: -webkit-radial-gradient(center, ellipse cover,  #77b7ef 0%,#000000 100%);
                /* Chrome10+,Safari5.1+ */
                background: -o-radial-gradient(center, ellipse cover, #77b7ef 0%,#000000 100%);
                /* Opera 12+ */
                background: -ms-radial-gradient(center, ellipse cover, #77b7ef 0%,#000000 100%);
                /* IE10+ */
                background: radial-gradient(ellipse at center,  #77b7ef 0%,#000000 100%); /* W3C */
                filter: progid:DXImageTransform.Microsoft.gradient( startColorstr='#77b7ef', endColo
                rstr='#000000',GradientType=1 ); /* IE6-9 fallback on horizontal gradient */
                background-size: 160% 160%;
                background-position: center -160px;
            }
            .panel h1{
                margin-top: 0px;
            }

            .panel h1, .panel p, .panel a{
                color: #fff;
            }
        </style>
    </head>
    <body>
        <div class="panel">
            <h1>Intro</h1>
            <p>Cras mattis consectetur purus sit amet fermentum.</p>
            <p><a href="#">read more</a></p>
        </div>
    </body>
</html>
```

You can see the finished radial gradient in Figure 1-27.

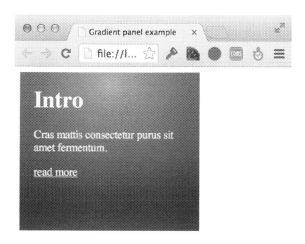

Figure 1-27. *Our finished gradient*

Summary

This chapter explained how responsive design techniques can enable you to build web sites that work well across a wide variety of different devices. It is important to remember that responsive design is not simply about making a web site work across mobile and desktop devices, but also about building a site that is flexible enough to function well across a wide variety of devices. You can't predict how future devices that will access your site will display, therefore, for your programming it is better to think of devices in terms of large, medium, small, and extra small rather desktop, tablet, and mobile.

In addition to getting an understanding of where to use responsive design, you should now be able to recognize times where using responsive techniques would not be suitable. A good example of this is a desktop replacement application like Google Docs, which has a lot of functionality that a smaller device does not have or the space to show the user.

Having gotten a sense of responsive design and what it can offer your site, it is a good idea to look at some existing responsive sites to get an idea of what you are able to achieve when using these techniques. This chapter also looked at a couple of examples of responsive design being used. However, with the explosion in popularity of responsive design, there are many more good examples out there. The AWWWARDS site has a really good listing of different responsive sites, which can be found at: http://www.awwwards.com/websites/responsive-design/.

What makes responsive design even possible is of course the improvements that have been made in the browsers with both HTML5 and CSS3. The new semantic tags that come as part of HTML5 enable us to bring more meaning to our HTML, which not only helps us as developers but it also enables screen readers to understand the structure of the page. CSS3 has also brought many improvements that allow us to have greater control of how we style our pages.

In the next chapter we will be exploring how we can effectively test our responsive site. We will initially start out by testing our site within our browsers, looking at how our site works with our browser window resized to different widths. We will then start looking at how we can test on different devices, starting with using the simulators and then progressing to looking at how we can test on real devices.

CHAPTER 2

Testing a Responsive Site

Having been introduced to responsive design and some of the new features found in both CSS3 and HTML5 in Chapter 1, this chapter will look at how to test responsive sites as you work on them.

It is likely you have already done some browser testing of your sites to ensure that you support the browsers your users are using. However, when it comes to testing a responsive site, it can be trickier as there is a much larger range of devices that need to be supported.

You need to know how to test your responsive sites in an effective way, and with this in mind this chapter will explain:

1. How to test responsive site in the web browser

2. How to test on a device

Testing Responsive Design in the Browser

During the development life cycle of a web site, it is likely that the first place you turn to test your site is the same browser you would use to surf the web. With responsive design, as long as your browser supports media queries (IE9+, Chrome, Firefox, Opera, Safari), you can continue to do this, turning to the other browsers when you reach the point where you need to cross-browser test.

To get started testing your responsive site, the first step is to load the URL of a responsive site into your browser. For this example, let's look at my blog at `www.jonathanfielding.com` (see Figure 2-1).

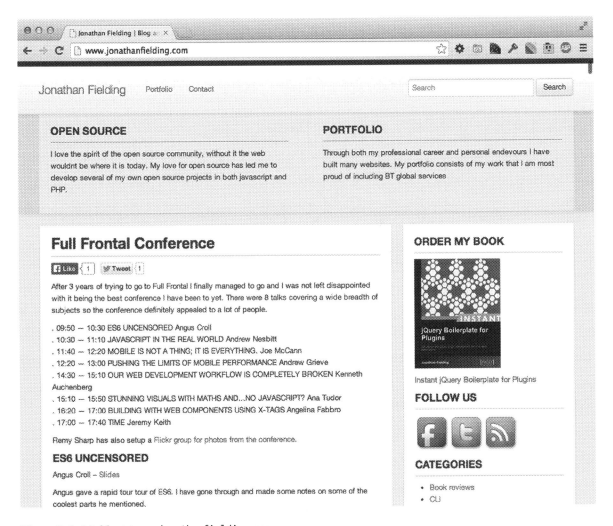

Figure 2-1. *My blog at www.jonathanfielding.com*

Because this site is responsive, the browser can be resized to test the mobile view (see Figure 2-2).

Figure 2-2. *My blog resized on a smaller device*

There it is, my web site in the desktop and mobile views. This simple resizing of the window process is the same in all browsers that support media queries.

Browser Specific Testing Features

I mentioned previously that you don't need to change your browser to test a responsive site. Some browsers provide additional developer tools that aid us in testing a responsive site. Although you don't need to switch browsers for your core development, it is useful to be aware of the different tools that browsers offer so where you feel there is a benefit to your workflow, you can switch browsers to take advantage of the particular tool.

Google Chrome

In Chrome you are able to emulate some of the most popular devices by following these steps:

1. Open the Developer tools, there are two ways in which you can do this, the first is to right-click your page and click Inspect element. The second method is to click on the menu button found to the right of the url field and select Tools ➤ Developer Tools.

2. Click the Show console icon to the right of the Developer Tools or press the Esc key on your keyboard. This will open the Console drawer, as shown in Figure 2-3.

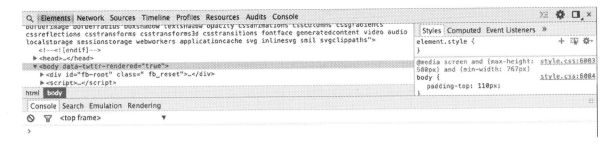

Figure 2-3. *The Console drawer open in Chrome's Inspector*

3. With the Console drawer open, you can now select the Emulation tab. As you can see in Figure 2-4, the Device line indicates it will default to Google Nexus 4.

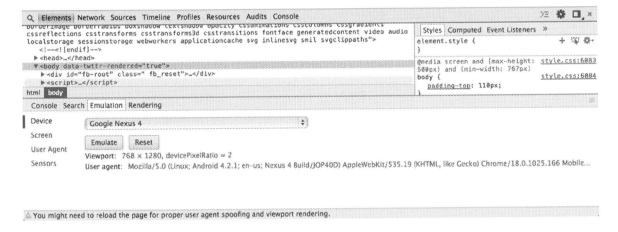

Figure 2-4. *The Emulation tab, preselected with a default device*

4. Using the drop-down menu, you have the option to emulate a specific device. Select the Apple iPhone 4 and click Emulate (see Figure 2-5).

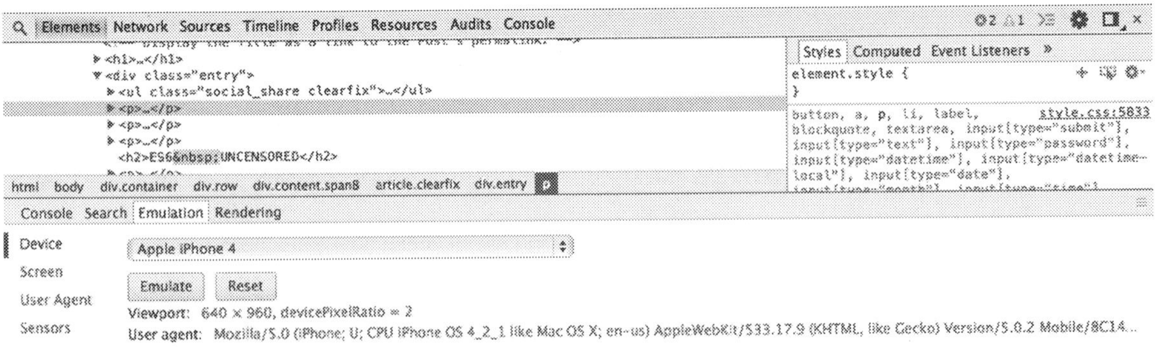

Figure 2-5. *Selecting the iPhone in the Emulation tab*

5.   Having selected the device to emulate, you will see the viewport has now automatically narrowed, and when you move your mouse cursor over the viewport, it will turn into a circle to signify your finger (see Figure 2-6).

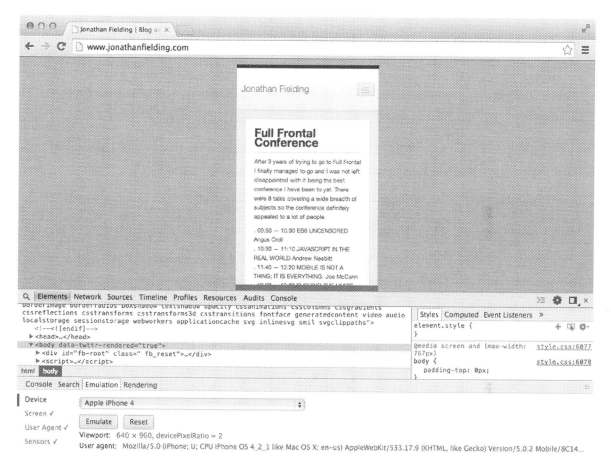

Figure 2-6. *With a device selected and emulation enabled, the browsers viewport changes*

▓ **Note**   Emulation in Chrome is not true device emulation but instead will simply emulate some of the key features of the device. These include the viewport size, device pixel ratio, user agent, and touch events. This means that any browser-specific bugs will not show because you are still testing within Chrome.

Firefox

Firefox takes a slightly different approach to this. Rather than emulating specific devices, you can enter responsive design mode, which allows you to test common viewport widths.

1. Open the developer tools. The easiest way to do this is to right-click the web page and click Inspect element.

2. Enter responsive design view; this is achieved using the icon tab on the far right.

3. Now that you are in responsive design view, you can see the site in a smaller viewport. You have the option to switch to landscape view, enable touch events, or change the viewport size to other commonly used viewport sizes. You can also resize the viewport and then save the new viewport size as a preset. You can see the Firefox interface in Figure 2-7.

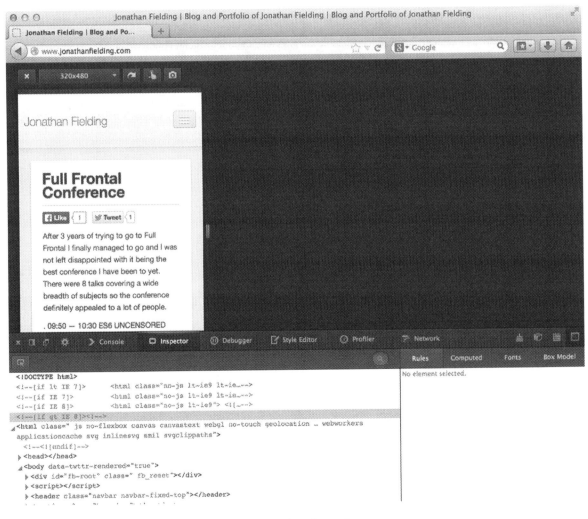

Figure 2-7. *The Firefox inspector with the Responsive Design view active*

Testing on a Device Simulator

So far you have been testing sites by resizing the browser window or using the tools built in to browsers for testing responsive sites. Although this is effective for viewing how media queries are working, it doesn't provide the full picture of how they will affect a site on mobile devices. We will now look at how we can test our project on device simulators and actual devices.

Before you get started with testing on real mobile browsers, you need to determine which browsers you are going to support. This may be different for each web site you build based on your site's target audience, so if you already have some analytics on the browsers your users are using, this is a good start. Additionally, if your web site is targeting a specific country, it is easy to find statistics on what percentage of users use each platform by looking at the StatCounter GlobalStats site (http://gs.statcounter.com/).

There are currently five main smartphone operating systems:

1.   iOS

2.   Android

3.   Windows Mobile

4.   BlackBerry OS

5.   Firefox OS

Having decided on which browsers you want to test on, let's look at how to test on real mobile browsers. There are two options: the first is to use simulators and the second is to get some actual devices to start testing on.

Simulators

Simulators provide a fantastic start to testing your responsive site. They are able to run on your local machine, often with the capability to access all your local files and files on the network you are on.

iOS Simulator

If you are using a Mac you can download the Mac developer toolkit, Xcode, from the Apple App Store. Included with this is the iOS Simulator, which can be used to test responsive sites. To get started with the iOS Simulator, you need to follow the following steps:

1.   Download Xcode from the Apple App Store.

2.   Open Xcode.

3.   Use the menu bar to navigate to Xcode ➤ Open Developer Tool ➤ iOS Simulator.

4.   Open Safari by clicking the Safari icon in the dock.

You can now access any web site, including local sites stored in your Hosts file. If you simply want to test an HTML file, you can even just drag and drop it into the iOS Simulator window.

Unfortunately, it is not possible to test sites in Mobile Safari on Microsoft Windows as Apple does not yet make a version of iOS Simulator compatible with the operating system.

Android

The Android emulator is available as part of the Android SDK (software development kit) on both Windows and Mac.

Mac

1. Download the Android SDK from `http://developer.android.com/sdk`.

2. Extract the zip file to `~/bin/Android` (~is the Unix shorthand for your user directory, so if your username is Jonathan, the full folder path would be `/Users/jonathan/bin/Android`).

3. Open your terminal.

4. Navigate to the SDK, which is located at `~/bin/Android/sdk/tools`. You can navigate to this path using the change directory Unix command `cd`, so the full command you enter into your terminal would be `~/bin/Android/sdk/tools`.

5. Run the SDK Manager by running the `./android` command in your terminal. This will load another application (be aware this application may take a while to load and unfortunately does not give any indication of the status of it loading).

Windows

1. Download Android SDK from `http://developer.android.com/sdk`.

2. Extract the zip file to C:\Program Files\Android.

3. Launch the SDK Manager.exe.

Shared Steps

1. You will now be able to select the SDK version you want to test. In this case I have selected Android 4.3. Then simply click Install, reading and accepting any licenses as required.

2. You then need to select Tools ➤ Manage AVDs on the menu bar. Then click the New button to create a new Android Virtual Device.

3. You will now need to enter the settings for your Simulator (see Figure 2-8).

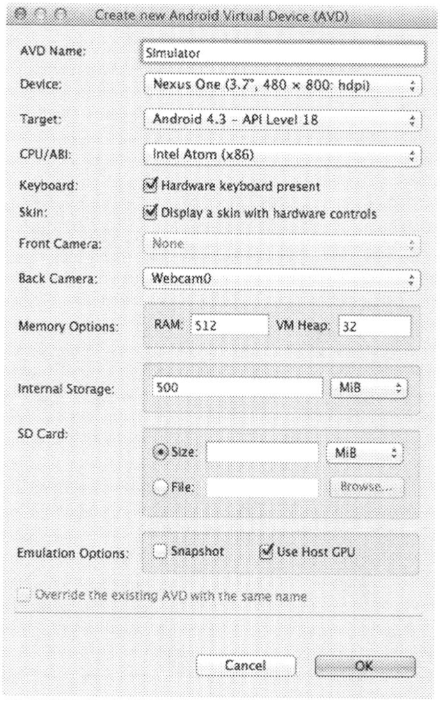

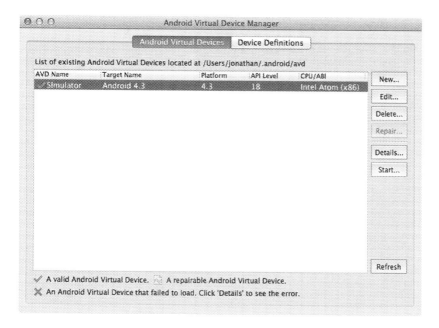

Figure 2-8. *The create a Simulator prompt allows you to configure your simulator*

4. You can now select your simulator and click Start (see Figure 2-9).

Figure 2-9. *Android Virtual Device Manager lists the available Simulators*

5. With the Android emulator installed, you can now simply use the emulator as you would with a normal Android device (see Figure 2-10).

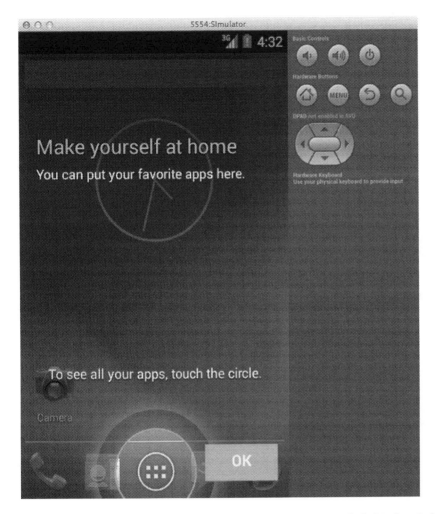

Figure 2-10. *The Android Simulator, with the hardware buttons included in the window*

Firefox OS Simulator

The Firefox OS Simulator runs as an add on for Firefox, and as of Firefox 26.0 it is really simple to install.

1. Launch Firefox and open the URL about:app-manager. You will be presented with the built-in App Manager, as shown in Figure 2-11.

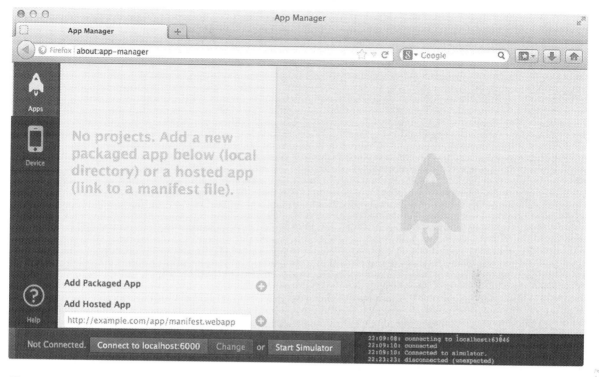

Figure 2-11. *The Firefox App Manager tool can be used to launch a Firefox OS Simulator*

2. You can now click Start Simulator. Because there is no simulator installed, you will be given the option to install the simulator, so click Install Simulator to continue, as shown in Figure 2-12.

Figure 2-12. *The App Manager allows you to install the simulator if it is not already installed*

3. You will now be taken to a web page to install a simulator, simply follow the instructions to install the latest version.

4. Once installed, go back to about:app-manager and refresh the page. Click Start Simulator and then select the version of the simulator you wish to start. If it still says Install Simulator, you should try to install a different version (see Figure 2-13).

Figure 2-13. *The option to choose from different versions of the Simulator to install*

5. After a short loading time, you will find yourself at the Firefox OS home screen, where you can select the web browser. The OS Simulator is shown in Figure 2-14.

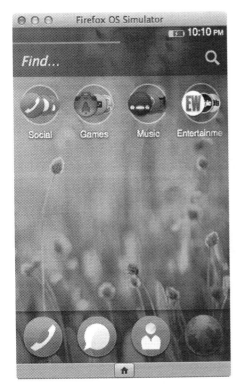

Figure 2-14. *Firefox OS Simulator home screen, with the browser found in the bottom right-hand corner*

6. Upon loading the browser, you can enter your web site URL and start testing your site. The browser is shown in Figure 2-15.

Figure 2-15. *Firefox running on the Firefox OS Simulator*

BlackBerry OS Simulator

BlackBerry Limited provides emulators for BlackBerry OS that run on both Windows and Mac, and they are really simple to install. However, you will need to also install VMware Player on Windows or VMware Fusion on Mac if you do not already have these applications, which can be found at www.vmware.com.

1. Download the emulator at http://uk.blackberry.com/sites/developers/resources/simulators.html.

2. Run the Installer.

3. Run the Virtual Machine in VMware, as shown in Figure 2-16.

Figure 2-16. *BlackBerry simulator running in VMware*

Windows Phone Simulator

The Windows Phone Simulator is part of the Windows Phone SDK, which is currently only available for Windows 8+. Unfortunately, running the Windows Phone Simulator also has specific hardware requirements, which can be found at `msdn.microsoft.com/en-us/library/windowsphone/develop/ff626524(v=vs.105).aspx`.

1. Download the Windows Phone SDK from `http://dev.windowsphone.com/en-us/downloadsdk`.

2. Run the SDK installer (this requires 6.5GB of hard drive space).

3. Upon completion of the installation, you will be told you need a license for Visual Studio, so you can either cancel and use the trial or register for a free license at `http://www.visualstudio.com/en-US/products/visual-studio-express-vs`.

4. Check for available updates to the SDK.

5. Open the command line (cmd) by right-clicking and clicking Run as administrator.

6. Run the command:

    ```
    "C:\Program Files (x86)\Microsoft XDE\8.0\XDE.exe" /vhd "C:\Program Files (x86)\Microsoft
    SDKs\Windows Phone\v8.0\Emulation\Images\Flash.vhd" /name WP8SDK
    ```

7. With the emulator now open, you should now be able to run Internet Explorer in the
    Simulator, as shown in Figure 2-17.

Figure 2-17. *Internet Explorer running on Windows Phone Simulator*

8. To make opening the simulator easier in the future, create a .bat file with the command.

Physical Devices

So far I have focused on how to test a site on development machines by both testing a site in a browsers and using the phone simulators. Although testing a site these ways can be very practical and allows you to quickly do initial tests, they don't provide a true reflection of how the site will work on real devices.

One of the reasons for this is that on development machines you are only simulating the different input methods the device uses using a keyboard and mouse. By testing on real devices, you are able to test using the input methods users would be using. Without testing a site on a physical device, you might not notice issues with the usability. Common issues you might not notice would be buttons being too small to tap or text that is unreadable on the small display.

With this in mind, it is really important to test responsive sites on as many devices to which you have access. However, if you are just starting your device collection, it can be really difficult to choose which devices to purchase, especially if you have a limited budget. In this situation, it makes sense to take a look at the devices your users are using and, when selecting the devices you need, ensure you cover your bases. Devices should cover the most popular operating systems as a minimum, with a mixture of high end and low end if possible.

Debugging Web Sites on Devices

When testing web sites across a variety of different devices, you need to be able to debug any issues that users might face. The way to do this debugging is dependent on the operating system of the device.

Debugging Sites on iOS

With the release of iOS6, Apple introduced a remote debugging feature to iOS that enables developers to connect the Mac Safari Web Inspector to the site open in Mobile Safari. To enable this, you need to open the iOS Settings ➤ Safari settings ➤ Advanced settings and turn the Web Inspector on. In Figure 2-18 you can see the Web Inspector setting enabled.

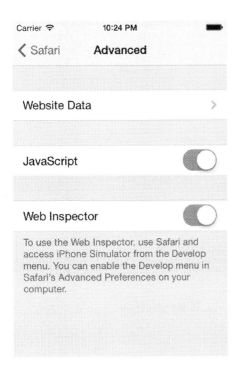

Figure 2-18. *Advanced settings for iOS Safari with Web Inspector enabled*

You also need to ensure that the Develop menu item is enabled on your Mac Safari. To do this, simply open Safari and check if the Develop item appears on the top menu. If this is not visible, you will need to open the Safari preferences under the Advanced tab. To enable the Develop menu, simply check the check box Show Develop menu in menu bar, as shown in Figure 2-19.

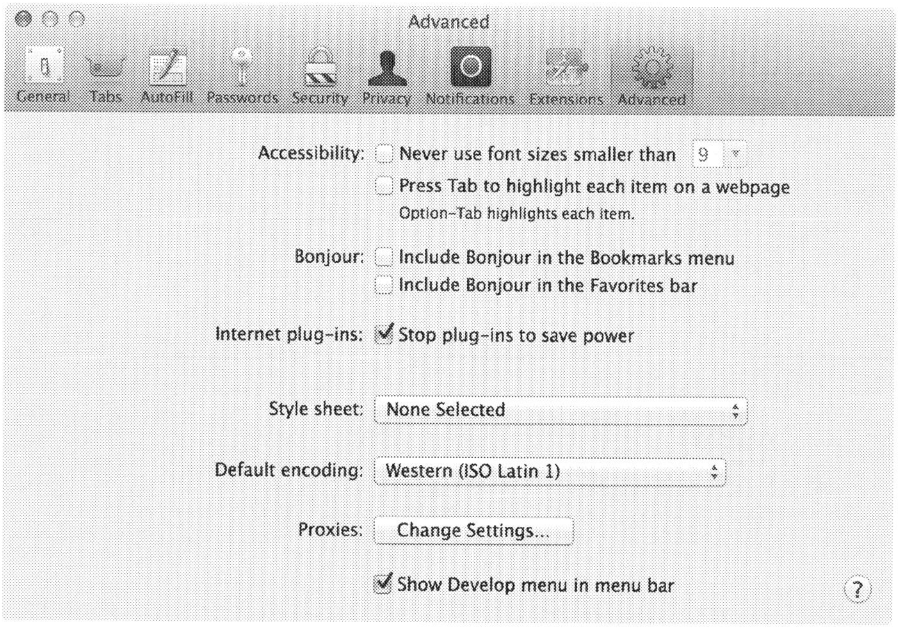

Figure 2-19. Safari preferences with Develop menu enabled

With both Mac Safari and the iOS device now set up, you can start to connect the two together so you can debug your site. To do this, first plug your device into your computer using the USB cable. After doing this, you can open your site in Mobile Safari. To then bring up the Inspector on your Mac, simply open the Develop menu where your device will show up. Upon selecting your device, you will then be presented a list of pages you can choose to debug, as illustrated in Figure 2-20.

Figure 2-20. *The Develop menu in Safari*

Upon selecting the site you want to debug, the Safari Inspector panel will open, giving you full access to the site code. From here debugging is the same as if you were debugging on desktop Safari, highlighting an element in the source code will highlight the corresponding element on the iOS device. The Safari Inspector panel is illustrated in Figure 2-21.

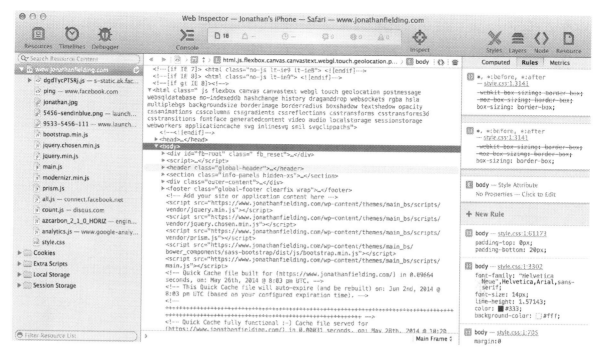

Figure 2-21. *Safari Inspector panel*

Debugging Sites on Android

Similar to iOS, you can debug web sites running in Chrome on Android from your development machines.

The first step is to configure your Android device so it allows remote debugging. The way you do this is dependent on the version of Android your device is running.

For Android 4.2 or newer, go to Settings ➤ About phone and tap the build number seven times (sounds a bit like the Konami code of old!), then return to the previous screen. Then navigate to the previous screen where the new menu option, Developer options, will have appeared. Under Debugging you can now enable USB debugging. The setting is highlighted in Figure 2-22.

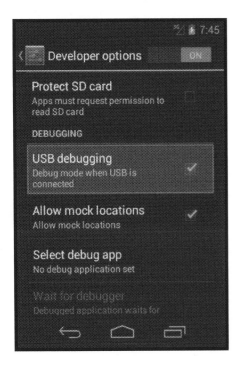

Figure 2-22. *The Android Developer options with USB debugging enabled*

For Android 4.0 or 4.1, go to Settings ➤ Developer Options. Under Debugging, you can now enable USB debugging. The setting is highlighted in Figure 2-22.

If you are using Windows, at this stage you will need to install the USB device drivers for connecting the Android device. These are available to download at http://developer.android.com/tools/extras/oem-usb.html.

It is at this point you need to change a setting in Chrome to enable remote debugging support. To do this, enter the URL about:inspect into your web browser. This will show you the settings page for the Chrome DevTools. You can then enable device discovery by checking the check box Discover USB devices, as shown in Figure 2-23.

Remote Debugging Chrom
Inspect with Chrome Deve
chrome://inspect/#devices
DevTools
Devices
Devices
Discover USB devices
Port forwarding...
Pages
sdk #EMULATOR-5554
Extensions
Apps
Shared workers
Other

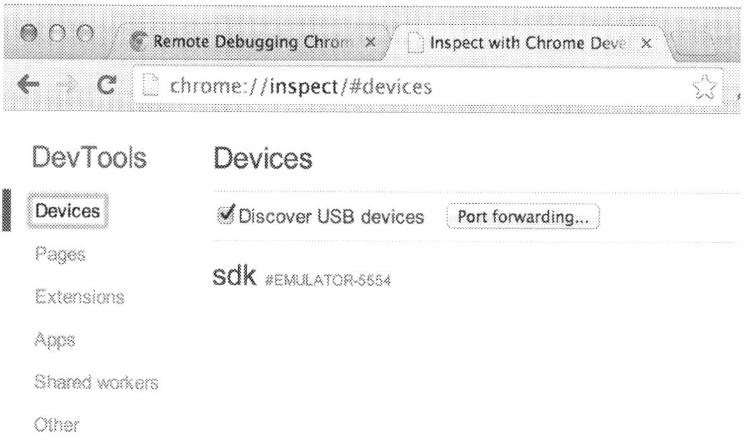

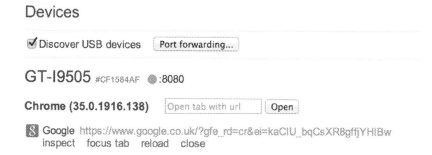

Figure 2-23. *Enable device discovery in Chrome*

You are now at the stage where you can connect your device by USB. When connecting, you may see an alert on the device requesting permission for USB debugging. To avoid this in future, you can check the Always allow from this computer check box before clicking OK.

You can now open your site in Chrome on your device. This will then appear on the `chrome://inspect` page underneath the device you have plugged in to your computer. This is illustrated in Figure 2-24.

Devices
Discover USB devices
Port forwarding...
GT-I9505 #CF1584AF :8080
Chrome (35.0.1916.138)
Open tab with url
Open
Google https://www.google.co.uk/?gfe_rd=cr&ei=kaCIU_bqCsXR8gffjYHIBw
inspect focus tab reload close

Figure 2-24. *Choose a tab on your device you want to inspect*

With a page loaded on your device, you can now click the Inspect link below the name of the site, which will open the Inspector. This is the normal Chrome Inspector you used to inspect web sites on your desktop (as shown in Figure 2-25). In addition all the developer tool plug-ins you have installed on your browser can also be used to debug your site.

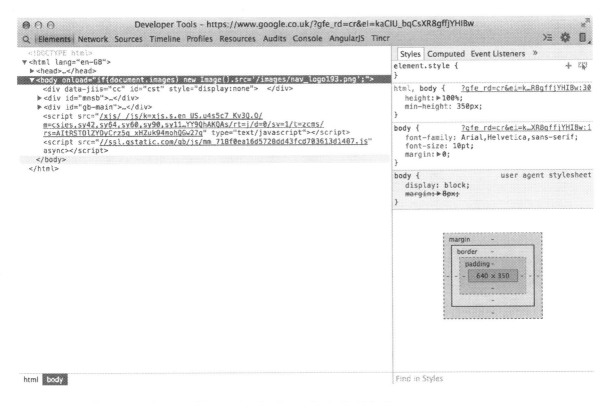

Figure 2-25. *Chrome Developer Tools inspecting the site on the Android device*

Open Device Labs

If you don't have the budget to buy any devices of your own, you can look if there are any Open Device Labs (http://opendevicelab.com/) near where you work or live. Open Device Labs is a community movement that establishes pools of devices that anyone can go and test on. They typically have a range of different devices, which will enable you to get a good picture of how your site works across them.

Online Solutions

You might be in the situation where you are not able to get your hands on devices and do not live close to an Open Device Lab. In this case there are also online solutions that will allow you to test across various devices.

The first of these online solutions is Perfecto Mobile (www.perfectomobile.com/). Perfecto Mobile is not a simulator but instead you are remotely controlling real devices. What this means is that you get a truer likeness of what the users of your site will experience when using your site.

A second solution is BrowserStack (www.browserstack.com), which allows you to test your web site across a wide number of different browsers. In addition to allowing you to test and debug your responsive site, BrowserStack also allows you to quickly generate screenshots of your phone across different browsers and devices. It is also worth mentioning that you do not need to make your site publically available to use BrowserStack, because it installs a browser plug-in that will proxy your local sites through to their servers securely.

Summary

Testing web sites is critical to building sites that work across a wide variety of different devices. Therefore, ensuring that you have a strategy in place as to how you will test your site is very important.

When planning the strategy you will use when testing your site you should ensure you take into account both the browsers your users are using and the devices they are using them upon.

This chapter explored how to test across these different platforms, including how you can initially test within your browsers and then move on to testing on real devices or simulators. Your strategy should take both into account, because you can't simply expect web sites to work on real devices if you have only tested on desktop browsers. Third-party tools like Perfecto Mobile and BrowserStack can be valuable parts of this strategy because they give you greater access to extra browsers you can test on.

In the bigger picture of web development, you need to ensure that you give adequate time to testing your site. Testing is not something you can simply do at the end of the process but instead should be an integral part of how you work, and you should be able to test a particular feature as it is implemented.

Thorough testing enables you to ensure that things don't get missed and that you have seen the different experiences the user gets from device to device.

In the next chapter, we will explore the power of media queries, and their importance to responsive design. You will gain a comprehensive understanding of not only what media queries are, but also the flexibility that they give you in building a site that can respond to the users browser environment.

CHAPTER 3

The Power of Media Queries

Chapter 1 introduced CSS3 with one glaring omission: media queries was not discussed. And for good reason; media queries are such a big area of responsive development they deserve their own chapter.

Media queries are core to responsive design because they allow developers to target specific CSS styles based on the capabilities of the device. The most common capability to target is the viewport width; however, there is much more to media queries than this, and I will explain these capabilities in this chapter.

This chapter will cover:

- An introduction to media queries
- Using media queries in CSS
- Mobile first vs. desktop first
- Targeting high pixel density displays

An Introduction to Media Queries

Media queries form the foundation of responsive design, allowing you to change the look and feel of the web site based on a query you have specified. A media query can be split into two types of components: media types and media expressions.

To start this introduction to media queries, let's look at media types, which were introduced as part of the CSS2.1 specification.

Media Types

Prior to the new CSS3 draft specification, CSS2.1 introduced media types, which allow developers to add media-dependent style sheets targeted toward different types of devices. There are ten different media types in total, three of which you are most likely to already have encountered: all, screen, and print.

If you have encountered media types in the past, it is likely you have seen them used to enable or disable style sheets based on a device type. An example of this is:

```
<link rel="stylesheet" type="text/css" href="all.css"    media="all" />
<link rel="stylesheet" type="text/css" href="screen.css" media="screen" />
<link rel="stylesheet" type="text/css" href="print.css"  media="print" />
```

In addition to screen and print style sheets, there are many other media types that enable support for a wide variety of other devices:

1. *all*: all devices

2. *aural*: speech synthesizers

3. *braille*: braille tactile feedback devices

4. *embossed*: paged braille printers

5. *handheld*: small or handheld devices

6. *print*: printers

7. *projection*: projected presentations, like projectors and projected slides

8. *screen*: computer screens

9. *tty*: media using a fixed-pitch character grid, like teletypes and terminals

10. *tv*: television-type devices

Aside from being able to specify a different style sheet for each media type, it is also possible to include these styles in your style sheet by using the following syntax:

```
@media print {
        /* print styles go here */
}
```

There are a couple of benefits from including the different media type queries within your main style sheet:

1. It reduces the number of HTTP requests. An increase in the number of HTTP requests can lead to reduced performance of loading a site.

2. Separate style sheets can increase the time that the page is blocked from rendering, as most browsers will wait until all the individual style sheets are downloaded before they will render the content.

An experiment by Stoyan Stefanov found that not only do browsers download the print style sheet, most browsers also wait for it to download before rendering (even though its not strictly needed to show the page to the user). This includes mobile browsers where users are unlikely to print.[1] Therefore, the benefit here is that you are reducing this blocking by reducing the number of style sheets the browser has to load.

When applying media types, consider that browsers will only declare one media type at any given time. This means that if the browser implements the handheld media type, then your styles for the screen media type will not be applied despite the assumption that a handheld device has a screen.

With media types, you are dependent on the browser to implement the media type you expect for the device. A good example of where browser vendors have not always implemented media types as expected is in the case of browsers on a television. Although there are some browsers that correctly support the television media type (including Opera), some television browsers incorrectly apply both tv and screen media types simultaneously. This means that if you have targeted styles specific to your desktop experience using a screen media type, they could be unexpectedly applied on a television, which would be incorrect according to the specification that states:

> *A user agent can only support one media type when rendering a document.*[2]

---

[1] See `http://www.phpied.com/5-years-later-print-css-still-sucks/`.
[2] W3C Media Types Spec, `http://www.w3.org/TR/CSS2/media.html`.

Media Queries

Media queries were added in CSS3 as an extension of media types with the aim of giving developers more control over how their web sites are displayed on different browsers and devices. The idea is that rather than having to build and maintain multiple versions of each page for different devices, you can instead adapt a single web site in your CSS based on the attributes, properties, or characteristics of the device.

Unlike media types that simply tell you the type of the device, media queries add a level of logic to CSS that says if a condition is met, then the styles should be applied, otherwise they should be ignored. This means that rather than simply targeting a device by type, you can now target the individual characteristics of the device.

What Can Media Queries Test for?

There are a variety of different types of query for which a media query can test. These are discussed in the sections that follow.

width | min-width | max-width

The width query allows you to test against the width of the browsers viewport. This enables you to target styles at specific browser widths. Not only are you able to test against a set width, but you are also able to target either the minimum width or maximum width of the browser viewport. This means you can use this query to match a wide variety of different device widths. The width media expression is one of the most used media expressions for adapting sites to be responsive.

height | min-height | max-height

The height query allows you to test against the height of the browsers viewport. Similar to the width query, you are able to target an exact height, minimum height, or maximum height. Although the height query is used less often than the width query, the height query can be especially useful where you want to ensure specific content is viewable (or not viewable) to your users when the page first loads, as you can use it to adjust the height of your content to best suit the height of the viewport.

device-width | min-device-width | max-device-width

The device-width query allows you to test against the width of the device. You are able to target either an exact width, minimum width, or maximum width. The difference between width and device-width is that width is related to the width of the browser, whereas device-width is related to the width of the screen of the device. Although there are some use cases for using device-width, the problem is that if the user resizes the browser on a desktop, the site wouldn't resize to fit. Additionally, if you are using the viewport meta tag and setting width to be equal to device-width, you should just use the width query.

device-height | min-device-height | max-device-height

The device-height query allows you to test against the height of the device. You are able to target an exact height, minimum height, or maximum height. The difference between device-height and height is that device-height relates to the height of the device's screen, whereas height relates to the height of the viewport. This distinction is important on devices where you are able to resize the browser window.

aspect-ratio | min-aspect-ratio | max-aspect-ratio

The aspect-ratio query allows you to test against the aspect ratio of the device's viewport. The aspect ratio of a device is the ratio between the length of the longer side of the device vs. the length of the shorter side of the device. The aspect-ratio query can be especially useful when you want to target assets to match a device's aspect ratio, including showing video, which is best optimized to the user's device.

device-aspect-ratio | min-device-aspect-ratio | max-device-aspect-ratio

The device-aspect-ratio query allows you to test against the aspect ratio of the device. The difference between device-aspect-ratio and aspect-ratio is that device-aspect-ratio relates to the aspect ratio of the device's screen, whereas aspect-ratio relates to the aspect ratio of the viewport. This distinction is important on devices where you are able to resize the browser window, as the aspect-ratio is as fluid as the size of the viewport, whereas the value for device-aspect-ratio will not change.

color | min-color | max-color

The color query allows you to test against the color capabilities of the device based on the numbers of bits per color components.

color-index | min-color-index | max-color-index

The color-index query allows you to test against the number of colors a device supports, and the value must be an integer and cannot be negative.

monochrome | min-monochrome | max-monochrome

The monochrome query allows you to test against the bits per pixel on a monochrome device, which uses 1 for true and 0 for false.

resolution | min-resolution | max-resolution

The resolution query allows you to test against the pixel density of the device. The resolution query accepts three different types of values: dpi (dots per CSS inch), dpcm (dots per CSS centimeter), and dppx (dots per pixel). The preferred option is to use dppx, which was a more recent addition to the specification than both dpcm and dpi. The benefit of dppx over its predecessors is that it is directly related to pixel density of the screen so it is much easier for developers to understand.

scan

The scan query allows you to test against the scanning process of a device. This is very specific to televisions, which can have progressive or interlace scanning. The difference between these is that a *progressive* display draws all the lines on the display at once, and an *interlace* display draws all the odd lines, then draw the even lines, to trick the eyes into thinking they are seeing all the lines at once.

grid

The grid query allows you to test whether the device is a grid device or a bitmap device, with two possible values. If the value is set to 1, the query will enable the CSS if the device's display is grid based, an example being a phone display with only one fixed font. Alternatively, you can check for all other devices by setting the value to 0.

orientation

The orientation query allows you to test whether the device is landscape or portrait and apply your CSS appropriately. A typical use case for the orientation query is where you might want to switch between a single column in portrait to two columns on landscape.

░ **Note** The types of queries that you can use are dependent on the media type of the device. The reason that not all media types support all the queries is that it doesn't always make sense, for example, if the user is using an aural device, queries that refer to the viewport or the screen such as width and device width wouldn't make sense.

Syntax of a Media Query

Now that you have familiarized yourself with media types and media queries and their uses, let's explore the methodology of writing them.

A media query is made up of at least the media type and can additionally have one or more media expressions, which return either true or false. For the CSS to be applied, the media type should match the device the page is loaded on and all the media expressions must return true. The media queries can be as specific or ambiguous as you want, allowing you to ensure your CSS is applied exactly in the way you expect. The best way to look at the syntax of writing media queries is to dive into some examples.

The first example looks at how you can add CSS to devices with a small viewport; typically a mobile phone. If you want to only enable your CSS on a small viewport, you need to add a rule that defines an upper limit for the width of the viewport the CSS will be applied to. In this case, you would add a max-width rule and set the value to 767px. A simple example of this would be:

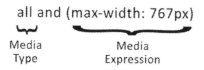

In this example, the media type is set to all, which means that it applies to all the media types. There is then a media expression with max-width set to 767px, because you want to target extra small devices (e.g., mobile phones), which in this case is defined as less than 767px. The reasoning here is that many of the devices that might be classified as small devices, such as the iPad, have a minimum width of 768px. The logic behind this media query says that for all devices, if the width of the viewport is less than or equal to 767px, the CSS styles are applied.

If you only wanted to apply the CSS to screen devices, you could change the media type used in the media query to screen. This change is reflected in this updated example:

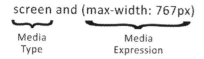

The logic to this media query is similar to that of the previous example, however, the key difference is that you have changed the media type to screen. The logic, therefore, is that for all devices of the type screen, if the width of the viewport is less than or equal to 767px, then the CSS is active.

The "Not" Logical Operator

If you wanted to apply CSS to all media types other than screen, you can take advantage of the not logical operator. The not logical operator in media queries tells the browser to reverse the results of the expression. With the screen example, you can simply add the not logical operator to the beginning of the expression:

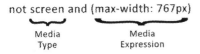

So for this example, the logic is that if the browser is not a screen device with a width less than or equal to 767px, then the style sheet will be activated.

The "Only" Logical Operator

The only logical operator is used to prevent an older browser that does not support media expressions from trying to process the media query. Without the only operator, the older browser will read the media type, however, it will not understand the media expressions; therefore, the media expressions are ignored and the styles are applied.

The reason for this behavior is that the media attribute was originally used for media types prior to being used for media queries. Although the CSS specification has extended to include media queries in CSS3, you still need to support older browsers that use the older specification. A media query using the only logical operator simply prepends the media type operator with only. This example updates the earlier media query for testing for extra small devices:

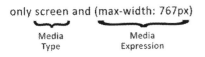

The logic to the media query in this example is exactly the same as before, however, you have now added the only logical operator, which will prevent the styles wrapped in this media query from being applied incorrectly in older browsers.

Using Multiple Expressions

One of the things that makes media queries really powerful is the ability to use multiple media expressions together. What this means is if you want to target small devices, like tablets, without affecting the extra small devices, you can do so, using two media expressions rather than one.

To chain the expressions, you need to use the and keyword in between the media expressions. This example uses a min-width of 768px and a max-width of 1023px to determine whether the device is a small device:

The logic for this media query is that if the media type is screen, the viewport is equal to or greater than 768px, and is less than or equal to 1023px, then the style sheet will be activated.

Chaining Media Queries

So far the examples have simply been using individual media queries; however, by chaining the media queries and allowing the CSS to be applied in multiple circumstances, you create the benefit of CSS being applied when any of the queries return true. Each media query can have its own media type and its own media expressions, meaning that the separate media queries can target different media features, types, and states. To use multiple media queries, simply separate them by adding a comma in between each query and then each of queries will be individually assessed to see if they are true, as shown in this example:

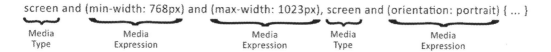

In this example, there are two media queries. The first media query will be true if the width of the browser is equal to or greater than 768px and is less than or equal to 1023px. The second media query will be true if the orientation of the device is portrait. Now if either of these two media queries is true, then the styles will be activated.

A common example of where you might want to use multiple media queries is to target a feature that is implemented differently in different browsers. An example of this is when you are using the min-resolution expression, as shown in this code:

```
@media only screen and ( -webkit-min-device-pixel-ratio: 2 ),
only screen and ( -o-min-device-pixel-ratio: 2/1 ),
only screen and ( min--moz-device-pixel-ratio: 2 ),
only screen and ( min-device-pixel-ratio: 2 ),
only screen and ( min-resolution: 192dpi ),
only screen and ( min-resolution: 2dppx ) {

  /* High resolution styles here */

}
```

In the early days of CSS3 media queries, there was the need to implement a way to target high pixel density devices, which lead to WebKit implementing the device-pixel-ratio expression under their vendor prefix. As the specification has matured, the correct implementation is to use a "resolution" expression; however, to support these older browsers, you need to use multiple media queries.

Using Media Queries in CSS

Now that you have explored the syntax of writing media queries, it is time to look at how you can apply them to a page. The three methods are:

1. Separate style sheets for each media query

2. Use @import in the main CSS file to load CSS files conditionally

3. Use the media queries inside CSS file

Separate Style Sheets

Typically when using screen or print style sheets in the past, there was a style sheet for each with the rules of which to apply to which media type. Similarly, you can do this with media queries to enable and disable a style sheet conditionally. To do this you can use the media attribute on the link tag used to include the style sheet. This is the same attribute you may have previously used to add a media type rule to your style sheet. When adding the rule, simply drop it into the media attribute, as shown in this example:

```
<link rel="stylesheet" media="screen and (min-width: 768px) and (max-width: 1023px)
" href="tablet.css" />
```

In this example the media query is taken for checking whether the user is on a small device and this is simply added to the media attribute.

The benefit of using separate style sheets is that it allows you to compartmentalize code easier. Please bear in mind that all style sheets in a media query are downloaded to the user's device and are simply not active if unneeded. This means that by using separate style sheets you are increasing the number of HTTP requests made to the server.

Use @import

If you want to use separate style sheets for each media query but do not want to have to define them in the HTML, you can use the CSS @import syntax with a media query applied. The @import syntax can be broken down into three parts:

1. The @import declaration

2. The URL to CSS file to include

3. One or more media queries

Putting this together, you end up with the following:

```
@import url("tablet.css") screen and (min-width: 768px) and (max-width: 1023px);
```

In this example you have taken the media query for checking whether the user is on a small device and simply added it to an @import syntax used to load the `tablet.css` file.

Similarly to using separate style sheets linked to the page in your <head> tag, style sheets loaded via @import increase the number of HTTP requests. However, in addition to this, the @import can prevent style sheets from being downloaded concurrently.

Using Media Queries in CSS

Rather than separate the CSS into separate style sheets, you can define the media queries within the site's style sheets. This allows you to define new styles and apply overrides to existing styles for when the condition is true, taking advantage of the cascading nature of CSS.

To write a media query in the CSS document, you can use the @media syntax. A breakdown of how to use this syntax is:

1. The @media declaration

2. One or more media expressions

An example of the @media syntax would therefore be:

```
@media only screen and (min-width: 768px) and (max-width: 1023px){
        /* Your styles. */
}
```

Although this is only a simple example, it shows you how easy it is to include a media query within the CSS files. Unlike both @import and separate files added to your <head>, using media queries within the main CSS document has the same benefits as including your media types within the main CSS document, these being reduced HTTP requests and reduced blocking.

Mobile First vs. Desktop First

Developers often will code in the way they are most comfortable with—humans are creatures of habit, after all, and despite what some believe, developers are human. Therefore, when responsive web design came along, the most common approach was to build your desktop site first and then adapt it for mobile applications using media queries; after all the majority of their users were still coming from desktop uses and developing for desktop is what developers were used to.

This kind of methodology is called *graceful degradation*, the idea being that you should create the best possible experience first and then start taking account for degradation as the capabilities of the browser decline. For a responsive site, this meant that as the viewport was shrunk, the web site would scale back, removing both content and features.

There is, however, another methodology that better suits responsive design called *progressive enhancement*. Progressive enhancement isn't a new idea; it was first suggested by Steven Champeon in 2003 at the South by Southwest Interactive conference in Austin. In a follow-up article written for Webmonkey, Steven said:

> *Instead of trying to mix presentation into markup that lowest common denominator browsers can't handle anyway, strip it out. Make sure only capable browsers even request it in the first place. The more we know about what browser supports what, the better off we are when it comes down to setting up our markup and styles.*[3]

What Steven was saying was to build your sites for the browser with the least capabilities and then progressively improve the site by adding new features and content. If you want to apply this methodology to a responsive site, you should be looking to build the mobile site first. You can then enhance the sites as the capabilities of the device improve. This kind of progressive enhancement is called *mobile-first responsive design*.

When graceful degradation is compared with progressive enhancement, it appears at first that they are simply opposite sides of the same coin. With graceful degradation, we simply start by building the best possible site and then degrade the experience, and with progressive enhancement we start by building the experience for the least capable browser and then progressively enhance the experience for the desktop.

In reality, when we build sites that are desktop first, we often add lots of features to the web sites. These might provide a great user experience for the desktop users, however, often there are features that do not scale well. The problem then becomes how to get that part of the site to work on mobile applications. This is very much the point that Luke Wroblewski made on his blog in 2009:

> *Mobile devices require software development teams to focus on only the most important data and actions in an application. There simply isn't room in a 320 by 480 pixel screen for extraneous, unnecessary elements. You have to prioritize. So when a team designs mobile first, the end result is an experience focused on the key tasks users want to accomplish without the extraneous detours and general interface debris that litter today's desktop-accessed Web sites. That's good user experience and good for business.*[4]

---

[3]Steven Champeon, Webmonkey. http://www.hesketh.com/thought-leadership/our-publications/progressive-enhancement-and-future-web-design.
[4]Luke Wroblewski, http://www.lukew.com/ff/entry.asp?933= November 3, 2009.

What he was saying is that by focusing on mobile first, we can build better experiences for our users. We don't clutter our interfaces with unnecessary features as we have to prioritize the features that matter to the users. Mobile uses also enable us to add additional features, through the way in which they extend the capabilities of the browser, for example, precise geolocation information and touch events. This means that while mobile browsers may be limited in some ways, they offer extra features of which we can easily take advantage.

When we are happy with our mobile build, we can then proceed to extend the viewport and progressively enhance the site, using techniques such as feature detection to allow us to target features at a browser that support them.

Looking at Building a Site Mobile First

Now that you know about the benefits of building responsive sites mobile first and the methodology behind this, let's look at building a mobile-first site.

To get started with mobile first, you need to put together some basic HTML. For this example you will type some HTML that could be used for a blog post, consisting of a header, the article, and a list of related posts, this is shown in Listing 3-1.

Listing 3-1. HTML for our mobile first example

```
<!DOCTYPE html>
<html>
<head>
        <title>Mobile First</title>
        <meta name="viewport" content="width=device-width">
        <link rel="stylesheet" type="text/css" href="mobile-first.css">
</head>
<body>
        <header>
                <h1>Blog</h1>
        </header>
        <div class="content" role="main">
                <article>
                        <h2>Article title</h2>
                        <p>02/12/2013</p>
                        <p>Praesent commodo cursus magna, vel scelerisque nisl consectetur et. Cras
                        justo odio, dapibus ac facilisis in, egestas eget quam. Vivamus sagittis lacus
                        vel augue laoreet rutrum faucibus dolor auctor. Etiam porta sem malesuada
                        magna mollis euismod. Cras mattis consectetur purus sit amet fermentum. Duis
                        mollis, est non commodo luctus, nisi erat porttitor ligula, eget lacinia odio
                        sem nec elit. Vestibulum id ligula porta felis euismod semper.</p>
                </article>
                <aside>
                        <h2>Related Articles</h2>
                        <nav>
                                <ul>
                                        <li><a href="#">Article item 1</a></li>
                                        <li><a href="#">Article item 2</a></li>
                                        <li><a href="#">Article item 3</a></li>
                                </ul>
                        </nav>
                </aside>
        </div>
</body>
</html>
```

If you load this into your browser, you get a simple single-column page without any styles, as shown in Figure 3-1.

Blog

Article title

02/12/2013

Praesent commodo cursus magna, vel scelerisque nisl consectetur et. Cras justo odio, dapibus ac facilisis in, egestas eget quam. Vivamus sagittis lacus vel augue laoreet rutrum faucibus dolor auctor. Etiam porta sem malesuada magna mollis euismod. Cras mattis consectetur purus sit amet fermentum. Duis mollis, est non commodo luctus, nisi erat porttitor ligula, eget lacinia odio sem nec elit. Vestibulum id ligula porta felis euismod semper.

Related Articles

- Article item 1
- Article item 2
- Article item 3

Figure 3-1. *Our mobile first example site before we have applied any styles*

Because you are building mobile first, you will concentrate on building the main CSS to style the page first. You will be applying the following styles:

1. `body`: Both margin and padding set to 0px, the font size set to 14px, and the line height set to 18px

2. `header`: Add background color and padding

3. `h1`: Set the color to white

4. `aside` and `article`: add margin of 20px to both the left and right

5. `article`: add a border to separate the article from the related articles

After putting this together, it will look along the lines of the code I put together for Listing 3-2.

Listing 3-2. The base CSS for our example mobile first site

```
body{
    margin: 0;
    padding: 0;
    font-size: 14px;
    line-height: 18px;
}
```

```
header{
        background: #304480;
        padding: 10px 20px;
}

h1{
        color: #fff;
}

article, aside{
        margin: 0 20px;
}

article{
        border-bottom: 1px solid #304480;
}
```

If you take a look at the site with these additional styles applied, you will see that you have a site that works quite well on our extra small devices, as shown in Figure 3-2.

Figure 3-2. The site, as it looks on browsers with a extra small viewport

If you simply stretch your browser to the widths of your screen, however, the site doesn't look so good, as shown in Figure 3-3.

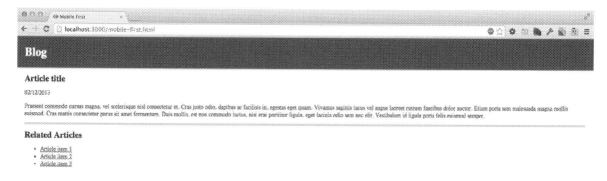

Figure 3-3. *Our mobile first site, shown on a larger viewport*

A single column site works well on mobile, however, on larger viewports, it makes sense to show the related articles list as a sidebar and to limit the width of the site.

As you increase the viewport of the site from the extra small device view, you reach the width of the small devices, an example of which is a tablet. For this example you will take the minimum width of an iPad, which is 768px, as a basis for the small device view and use it for the media query. The media query will therefore target a min-width of 768px, as shown in Listing 3-3.

Listing 3-3. Our media query targetting our small devices

```
@media screen and (min-width: 768px){
        header, .content{
                width: 728px;
                margin: 0 auto;
                padding: 10px 20px;
        }

        article, aside{
                float: left;
                margin: 0px;
        }

        article{
                width: 80%;
                border-bottom: 0px;
        }

        aside{
                width: 20%;
        }
}
```

As you have already done all of the shifting around to make the site work on a tablet, you simply need to increase the width of the page to take advantage of larger viewports, the code for which is shown in Listing 3-4.

Listing 3-4. Our media query targeting our larger viewports

```
@media screen and (min-width: 1024px){
        header, .content{
                width: 940px;
        }
}
```

Now if you look at this in the browser, you will see that the site is now styled into a nice two-column layout with related articles showing in the sidebar, as shown in Figure 3-4.

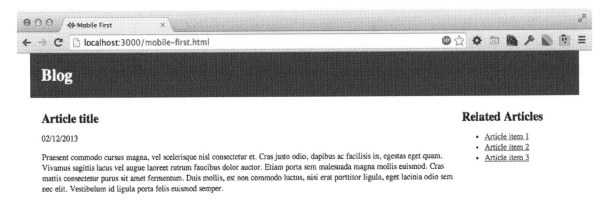

Figure 3-4. *Our completed site shown on a larger device viewport*

In this example we have built a simple responsive blog, built from a mobile first perspective. We built our core styles initially and then as our browser viewport increased in size we introduced new media queries to enable our site to respond to width of the viewport and take advantage of the increased space.

Caveats of Mobile First

There are caveats of building a web site using a mobile-first approach, the biggest being the level of browser support for media queries. On the whole, browser support for media queries is good, however, the earliest version of Internet Explorer to support media queries is Internet Explorer 9. This means with a mobile-first approach, Internet Explorer 8 and earlier will receive your mobile site. You might be happy to leave it at that, or you can instead choose to add a polyfill called Respond.js, which will enable limited media query support to Internet Explorer 8.

It can also be a challenge to get comfortable with building a site to the constraints of mobile; if you are like me and have spent your career building experiences using mouse events such as hover and clicks, you will notice their absence on smaller, touch-screen devices where instead you have finger taps and swipes.

Building from a mobile-first perspective, we should be thinking of the input types our users are using from the start, aiming to support a broad spectrum of ways our users might interact with our site. One of the problems we might find with supporting multiple input types properly is that with some actions, some browsers have tried to anticipate how we want our web site to work.

An example would be a mouse-hover interaction; on some touch-screen devices, browsers have implemented the hover event so that it can be toggled, with the hover state being turned on when you first tap on the element, and off on a second tap. The purpose for this is to allow the user to access content that would otherwise only have been accessible on hover (and you can't hover on a mobile device). This in itself adds extra challenges as the area that has a hover state may also be a link, meaning it should already have an action when the user taps on it. Unfortunately, media queries are unable to determine if a device is a touch device, and feature detection techniques are also unable accurately determine if the user is using a touch device. Therefore, we need to think of new ways in which to handle these interactions when building a web site.

Targeting High Pixel Density Displays

It is becoming increasingly common for mobile devices to have high pixel density. To the end user, the benefits of a display with a high pixel density are immediately clear, providing crisper text and sharper images. It's not only mobile devices that are benefiting from this revolution in display technology; notebook computer manufacturers are also offering higher quality displays on their premium machines.

With this in mind, when building a web site, you need to look at how you can take advantage of this change in display technology, and thankfully the browsers are not leaving us stranded, as media queries support testing the pixel density of the display using the resolution media feature.

When using media queries to target a device with a high pixel density display, you use the media query resolution feature to check for a minimum screen resolution. This feature supports three different types of units:

1. `dpi`: dots per CSS inch

2. `dpcm`: dots per CSS centimeter

3. `dppx`: dots per pixel unit, 1dppx = 96dpi

Although these are the supported units, the browser vendors are recommending developers to use dppx. Google Chrome currently gives the following warning if you are using `dpi`:

> *Consider using 'dppx' units instead of 'dpi', as in CSS 'dpi' means dots-per-CSS-inch, not dots-per-physical-inch, so it does not correspond to the actual 'dpi' of a screen. In media query expression: print, not all, (-webkit-min-device-pixel-ratio: 1.25), (min-resolution: 120dpi)*

https://github.com/h5bp/html5-boilerplate/issues/1474

This warning was shown when using a popular open source template called HTML5 boilerplate. As the warning notes, the dpi is dots per CSS inch, which can cause confusion to developers who not aware that the dpi in media queries is not the actual dpi of the screen.

Before I show some examples of how to implement media queries targeting high pixel density displays, you need to be aware of the browser support. As discussed earlier, CSS3 is still a draft standard, which means that each of the browsers has its own implementation behind a vendor prefix. Also some of the early implementations of media query resolutions use the device's physical resolution rather than its CSS resolution. Also although you should be using dppx as the unit with resolution queries, it was added to the specification later than dpi, so for compatibility with browsers not implementing dppx, you should also include dpi. This means that you need to take all of this into account when you write media queries, adding a level of complexity to when you read the media queries. In an attempt to cover as many browsers as possible, the following media query can be used:

```
@media only screen and (-webkit-min-device-pixel-ratio: 2),
only screen and (-o-min-device-pixel-ratio: 2/1),
only screen and (min--moz-device-pixel-ratio: 2),
only screen and (min-device-pixel-ratio: 2),
```

```
only screen and (min-resolution: 192dpi),
only screen and (min-resolution: 2dppx) {

  /* High resolution styles here */

}
```

To properly see how we can handle these high pixel density devices, let's look at a simple example to see how a logo would look without any media queries, and then write the media query to show a higher resolution image in its place.

To begin with let's write some simple HTML, using image replacement techniques to add a logo to the H1 on the page. Our HTML is shown in Listing 3-5.

Listing 3-5. HTML for the high-resolution image example

```
<!DOCTYPE html>
<html>
<head>
        <title>High Res Image Example</title>
        <meta name="viewport" content="width=device-width">
        <link rel="stylesheet" type="text/css" href="high-res-images.css">
</head>
<body>
        <h1>logo</h1>
</body>
</html>
```

Then you need to create the CSS. For now you will just create the CSS to show the logo for the standard resolutions. Let's add a border around the logo to show the size of the image clearly.

Listing 3-6. The base CSS for our logo, using the normal low res image

```
h1{
        width: 100px;
        height: 100px;
        text-indent: 100%;
        white-space: nowrap;
        overflow: hidden;
        background-image: url("low-res-image.png");
        border: 3px solid #d3000c;
        margin: 0px;
}
```

Now when you look at this on a device with a high pixel density display, you can see that there is some fuzziness caused by the upscaling of the image, as shown in Figure 3-5.

Figure 3-5. *Our lower resolution logo shown on iOS*

We can now look at how we can add media queries to handle loading a higher resolution version of the logo.

To load the higher quality version of the image, use the query you used earlier and then add some CSS to it to change the background image to the higher resolution version of the image. You also need to scale the background image to the size of the original image so that it fits in the same dimensions (Listing 3-7).

Listing 3-7. CSS media query to show the higher resolution logo on high pixel density displays

```css
@media only screen and (-webkit-min-device-pixel-ratio: 2),
only screen and (-o-min-device-pixel-ratio: 2/1),
only screen and (min--moz-device-pixel-ratio: 2),
only screen and (min-device-pixel-ratio: 2),
only screen and (min-resolution: 192dpi),
only screen and (min-resolution: 2dppx) {
        h1{
                background-image: url("high-res-image.png");
                background-size: 100px 100px;
        }
}
```

Now if you test this on a high pixel density device, you will see that the logo image is displayed with greater clarity, this is shown in Figure 3-6.

Figure 3-6. *Our high resolution logo shown on iOS*

This is only a simple example of how you can use media queries to improve how a web site is displayed on high pixel density devices.

Summary

There are a broad spectrum of devices available, and building a web site that can support them all can be very challenging. The devices developers need to support come in a variety of different types, from televisions to audio synthesizers, and as discussed in this chapter, since CSS2.1 specification, we now have the ability to target these using media types. Media types limit developers to simply targeting these different types directly, however, a wide variety of modern devices now use screen media type, which means that although it makes logical sense to developers that they should also fit into one of these other categories such as television or handheld, this is not the case.

This is where media queries come in. They allow developers to target styles with greater control than could be done with media types. Media queries allow developers to target a wide range of features of devices, including the screen width, screen height, and resolution. This fine-grained control means we can better target the wide variety of devices that are available.

Media queries form the foundation of responsive web design, so it is really important that developers have a good understanding of how to use them to optimize a web site to work across a wide variety of devices. Going forward, media queries will allow us to support the growing number of devices, and with new device categories being thought up all the time, by using media queries we are already well placed to support them.

In our next chapter you will learn about the different types of layout typically used in web design, with a focus on looking at the principles of working with fluid design and how we can implement fluid design as part of a responsive site.

CHAPTER 4

Using Fluid Layouts

Having already examined the use of media queries, this chapter will examine how to utilize these together with other aspects of CSS3 to build a better experience for your users, an experience that is both flexible and capable of working across a wider variety of devices.

This chapter will explore:

1. The different types of layouts.

2. Principles when working with a fluid design.

3. Building a fluid design using a CSS grid.

Types of Layouts

When it comes to the structural layout of the page, there are multiple types of layouts from which you can choose. The three most popular types of layouts are fixed width layout, fluid layout, and elastic layout, each having its own benefits and disadvantages.

When deciding upon which type of layout you want to use, it is important to consider the user's experience. For a responsive site, your layout choice needs to work well across a significant number of devices. With the sheer number in use, it is important to choose a layout type that allows you to provide the best experience to the most number of users. You also need to take into consideration the very possible chance that your site could be accessed on anything ranging from the smallest of smartphones to an 85-inch television in a living room.

Let's take a look at the different layout styles and consider the benefits and disadvantages of each, with the intention to learn how to pick the best bits from each in order to build a great experience for web site users.

Fixed Width Layouts

As the name suggests, fixed width layouts are built primarily with a wrapper that has a fixed width. This is then positioned on the screen, typically being centered in the browser viewport. Regardless of the size of screen being used to access the site, the fixed width layout will maintain its fixed width.

Historically, when developers built web sites, they were building from a design, which has a fixed width. Typically, designers would design sites to be 960px wide, as this was the ideal width for using grid layouts because this number is divisible by 3, 4, 5, 6, 8, 10, 12, and 15. When developers proceeded to build these designs, they would then build the site at 960px wide, striving to be as pixel perfect with the build as possible. The idea here was that they could make the design look as fantastic in the browser as what had been presented to the client as flat designs. An example of a typical three-column fixed layout, with two sidebars and a main content area, is shown in Figure 4-1.

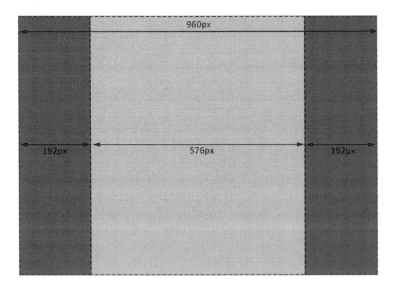

Figure 4-1. *An example of a 960px wide, three-column fixed layout*

If you look at how a typical fixed width layout is made up, you would normally have a wrapper with a fixed width of 960px, and inside of this you would then have your web site content, usually having the width defined in pixels. In the example in Figure 4-1, there is a main content area with a width of 576px with two 192px columns on either side.

Fixed width builds are still incredibly popular, and when you factor in the ability to create content including images that perfectly fit the design, it is easy to understand why. A current example of a fixed width web site for Samsung is presented in Figure 4-2.

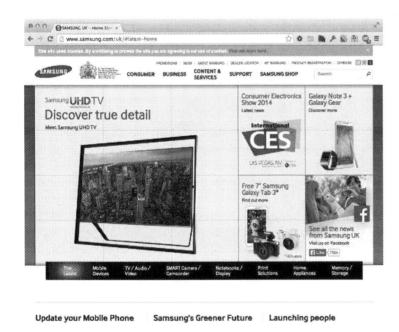

Figure 4-2. *The Samsung web site is a good example of a fixed layout*

The Samsung web site is built to be 960px wide, enabling the site to target a wide variety of popular viewports. Although not responsive, the site is still usable on a mobile device; it initially loads full screen with the full site visible, then, to interact with the site, the user is able to take advantage of the browser built-in user interactions of pinch, pull, and double-tap to zoom and navigate the content. Although this is usable, it doesn't provide the fantastic user experience that we have come to expect on our mobile devices.

If you take a look at the Samsung site in Mobile Safari on an iPhone, you would see the image shown in Figure 4-3.

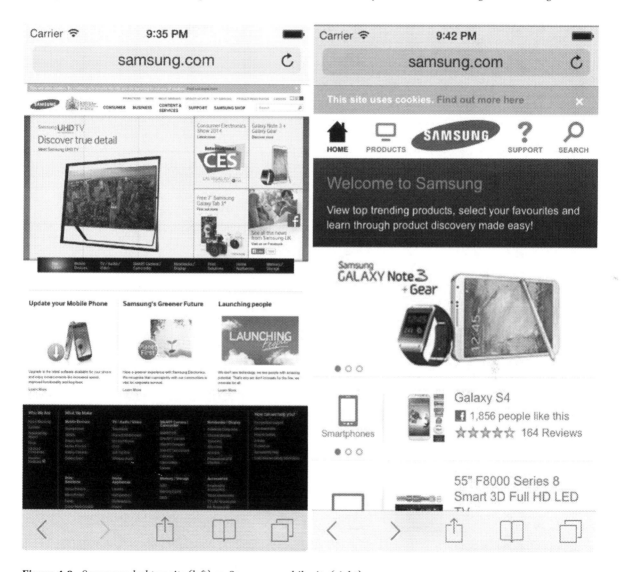

Figure 4-3. *Samsung desktop site (left) vs. Samsung mobile site (right)*

Samsung does provide a specific mobile site, which is shown in Figure 4-3, however, it does not share the same content as the desktop site. This means that users could still end up using the desktop site on their mobile devices to access content that is unavailable otherwise.

One of the main issues of fixed width design is that you are making a judgment call regarding what width your sites should be designed and built to. The limitation of making this kind of decision is that there is a huge range of browser widths to support. The result of this is that on a browser window smaller than the chosen fixed width you get horizontal scrolling, and on larger browser windows you have excess space to the sides of your site that could be better utilized.

When Apple launched the iPhone in 2007, the majority of web sites were fixed width so developers tried to compensate for this by making sites by default start zoomed out (as per Samsung), meaning that users would be able to see the full width of the site despite it being too big for their devices. Although this offered a better experience than only getting to see a corner of a site, it still could be quite frustrating to navigate a large site.

Using a fixed width design isn't necessarily a bad decision, and it is important to consider what your web site will be used for and its target audience. A fixed width site makes sense for sites where you want to retain the same layout and proportions across all viewports.

Elastic Layouts

Elastic layouts do not define widths in pixels but instead are measured in ems. The em unit is a multiple of the font size, so if you set your font size to 16px, then a width of 2em would be equal to 32px. This means that the if the user changes the font size while viewing the site, the layout of the site will also change proportionally to the increase or decrease in font size.

Elastic layouts give the developer more control because the design proportions stay intact when the user resizes the text in the browser. What this means is that if a user needs to increase the font size used on your site, the experience they receive on your site is no different from that of a user viewing the site at the original font size. The elements of the site resize in proportion to the font size. This means that elastic layouts work really well at enabling developers to ensure that their sites are accessible to all users.

If you take the original fixed width web site design, using a base font size of 16px, you can easily convert the layout to use em instead of pixels by dividing each of the pixel column widths by the font size, in this case 16. Figure 4-4 shows the same layout used in Figure 4-1 for the fixed layout example converted to an elastic layout.

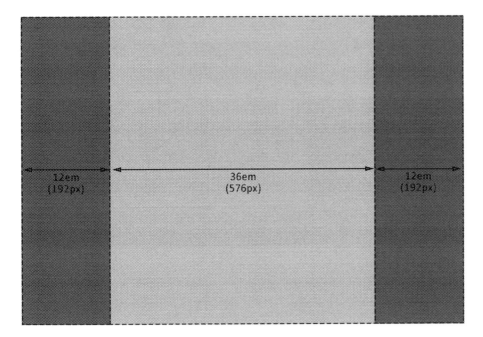

Figure 4-4. An example of a 960px wide, three-column elastic layout with em conversion

The example now has the column width defined in ems rather than pixels. The calculation from pixels to ems is very easy to perform:

Width in pixels / base font size = Width in em

Using this simple formula, you can easily calculate the widths of your elements in ems. In Figure 4-4 you can see how to calculate the element widths by substituting the pixel widths into the calculation:

576 / 16 = 36em
192 / 16 = 12em

It is important to be aware that ems can have a decimal value, so if your calculation doesn't result in a round number, it isn't a problem.

An example of a site that uses elastic layouts is the Northern Ireland Community Archives microsite about the Plantation of Ulster, as shown in Figure 4-5.[1]

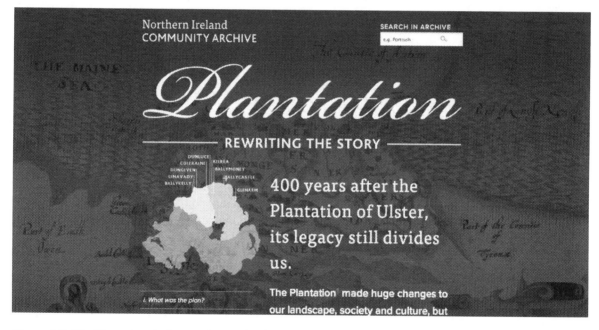

Figure 4-5. *The Plantation site is a good example of an elastic layout*

This web site uses ems to define the widths of both the outer wrapper and the columns of its layout. If the base font size is increased, the whole site then resizes to accommodate the larger text, as shown in Figure 4-6.

---

[1]http://niarchive.org/trails/plantation-rewriting-the-story/.

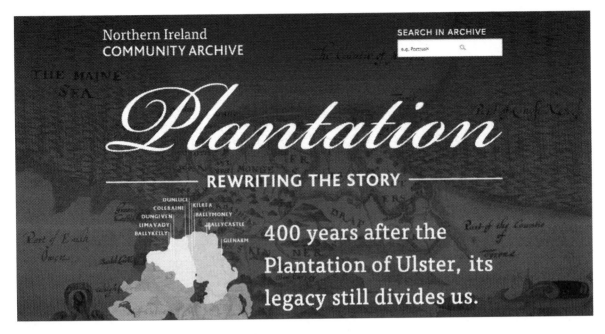

Figure 4-6. *The Plantation site after increasing the base font size*

One of the initial problems with elastic layouts is that because the width of the site is based on the base font size, if the user increases the font size beyond a certain point, the site will become very large in the viewport, potentially causing the browser to have horizontal scrollbars.

Another problem with elastic layouts is that they are essentially still a form of fixed width layout, by which I mean that the elasticity is based on the base font size, so unless the font size is changed by the user, the site will stay the base width the developer intended. What this means is that while elastic layouts offer a more accessible approach than a pixel-based fixed layout, the layout still appears to snap into position at each of the breakpoints because the CSS inside each of the media queries is applied; thus, there is no fluidity between them as the site adapts to different sizes.

One of the reasons that elastic layouts are not more popular is because of the difficulty that is posed by having to calculate the widths in ems. It isn't immediately clear what a width of 36em would be in pixels until you look at the base font size. With a base font size of 16px, the width would be 576px; however, by simply changing the base font size to 14px, the width would be reduced to 504px. Having to perform this (albeit, simple) calculation adds an extra step for the developer.

Another issue you might face is that ems are calculated relative to the parent; therefore, if the parent defines a different font size than the body, you might find the width of the element is not what you would expect. This is because you have likely calculated the width based on the font size of the body; to fix this you simply redo the calculation based on the font size of the parent element. To avoid this issue completely, one option is to use rem rather than em for the font size, which means all of the font sizes will be relative to the base font size regardless of the font size of the parent's elements, the caveat being that rem does not work in legacy browsers such as Internet Explorer 8 and earlier.

Fluid Layouts

Fluid layouts, also known as liquid layouts or relative layouts, change in width dependent on the user's viewport. Unlike fixed layouts, where widths are defined in pixels, you instead define the widths as percentages, where the percentage is referencing its portion of the viewport, as shown in Figure 4-7.

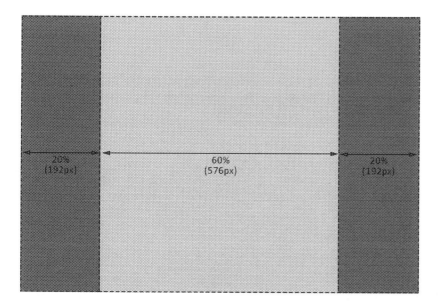

Figure 4-7. *An example of a fluid web site, with browser currently open at 960px wide*

If you take the example in Figure 4-1 of the fixed width layout and turn the dimensions into percentages, you would have two columns with a width of 20 percent and a single column with a width of 60 percent. With a browser viewport at 960px, the equivalent pixel values are the same as those in the fixed example (pixels shown in brackets), as shown in Figure 4-8.

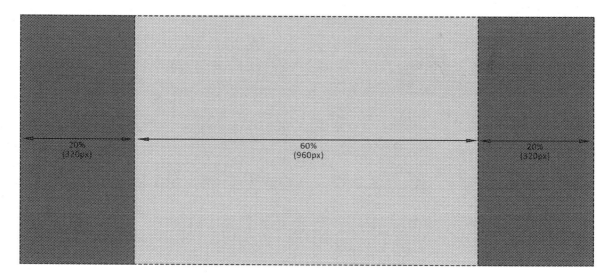

Figure 4-8. *An example of a fluid web site, with the browser open at 1,600px wide*

If you were then to resize the browser to have a viewport width of 1,600px, the web site would simply naturally scale up to the full width of the browser. The smaller columns would now have a width of 320px and the larger column a width of 960px. The benefit of this is that the content naturally fills the page, potentially scaling up any images and flowing the text to fill the available space.

Yahoo! recently redesigned the Flickr site using a fluid layout approach (as shown in Figure 4-9), taking advantage of the additional space available to allow them to increase the size of the images, and depending on the screen size, increase the number of images per row. The benefit here is that users of the site could browse through more images quicker and be more engaged with the site.

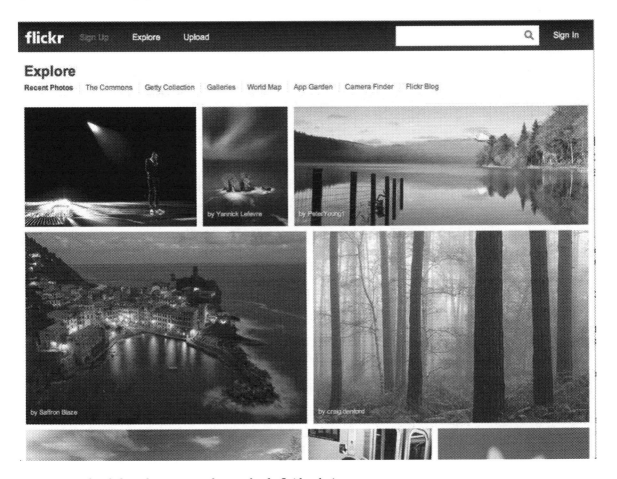

Figure 4-9. The Flickr web site is a good example of a fluid web site

If you were to resize the browser window, the Flickr site simply scales with the browser, making better use of the available space. Images either increase in size or allow for more in a row, utilizing the users' viewing space and maximizing the amount of material they are able to view at any given time. You can see this wider view of the Flickr site in Figure 4-10.

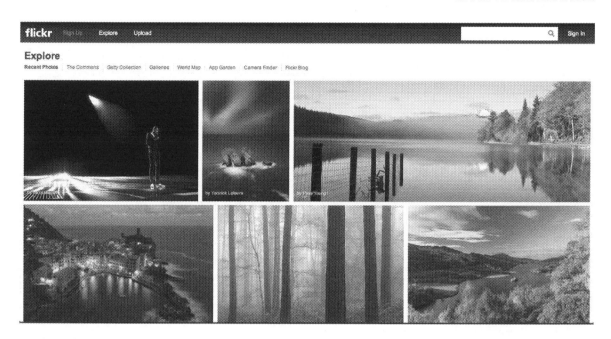

Figure 4-10. *The Flickr web site when viewed on a wider screen*

The benefit to Flickr of using a fluid layout is clear; the imagery can fill up all available space, allowing the user to properly appreciate the photos. The improvement of the experience to the users can also be measured by the increase in engagement the site has received. Although Yahoo! has not released any firm figures, a Flickr user named Thomas Hawks[2] did some research on his own. Within six days of the redesign launching, 80 million new photos had been uploaded to the site, in comparison to the six days prior to the redesign, when users had uploaded only 47 million images.

A fluid layout is not only beneficial to sites like Flickr, which is solely imagery, but it also of benefit to sites where content is tiled. An example is Pinterest, which, although also quite heavy on images, has other content displayed. For Pinterest, users will often skim through the boards that interest them, looking for things that grab their attention, and by using a fluid layout, Pinterest is able to show the maximum amount of content the user is able to view at that time, allowing them to find what they want, faster. The fluid width, tiled interface of Pinterest is shown in Figure 4-11.

---

[2]http://thomashawk.com/2013/05/flickr-users-uploading-71-more-photos-to-flickr-since-new-design-rolled-out.html.

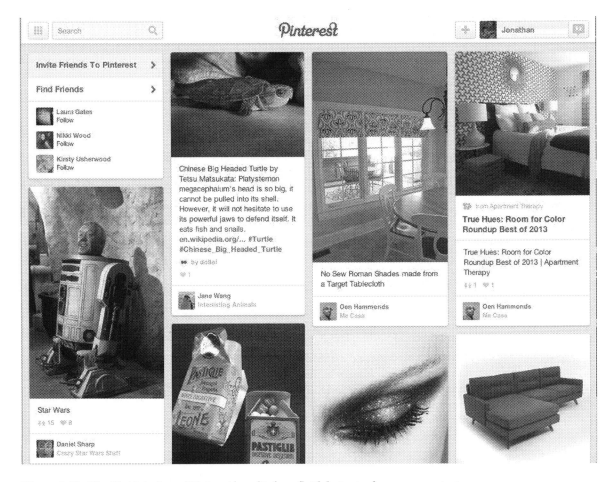

Figure 4-11. *The tiled interface of Pinterest benefits from fluid design to show more content*

One of the benefits of using a fluid layout is that it can be a lot more user friendly simply because of the way it adjusts to the user's device. Rather than having excess white space, a fluid layout can take advantage of the space available, allowing content to fill all the available space, and on larger devices, it allows the content be more spaced out with extra breathing room.

Although fluid layouts are incredibly powerful, they do have some disadvantages, the most important of which is that they can result in issues in the way the content is rendered. Because a fluid layout could be viewed at any browser width, you may find that you face issues with how your images look. Although it is possible to scale your images as the browser resizes, it is important to be aware that some images will not scale well. Images containing focal points will suffer, as scaling them down will not only lose the impact, but also make the focus too small. Similarly, a low-resolution picture, when scaled up, could significantly degrade in quality.

Aside from issues with content rendering, a fluid width site may face issues with some of its interactive functionality. It is common for web sites to use JavaScript to augment the user's experience, for example, to display equal height columns. The problem comes with when the user resizes the browser; the text reflows and the columns then become too tall or too short. Therefore, the JavaScript needs to be adapted to recalculate the heights upon resizing.

Why Use Fluid Layouts for Responsive Design

Having explored fixed, fluid, and elastic layouts, it is important to get a good understanding of the benefits and disadvantages of each approach. I have not, however, really discussed how this all relates to responsive design.

In Chapter 3, I explained how you can use media queries to adapt your web sites to different viewports. The problem with doing this is that with both fixed and elastic layouts, they snap between two or more different layouts that are adapted to different screen sizes. Rather than being responsive to all sorts of different devices, they are instead adapted to work across a few different common screen sizes.

But devices no longer conform to a few different common screen sizes; instead developers now face browsers with viewports of any dimension, viewed on devices ranging from an 85-inch television to a 3.5-inch mobile phone screen. Developers must have the mindset of wanting their web sites to look great regardless, not just on a few choice screen sizes. If the user were to resize their browsers, you would want the resize to be smooth and flowing, with the layout simply working at any given resolution.

When considering your choice of layout style, you should ensure that you are familiar with the alternative options available, which is why I have covered the advantages and disadvantages in the previous sections. When building web sites, you should feel comfortable with your choice of layout style and adapting them to suit your needs, not be restricted by them. That being said, responsive design really requires a fluid layout to deliver the best user experience across the widest range of devices with minimal interruptions between different viewport sizes. This doesn't mean you can't have breakpoints, which causes the layout to snap to change it to better take advantage of the available screen space. This is, in fact, encouraged; you will want to be able to take advantage of the space you have available the best way you can.

Principles When Working with a Fluid Design

Building a fluid design can bring a wide variety of benefits to responsive design; however, there are some important principles to bear in mind to ensure your web site remains usable regardless of the size of the viewport.

The key principles you should try to follow are:

1. Do not use fixed heights.

2. Do not necessitate horizontal scroll bars.

3. Think about how your images look at different sizes.

4. Think about wrapping content.

5. Think about spacing.

6. Think about the length of your lines of text.

Let's explore these in more detail, looking at potential ways around the problems you might encounter.

Do Not Use Fixed Heights

If you are used to building fixed layouts, you most likely have encountered the problem where you have defined a fixed height for an element, but when the content was changed, the height either had excess spacing or the content overflows outside the defined height.

With the variable widths that come with fluid design, this issue is a lot more common, as the way in which the content wraps will change based on the size of the viewport, so setting a fixed height in the CSS becomes impractical.

Unfortunately, sometimes it is integral to the design to show content in equal columns, each with its own background color. This can be tricky to achieve without defining the height in the CSS; so the options are either to create faux columns in the CSS or use JavaScript to dynamically set the height of the columns.

Using CSS to Create Faux Columns

It is possible to create the effect of columns simply by using some CSS.

For a two-column layout, where you know that one column will always be taller than another, simply set the parent element's background color to that of the shorter column. Then by setting the background color of longer column's element, you have created the effect of having two columns. Let's take a quick look at the code to handle this, starting with some simple HTML:

```
<div class="col-container">
        <aside class="col">
                Sidebar
        </aside>
        <div class="col main">
                Main Content Area
        </div>
</div>
```

As mentioned, you will apply the background for the columns to the column container and to the main content column. To achieve the column effect, you would also defined the columns as a width of 50 percent, floated left so they sit next to one another:

```
.col-container{
        background: #000;
        color: #fff;
}

.col-container:after{
        content: ' ';
        clear: both;
        display: block;
}

.col{
        float: left;
        width: 50%;
}

.col.main{
        background: #999;
}
```

It is important to note that you have added a pseudo-element to the column container to clear the floated columns. This is necessary so that the browser calculates the height of the column container itself. If your site is already using the clearfix class for this, you could choose to add this to your column container rather than add a pseudo-element specific to that element.

If you check this out in your browser, the layout has the two columns with equal height as expected, as shown in Figure 4-12.

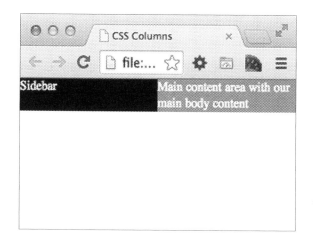

Figure 4-12. *Two columns with equal height using CSS*

Although this is pretty simple, this method for two columns works across all browsers and is very effective, with the caveat being that this approach only works well for two columns and it requires that you know which is the taller column.

In the case where you have more than two columns, you could choose to use a CSS3 gradient on the parent to achieve the same effect. However, bear in mind this approach will only work in Internet Explorer 10 or later. Extending the example from above, you would add an additional column to the HTML:

```
<div class="col-container">
        <aside class="col">
                Sidebar
        </aside>
        <div class="col main">
                Main content area with our main body content
        </div>
        <div class="col">
                Related content
        </aside>
</div>
```

You can then simply adapt the existing CSS as you no longer need to add a background to the main column. Therefore, you can remove that part of the CSS. You will then add the CSS3 background gradient to the column container. In the example that follows, you only include the W3C CSS3 property, and it is important for live code to add the prefixed versions to ensure browser support:

```
.col-container{
        background: linear-gradient(to right, #000000 0%,#000000 33%,#a0a0a0 33%,#a0a0a0 66%,#a0a0a0 66%,#707070 66%);
        color: #fff;
}
.col-container:after{
        content: ' ';
        clear: both;
        display: block;
}
```

```
.col{
        float: left;
        width: 33.3%;
}
```

When looking at the results of running this in the browser, the new column appears with the correct background color, as you can see in Figure 4-13.

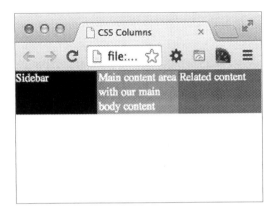

Figure 4-13. *Three columns with equal height using CSS*

If you need support for older versions of Internet Explorer or you want to support a dynamic number of columns, you should perhaps look at using JavaScript.

Using JavaScript

Having already looked at how to use CSS to create a faux columns effect, let's look at how to use JavaScript to create columns of equal height. The JavaScript approach does not try to fake the appearance of columns, but instead makes all the columns the same height.

The approach to using JavaScript to create equal height columns is to loop through each of the columns, find which is the tallest column, and then set all the columns to the height of the tallest.

To demonstrate this, let's look at a simple example, beginning with some HTML:

```
<div class="col-container">
        <aside class="col nav">
                Sidebar
        </aside>
        <div class="col main">
                Main content area with our main body content
        </div>
        <div class="col related">
                Related content
        </aside>
</div>
```

You then need to style the columns so they each have a different background color:

```
.col-container{
        color: #fff;
}
.col-container:after{
        content: ' ';
        clear: both;
        display: block;
}
.col{
        float: left;
        width: 33.3%;
}
.col.nav{
        background: #aaa;
}
.col.main{
        background: #000;
}

.col.related{
        background: #999;
}
```

With this in place, the columns now all sit nicely, each with a unique background color; however, the heights of the columns are still unequal. You can see how this looks in Figure 4-14.

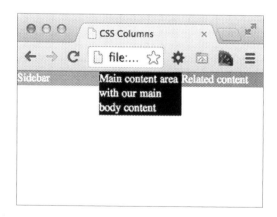

Figure 4-14. *Three columns with unequal height before adding the JavaScript*

To progress to making the columns equal, you will need to add some JavaScript. In the below example I have used document.getElementsByClassName, which is only supported by Internet Explorer 9 or later. However, you can use a polyfill to enable support for this method, one such polyfill is available in this Gist code: https://gist.github. com/eikes/2299607.

```
<script>
        var columns = document.getElementsByClassName('col'),
                height = 0;

        //Loop through columns and find the tallest columns
        for (var i = 0; i < columns.length; i++) {
                if(height < columns[i].clientHeight){
                        height = columns[i].clientHeight;
                }
        }

        //Apply the max height to all columns
        for (var i = 0; i < columns.length; i++) {
                columns[i].style.height = height + "px";
        }
</script>
```

The equal column JavaScript simply iterates through all of the columns to find the tallest element. It then iterates through the elements again to define the height. You can see the JavaScript working in Figure 4-15.

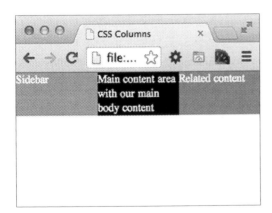

Figure 4-15. *Three columns with equal height after adding the JavaScript*

With a fixed, non-responsive design, simply running this JavaScript when the page has loaded is enough. However, with a fluid, responsive design, the user may resize the browser so the JavaScript then needs to be able to update the column height on resize:

```
<script>
        var equalColumns = function(){
                var columns = document.getElementsByClassName('col'), height = 0;
```

```
        //Reset the height of all the columns so that we can recalculate max height
        for (var i = 0; i < columns.length; i++) {
                columns[i].style.height = "auto";
        }

        //Loop through columns and find max height
        for (var i = 0; i < columns.length; i++) {
                if(height < columns[i].clientHeight){
                        height = columns[i].clientHeight;
                }
        }

        //Apply the max height to all columns
        for (var i = 0; i < columns.length; i++) {
                columns[i].style.height = height + "px";
        }
    }

    //Initially set the column heights
    equalColumns();

    //Update column heights on browser resize
    window.addEventListener("resize", equalColumns, true);
</script>
```

With this revised JavaScript, you have wrapped our equalColumns JavaScript up as a function and updated it so that it resets all the heights of the columns prior to recalculating the heights. The method is then run when the page loads and attaches it as an event listener to the resize event. With this now in place, if the user resizes the browser, the columns heights will adjust accordingly.

Do Not Necessitate Horizontal Scroll Bars

When using a site, it is typical for content to flow down the page, so being able to scroll two directions could therefore harm the user's experience.

There is a use case for creating a horizontal layout; however, in this case, you would avoid the use of vertical scrollbars and concentrate on providing a horizontal experience. An example of where you might want to build a horizontal layout would be an online portfolio for an artist or a photographer, such as C. L. Holloway's portfolio site, where he has created an art gallery–like experience by allowing the user to scroll horizontally.[3] It is important to note that although the developer of this web site chose to use horizontal scrollbars, the site has opted to avoid vertical scrollbars except where the viewport is too shallow to show all the content (at approximately 610px, which fits the most popular vertical screen resolutions nicely).

Think About How Your Images Look at Different Sizes

When implementing images on a site using a fluid design, it is important to look carefully at how the image will look at different sizes. You need to think about how you will scale your images, and this depends on whether you want to include the image on your page as an <img> tag or if you want to use the image as a background image.

---

[3]http://www.clholloway.co.za.

Scaling an Inline Image

To scale an inline image, you can simply apply a width to the image. If your site is responsive, you don't really know which width size to apply to an image, so instead of defining an absolute width you can set the max-width property with a value of 100 percent, as shown in the following code:

```
img {
        max-width:100%
}
```

With this in place, if an image is larger than its container, it will scale down; however, if the image is smaller than the container, it will stay the original size.

Scaling a Background Image

If you are scaling a background image, you can use the CSS3 background-size property. This can take three different values: cover, contain, and width/height values.

```
.image{
        background-size:80px 60px;
}
```

The problem with background-size is that although you can use relative widths to set the width of the element to be fluid, this is not quite as easy for the height of the element.

The first step is to define the div that will contain the background image:

```
<div class="image"></div>
```

Next you need to define the CSS. First, you will define the image container. Because you want the width to be relative, you will use a percentage value, in this case width: 100%. The height of the image needs to be proportional to the width of the image; this is not achievable with the height property because heights cannot be relative. Instead you can use padding. Because percentage padding is based on the width of the element, you can use this to define the height. This is unfortunately where it gets a bit complicated, as you will need to set the padding bottom so that it maintains the correct aspect ratio for the image.

With the correct width and height in place, you now simply need to add the image as a background image and set the background-size so it scales to the full width and height of the element:

```
.image{
        width: 100%;
        position: relative;
        padding-bottom: 125%;
        background: url(scalableimage.jpg) 0 0 no-repeat;
        background-size: 100% 100%;
}
```

With this in place, you can look at the image in the browser and see it is now proportional to the width of the page. Figure 4-16 shows how this looks in the browser.

Figure 4-16. *Scaling a background image with CSS*

Think About Wrapping Content

When building a fluid site, it doesn't always make sense for the elements to continually get smaller, because eventually the content could become unstable and unreadable. Reversely, as the viewport gets larger, it doesn't make sense to keep the content blocks all stacked on top of each other. The option in both circumstances is to think about how the content wraps at different viewports.

An example of this is when there is a sidebar with related content at the side of a web site. If the sidebar takes up 25 percent of the page width and the viewport is only 320px wide, then the column would only be 80px wide. Instead of maintaining the column structure, the sidebar could instead be moved below the main content of the page, freeing up extra space for the main content and allowing the sidebar column to also go full width.

Think About Spacing

When working with a fluid design, you use percentages for the widths of the elements, the benefit being that the browser is able to scale the widths based on the width of the viewport. Alongside working out the width of the elements as percentages, you also need to consider how to handle the spacing in between each of these elements.

One way in which the spacing could be added would be to use percentage values for the padding. The problem here is that on larger viewports the spacing would be too much and on smaller viewports the spacing would be too small.

Ideally you want to define the element widths in percentages and the element padding in pixels or ems. Unfortunately, by default, the way the browser renders the box model places padding on the outside of the widths, which means that when defining pixels for padding, the fluidity of the design breaks as horizontal scrollbars will appear, as shown in Figure 4-17.

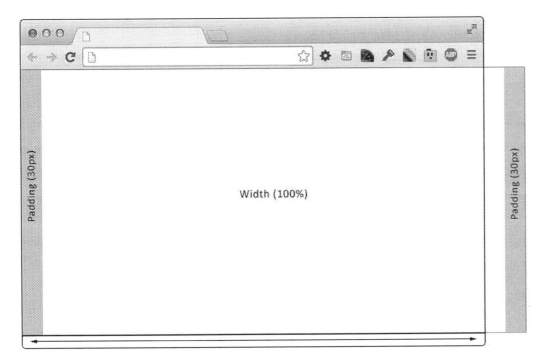

Figure 4-17. *Using pixel values for paddings, the Fluidness of the design breaks and horizontal scrollbars appear*

If you have been in web development for a while, you might be aware of *quirks mode*. Essentially, in older browsers the standards were not properly implemented, and when it came to Internet Explorer 6, it was decided that to implement the HTML and CSS standards, a fallback would need to be left in place for older sites that had not been updated to support these standards. This fallback is known as quirks mode, and it is triggered by not including a doctype on the first line of the HTML document.

In particular, in these older browsers, the box model was incorrectly implemented when compared against the standard. The W3C standard required that when the width or height of an element was defined, it excluded the padding, borders, and margins, which were to be applied to the outside of the width or height. In these older browsers, the implementation included the content, padding, and borders, all within the specified width or height.

The quirks mode implementation would be ideal for allowing you to add the spacing to your fluid design site, however, you don't want to be forcing your site into quirks mode to do it because you want your site to be standards compliant. With the arrival of CSS3, the control over how the box model works is given to the developers, and we are now able to determine how the box renders using the new box-sizing CSS property.

The box-sizing property gives us three values to choose from, and each will render a box with a different version of the box model. The values available for box-sizing are content-box, padding-box, and border-box.

content-box

The default style is specified by the CSS standard. The width and height properties are measured to include only the content area. The border, margin, and padding are added to the outside. An example is shown in Figure 4-18.

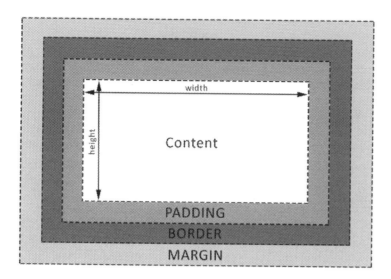

Figure 4-18. *The box model as applied by setting the CSS property box-sizing to content-box*

padding-box

With padding-box, the width and height properties include the padding size and do not include the border or margin. An example is shown in Figure 4-19.

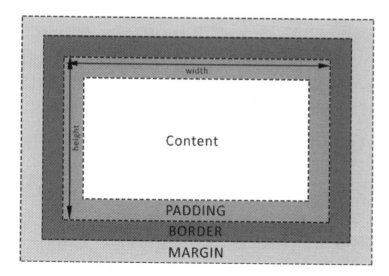

Figure 4-19. *The box mode asl applied by setting the CSS property box-sizing to padding-box*

border-box

Both the width and height properties include the padding and border but exclude the margin. If you have been developing for a while, you might be familiar with the workings of border-box because it is used by Internet Explorer when the document is in quirks mode. An example is shown in Figure 4-20.

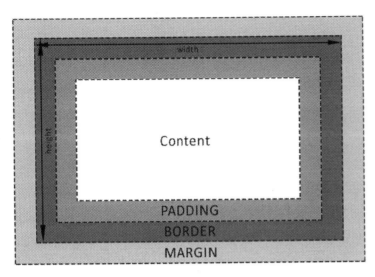

Figure 4-20. *The box model as applied by setting the CSS property box-sizing to border-box*

The border-box is the holy grail when it comes to responsive development as it allows us to add consistent padding to the elements while still using percentage-based widths.

It makes complete sense for a responsive site to use border-box for all elements. Not only does it maintain consistency, it also means you can use percentage widths for everything from divs to input fields. The way in which you apply border-box to all elements is to use the universal selector (*):

```
* {
        -webkit-box-sizing: border-box; /* Safari/Chrome, other WebKit */
        -moz-box-sizing: border-box;    /* Firefox, other Gecko */
        box-sizing: border-box;         /* Opera/IE 8+ */
}
```

Think About the Length of Your Lines of Text

When building a fluid site, it is very easy to simply allow a site to be full width, regardless of the browser size. However, often this can lead to very long lines of text.

Chris Coyier wrote a post on CSS Tricks in November 2013 regarding this particular issue:

Traditional thinking is that body copy (long text, multiple paragraphs, takes more than a glance to read ...) should be between 45 and 75 characters per line to be comfortable. Shorter is awkward, longer makes it easy to lose your place and find the next line.

This makes complete sense; at a quick glance, it is more comfortable to read lines that are not excessively long; it's for this same reason that newspapers use columns. In a fluid layout, it is very easy to allow the length of the lines of text to become too long. To avoid this, you would use a CSS property called `max-width`, which was introduced as part of the CSS2.1 specification.

The CSS `max-width` property allows you to define the maximum width an element can span, enabling you to control the length of the lines of text by defining a maximum width on either the containing element or the paragraph tag directly. When defining this maximum width, you can actually take into account the maximum number of characters per line by defining your `max-width` in ems. This means that the maximum width of your element will stay relative to the font size defined, so if the user were to increase the default font size, the element will scale appropriately. It is important to note that it can be tricky to use pixel widths to contain widths defined by em, so it is important to be consistent with how you define your widths.

You will similarly want to ensure that your lines of text do not appear too short. For this you can use the CSS property `min-width`, which was also introduced as part of the CSS2.1 specification. The `min-width` property allows you to specify a minimum width that an element can have and it overrides the values of both the `width` and `max-width` properties if the width of the element would drop below the `min-width` value. The `min-width` property won't help cases where the copy is too short for a single line of text; however, it does help prevent cases where you have multiple lines of text with only a couple of words on each line because the element is not wide enough. It is important to note that if the container has a width of less than the element, the element will then overflow outside its container. Additionally, if the container has the CSS property overflow set to hidden, the content of the element will be cropped, which of course is undesirable.

Browser support for both `max-width` and `min-width` is good with Internet Explorer 7 and later, Firefox, Chrome, and Safari, including the mobile versions, all of which support the property.

Building a Fluid Design Using a CSS Grid

At this point you now have a good understanding of the principles to follow when building a fluid design. Let's look at putting these into practice to build a fluid design. Having already built a responsive site in Chapter 3, when you learned about media queries, let's look at building a responsive CSS layout grid using fluid design principles.

Layout grids have their roots in publishing, where companies would lay out printed materials such as magazines and books by using a predefined grid. The aim of this was to allow them to achieve visual symmetry throughout the printed work. The objective of these invisible grids is to provide the reader with a simpler, consistent reading experience. Long before responsive design became the trend, the benefits seen from grids in prints prompted their transition in the form of CSS grids to the web.

CSS grids are typically built using columns; these are the grid's smallest unit of measurement and blocks can span one or more columns. Usually, a grid will have between 12 and 16 columns, and in between each column there will be gutters. The *gutter* is the spacing in between each column, which is generally defined as either padding or margins.

To allow me to easily illustrate how a grid might work, I put together an example of a fixed layout grid, which is shown in Figure 4-21. In this example, we have a four-column grid, each of the columns being 215px wide with 20px gutters applied either side of each column.

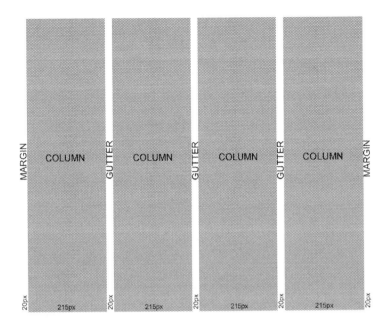

Figure 4-21. *An example of a fixed width grid*

The fixed width layout allows us to picture how our grid is spaced out however we want to be building our grid to be fluid. To achieve this we will instead define each of our columns to have a width of 25%, then to enable the gutters for our site we would use the box-sizing property to move the padding inside of our columns. At 960px wide total, each of the columns is 240px wide; however, if you were to scale this down to 320px, the columns scale with the browser with each column instead of being 80px wide each. This fluid grid is shown in Figure 4-22.

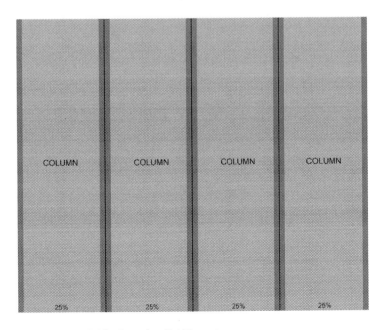

Figure 4-22. *Grid adapted to fluid layout*

Building a Grid

Although you could simply use a CSS grid framework, it is first important to have a good understanding of how grid frameworks work so you can make the most of them. Let's look at how to write a simple mobile first, responsive CSS grid.

In the simplest form, a CSS grid consists of the following:

1. Columns

2. Gutters

3. Rows

4. Wrappers

Let's look at these elements of a grid in more detail:

Columns

When developing a CSS grid, you need to decide upon the number of columns that the grid system will use, and as mentioned, it is very common for a grid system to have 12 or 16 columns.

Columns in a CSS grid are usually of equal width, positioned next to one another. Typically this is achieved by floating the columns left:

```
.col{
        float: left;
        width: 25%;
}
```

For the example CSS grid that you'll be writing, you will be using four columns. You might remember I mentioned earlier how you may want your content to span multiple columns, so in order to support this you'll need to make some tweaks. It is very easy to make a grid support spanning multiple columns by simply defining each of the supported widths. Previously I named a single column .col, however, to enable you to use a single selector to apply the shared styles to our additional columns, you will rename it ".col-span-x" where **x** is the number of columns the column should span.. The column names should reflect how many columns they will span:

```
[class*="col-span"]{
    float: left;
}

.col-span-1{
        width: 25%;
}

.col-span-2{
        width: 50%;
}

.col-span-3{
        width: 75%;
}

.col-span-4{
        width: 100%;
}
```

You may have noticed that here I have used a syntax of CSS that I have not covered in this book, one you might not have used before, called an *attribute wildcard selector*. The attribute wildcard selector used [class*="col-span"] allows you to target all the columns without having to add an additional class. In this example, I used it instead of writing:

```
.col-span-1, .col-span-2, .col-span-3, .col-span-4{
        float: left;
}
```

Up to this point you have created four columns, however, here you will want to be able to adapt your site based on the size of the viewport. When I discussed the principles of building a responsive fluid design, I mentioned how resizing some content too small could provide a bad user experience. You should therefore be able to control how many columns content takes up independently on smaller devices vs. larger devices. You can do this by improving the classes with media queries:

```
[class*="col-span"]{
     float: left;
}

.sm-col-span-1{
        width: 25%;
}

.sm-col-span-2{
        width: 50%;
}

.sm-col-span-3{
        width: 75%;
}

.sm-col-span-4{
        width: 100%;
}

@media screen and (min-width: 768px){
        .lg-col-span-1{
                width: 25%;
        }

        .lg-col-span-2{
                width: 50%;
        }

        .lg-col-span-3{
                width: 75%;
        }

        .lg-col-span-4{
                width: 100%;
        }
}
```

As you are building this CSS grid to be mobile first, you have defined the default column widths first and then defined classes for larger devices that will activate if the minimum width of the device is 768px. You have changed the original classes to be prefixed with sm- and lg-. The sm- prefixed classes target small devices and above, and the lg- prefixed classes target larger devices. The idea is that you apply the sm- prefixed column classes to the HTML elements to define the layout for smaller devices, and then use the lg- prefixed columns to override the column spans where appropriate.

Gutters

The gutters of a CSS grid are the spacing in between each of the columns; historically, this was achieved using margins. However, when working with a fluid design, you want the spacing to be part of the columns, so you can choose to use percentages for the column widths. Therefore, you should be using padding for the gutters in between the columns.

The disadvantage of using padding for the gutters is that it prevents you from adding a background color to the columns. The reason for this is that if you add a background color to the columns the background will also show up in the gutters. The only way around this is to add any background colors to the elements inside the column rather than to the column itself.

Previously I explained the CSS3 box-sizing property, which allows you to change how the box model works to allow you to control whether the padding is on the inside or outside of the width. For this grid you will want the columns to include the padding, which will be used for the gutters. To achieve this, the columns will have box-sizing set to border-box. If you have already applied this to the universal selector as I suggested earlier, you do not need to add the box-sizing again here:

```
[class*="col-span"] {
        box-sizing: border-box;
        padding-left: 15px;
        padding-right: 15px;
}
```

As you can see, you have also added the padding to the column. You have added the padding using the full padding-left, padding-right property names because this prevents you from overwriting any padding added to the top or bottom of the element that may have been specified elsewhere in the CSS.

Rows

The row is used to contain the columns. Because the columns are floated left, they are being taken out of the flow of the page; therefore, nonpositioned block elements before and after the floated element flow as if the element were not there. So, to prevent this issue, the row also has the job of clearing the floats used by the columns.

The usual approach to do this is to add a pseudo-element as part of the row that clears the floats:

```
.row:after{
        content: ' ';
        clear: both;
        display: block;
}
```

As demonstrated above, the pseudo-element is an empty block-level element with a clear: both applied.

Wrapper

Finally, you will add a wrapper around all the rows. It is used to add the additional padding to the left and right of the site:

```
.wrapper{
        padding-left: 15px;
        padding-right: 15px;
}
```

Putting the Grid Together

The previous examples focused on how to build a responsive blog so that it was possible to see the differences between those examples, and this new code will therefore build a responsive grid for a blog.

I have already explained the CSS that will make up this grid, so let's put it all together (Listing 4-1).

Listing 4-1. Sample HTML Used for the Grid

```
<!DOCTYPE html>
<html>
<head>
        <title>Responsive Grid</title>
        <meta name="viewport" content="width=device-width">
        <link rel="stylesheet" type="text/css" href="responsive-grid.css">
</head>
<body>
        <header>
                <div class="wrapper">
                        <div class="row">
                                <div class="sm-col-span-2 lg-col-span-4">
                                        <h1>Blog</h1>
                                </div>
                                <nav class="sm-col-span-2 lg-col-span-4">
                                        <ul>
                                                <li><a href="#">Latest posts</a></li>
                                                <li><a href="#">Popular posts</a></li>
                                        </ul>
                                </nav>
                        </div>
                </div>
        </header>
        <div class="content" role="main">
                <div class="wrapper">
                        <div class="row">
                                <article class="sm-col-span-4 lg-col-span-3">
                                        <h2>Article title</h2>
                                        <p>02/12/2013</p>
                                        <p>Praesent commodo cursus magna, vel scelerisque nisl
consectetur et. Cras justo odio, dapibus ac facilisis in, egestas eget quam. Vivamus sagittis lacus
vel augue laoreet rutrum faucibus dolor auctor. Etiam porta sem malesuada magna mollis euismod. Cras
mattis consectetur purus sit amet fermentum. Duis mollis, est non commodo luctus, nisi erat porttitor
ligula, eget lacinia odio sem nec elit. Vestibulum id ligula porta felis euismod semper.</p>
                                </article>
```

```
                          <aside class="sm-col-span-4 lg-col-span-1">
                                  <h2>Related Articles</h2>
                                  <nav>
                                          <ul>
                                                  <li><a href="#">Article item 1</a></li>
                                                  <li><a href="#">Article item 2</a></li>
                                                  <li><a href="#">Article item 3</a></li>
                                          </ul>
                                  </nav>
                          </aside>
                  </div>
          </div>
      </div>
  </body>
  </html>
```

Now let's putting together the CSS; so the CSS is easy to follow, let's separate the CSS grid from the site-specific styles that had been applied to make it look like a blog. The completed CSS code is shown in Listing 4-2.

Listing 4-2. The Completed CSS for the Grid

```
/*Grid styles*/
.wrapper{
        padding-left: 15px;
        padding-right: 15px;
}

.row:after{
        content: ' ';
        clear: both;
        display: block;
}

[class*="col-span"] {
    float: left;
    box-sizing: border-box;
    padding-left: 15px;
        padding-right: 15px;
}

.sm-col-span-1{
        width: 25%;
}

.sm-col-span-2{
        width: 50%;
}

.sm-col-span-3{
        width: 75%;
}
```

```
.sm-col-span-4{
        width: 100%;
}

@media screen and (min-width: 768px){
        .lg-col-span-1{
                width: 25%;
        }

        .lg-col-span-2{
                width: 50%;
        }

        .lg-col-span-3{
                width: 75%;
        }

        .lg-col-span-4{
                width: 100%;
        }
}

/*Site specific*/
body{
        margin: 0;
        padding: 0;
    font-size: 14px;
    line-height: 18px;
}

header{
        background: #304480;
        padding-top: 10px;
        padding-bottom: 10px;
        color: #fff;
}

ul{
        padding: 0px;
        margin: 0px;
}

ul li{
        list-style: none;
}

header nav{
        text-align: right;
}
```

```css
header nav a{
        color: #fff;
}

@media screen and (min-width: 768px){
        header nav{
                text-align: center;
                padding-top: 10px;
                border-top: 1px dashed #ccc;
                margin-top: 10px;
        }

        header nav li{
                display: inline-block;
        }
}
```

We can now look at how this looks on an extra small device (shown in Figure 4-23).

Figure 4-23. *Our site shown on an extra small device (in this example an iOS device)*

Having seen how our site looks on an extra small device, we should also take a look at how it appears on larger devices, we can do this by simply firing up our desktop browser and loading our site. Figure 4-24 shows what we would expect to see.

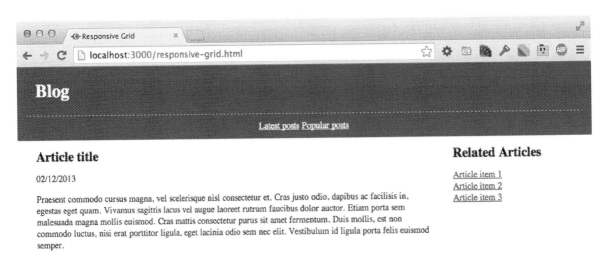

Figure 4-24. *Our site shown on a larger device (in this example a desktop browser)*

However, if you were to increase the viewport width further to 1,440px, you would then start to notice that the lines of copy in the article have started to become quite long. As discussed earlier, the optimum number of characters per line is between 45 and 75, and looking at the screenshot in Figure 4-25, you will notice the text is far beyond this.

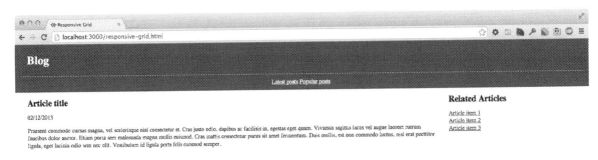

Figure 4-25. *Text beyond the optimum number of characters per line*

Preventing this isn't too difficult; you simply adapt the wrapper to have a maximum width, after which it will simply center the site:

```
.wrapper{
        padding-left: 15px;
        padding-right: 15px;
        max-width: 1200px;
        margin: 0 auto;
}
```

Now if you check the site on the large viewport, it now centers when the viewport is over 1,200px, as shown in Figure 4-26.

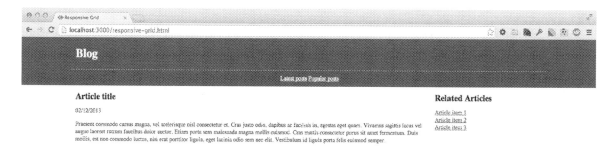

Figure 4-26. *Text now centering with larger viewport*

Improving the Grid

Having now completed this first responsive grid, you have learned the basic principles for building a CSS grid. If you were to take this further, there are many ways in which you could improve the grid to allow you to build better, more usable sites.

The first way would be to increase the number of columns. A typical grid uses between 12 and 16 columns, however, for simplicity here I opted for only four columns. Increasing the number of columns would be relatively straightforward, with each column simply being calculated using the following formula:

Column width = (100 / Total Number of columns) * column span

Rather than calculate this manually, you could choose to use Nicolaj Kirkgaard Nielsen's grid calculator.[4]

A second way in which you could improve the grid is to provide greater control of the number of columns across different viewport sizes. You already added media queries to allow targeting of the number of columns for small and large devices independently; however, you could add more fine-grained control by adding the ability to target medium-sized devices.

---

[4]http://gridcalculator.dk/.

Summary

Fluid layouts are a prominent feature of any responsive site as they allow web sites to make use of any available space. As highlighted in this chapter, this feature of fluid layouts is of particular importance to responsive design as we are developing for devices of all shapes and sizes.

Fluid layouts do impose some extra challenges on us as developers, however, so we looked at some principles to follow that ensure we are able to optimize our responsive sites for usability. In addition, these principles should guide you in being able to quickly and effectively build your site.

Having learned about fluid design, I explained how you could apply these techniques; in particular, I focused on building a fluid responsive CSS grid. This explained how to apply what you have already learned about media queries to fluid layouts.

Having looked at fluid layouts and learnt about how to build a basic grid ourselves, in the next chapter you will learn more about existing CSS grids and frameworks we can use to build our responsive sites.

## CHAPTER 5

Frameworks in Responsive Design

Responsive development, as I'm sure you can appreciate, does add additional work to a project, where developers need to consider all the different variations of a web site when viewed with different screen resolutions. A way in which we can reduce our workload when building a site is to use a responsive framework as a starting point.

When looking at fluid design as discussed in Chapter 4, I explained the basics of CSS grids and you learned how to develop your own. However, in the example provided, the grid was largely simplified, and developing a more complex grid could actually be quite time-consuming. Thankfully, as developers, we have a world of open source code available to us, and this chapter will explore some of the most popular grids and frameworks.

In this chapter on grids and frameworks, the topics I will explain are:

1. Grid systems

2. CSS frameworks

3. What is best for a particular web site

4. Prototyping a site using CSS frameworks

Grid Systems

In its simplest form, a grid system is a structure within which you can build the layout of your web site. Consisting of horizontal rows and vertical columns, it houses the content of the web site, which can span one or more columns. A grid system can offer significant benefits when building a site, allowing you to achieve consistency of spacing in your build, with which comes improved usability of the site because the text is easier to follow.

When looking for an open source grid system, you will notice that they are often very basic and simply include only the styles necessary to render the grid, leaving all the other decisions over how you build your site up to you. The grid systems explained in this chapter are all built to be responsive, so in addition to the basic grid, they also include the media queries that allow them to respond to the width of the browser viewport.

Despite the benefits of mobile first responsive design and a drive within the web development community to embrace it, a majority of standalone grid systems are still built desktop first. Therefore, when looking at grid systems, it is important to look at whether they are built to be mobile first.

This chapter will look at three of the popular mobile-first responsive grids. The grid systems examined are:

1. Fluidable (http://fluidable.com/)

2. CSS Smart Grid (http://dryan.github.io/css-smart-grid/)

3. csswizardry-grids (http://csswizardry.com/csswizardry-grids/)

Fluidable

Fluidable (http://fluidable.com/) is a mobile-first, responsive grid system developed by Andri Sigurðsson, which has fixed gutters and supports variable column widths. Figure 5-1 shows its home page.

Figure 5-1. *The Fluidable home page*

I asked Andri what his reasoning was behind developing his own grid system and he explained as follows:

I wanted a grid that could be configured for any number of columns, be fluid (use percentages), and on top of that, have fixed width gutters, which I feel is the only way to make a grid. From a design perspective, having your gutters shrink is just a big no-no. You want to be able to control when the gutters change. Then, when responsive design started came into the picture, using pixels just didn't make sense anymore. My final reason was that I really wanted something lightweight that I could use for smaller projects, like one-pagers and smaller sites where using a full fledged framework was overkill.

After speaking to Andri, it was very clear that in building his grid he was trying to achieve a lot of what we explored when building our own grid, however, having spent more time working on it, he has implemented a full 12-column grid (see Figure 5-2).

Figure 5-2. *Screenshot of the different grid arrangements shown on the Fluidable web site*

In looking at how the Fluidable grid is built, it is possible to see its capability to define how many columns the element spans for each different device type, meaning that when using this technology it is possible to easily control how the site looks down to an individual device type. The way this is achieved is through the naming conventions used for the elements' class names:

1. `.col-mb-x` Defines how many columns it should span on mobile

2. `.col-x` Defines how many columns it should span on a tablet

3. `.col-dt-x` Defines how many columns it should span on a desktop

For each of these, the x represents the number of columns the element should span. A similar approach was used in the example grid to allow mobile to have a different grid layout, however, it didn't go as far as to separate tablet from desktop. Fluidable does not have this limitation and instead offers the three different column class sets, as listed above. My only complaint with their implementation of this is the naming convention for the column class names is not consistent, with col-x being used for tablet, which isn't immediately clear.

From a technology point of view, Fluidable is built using the CSS preprocessor LESS (leaner CSS [CSS preprocessors will be discussed later in the book]), meaning it is also possible to customize your grid if you are using LESS by changing the values of the variables. Fluidable is configurable using five variables—@columns, @maxWidth, @gutterWidth, @screenTablet, and @screenDesktop—which allow it to be more flexible.

CSS Smart Grid

The next grid system is CSS Smart Grid by Daniel Ryan (`http://dryan.github.io/css-smart-grid/`). Daniel initially released CSS Smart Grid in 2011 on GitHub and after nine releases it was at version 4.0 at the time of writing. Figure 5-3 shows the home page and documentation site for CSS Smart Grid.

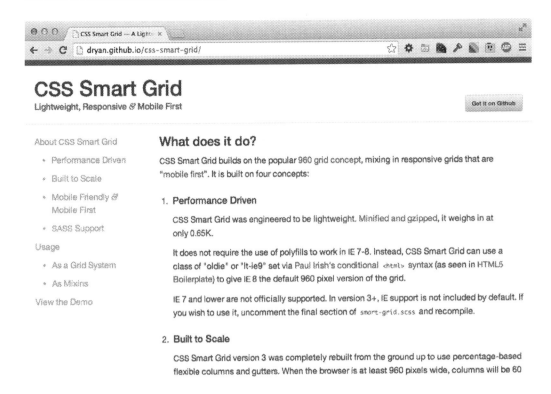

Figure 5-3. *The CSS Smart Grid home page*

I contacted Daniel to ask him why he chose to develop his own grid system rather than use an existing grid.

The grid I created was born in the summer of 2011 specifically for the Obama campaign. We wanted to be mobile first, but there weren't many robust grids at the time that took that approach. Then we had the issue that polyfilling @media queries was a real issue for us because all the JavaScript solutions used AJAX to load and parse the CSS. Our CSS was served over a CDN that didn't support CORS headers, so it was a no-go for us. The final requirement I had was that the grid needed to be lightweight and performant.

The most interesting point he raised was the issues he had with polyfilling media queries in the past, so I will explain how this was engineered as part of CSS Smart Grid.

CSS Smart Grid is cleverly engineered to support Internet Explorer 8 without the need for a JavaScript polyfill. This is achieved by using the conditional comments to add classes to the HTML tag, which can then be used to show the default 960 grid to Internet Explorer 8. By using this technique, the grid can still be built using a mobile-first approach and provide a desktop layout to Internet Explorer 8 without any JavaScript required.

Having already learned about what makes this grid standout, let's look at the actual grid to see how the grid itself compares to the other grid systems being examined here (see Figure 5-4).

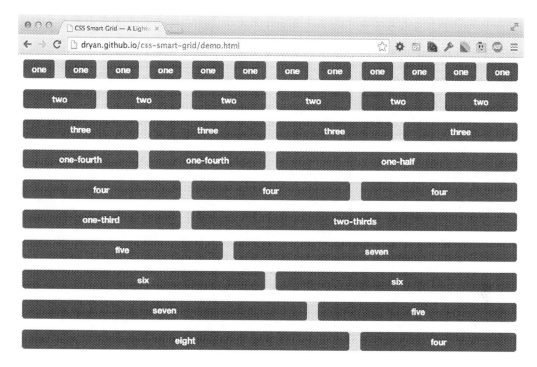

Figure 5-4. *Screenshot of the different grid arrangements shown on the CSS Smart Grid site*

The columns in CSS Smart Grid are defined by adding the class "columns" with an additional class to specify the number of columns it should span (e.g., one, two, three). This is supported right up to 12 columns. Alternatively, you can also use keywords to specify how wide an element should be, these are:

1. one-fourth: equal to 25 percent or three columns' width

2. one-half: equal to 50 percent or six columns' width

3. one-third: equal to 33.33 percent or four columns' width

4. two-thirds: equal to 66.66 percent or eight columns' width

An example of using the grid in practice is shown below. As you will see, a row is defined, along with two columns, each with a width defined using the keywords discussed above:

```
<div class="row">
    <div class="columns two-thirds">
        <p>Lorem ipsum</p>
    </div>
    <div class="columns one-third">
        <p>Lorem ipsum</p>
    </div>
</div>
```

Using these keywords adds extra flexibility to how you choose to label your columns, however, it is important to note that in the CSS it is doing the same as if you had simply used the numerical column class names.

The grid itself is built using the SASS (Syntactically Awesome Style Sheets) CSS preprocessor, and for CSS Smart Grid, Daniel has included the option to include the column widths as a "mixin" rather than use the classes in the HTML. The benefit to this is that the HTML appears less cluttered as you don't need to add as many classes to your markup. The disadvantage of this, however, is that you are tying your element to only work at that specific width, as you are defining the width in your CSS. If instead you were to use the column width classes in your HTML, you could easily change the size of your element simply by changing the class. In this respect, the block itself would be a fluid width; the column class would then simply give it a defined width. This makes your code more flexible as you can then use the same block of code in multiple places with different widths by simply changing the column width class used.

csswizardry-grids

The next grid is the csswizardry-grids by Harry Roberts (`http://csswizardry.com/csswizardry-grids/`). It is a mobile-first responsive grid available for download on GitHub (see Figure 5-5).

Figure 5-5. *csswizardry-grids home page*

I contacted Harry Roberts to ask him the reason behind the development of csswizardry-grids:

> *I wanted a pragmatic answer to a complex problem; most other solutions seemed like complex answers.*[1]

---

[1]Harry Roberts, January 17, 2014, Twitter @csswizardry.

The grid is built to be really flexible, with an additional benefit over the previous grids discussed, being that it allows you to define whether your columns should be centered or gutterless. This means that rather than try to offset the column evenly to center it, you can center a column simply by using a class. The grid also has the added flexibility to allow you to nest columns within other columns (see Figure 5-6).

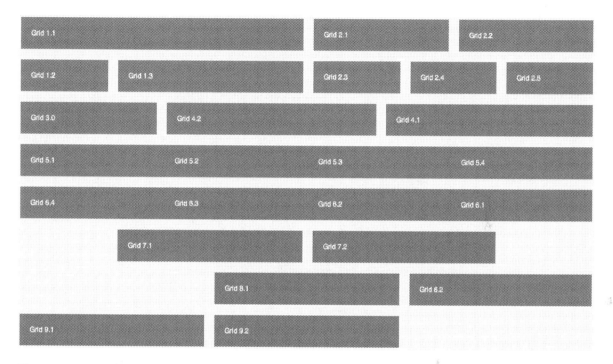

Figure 5-6. *Screenshot of the different grid arrangements shown on the csswizardry-grid site*

Similar to the CSS Smart Grid, this grid system uses a class-naming convention that refers to the column widths as fractions, examples being:

1. one-half

2. one-third, two thirds

3. one-quarter, two-quarters, three-quarters

This class-naming convention lends itself to being easier to read than the common span-X approach used by a large number of grid systems.

Again, in a similar way to CSS Smart Grid, csswizardry-grids allows you to use SASS with it (a CSS preprocessor that will be discussed later in this book), and you can simply extend the rules for the columns to your own CSS class selector, meaning that if you choose, you can avoid adding the extra classes into the HTML itself. This has the same advantages and disadvantages of using this approach as you would have using it with CSS Smart Grid.

One of the main disadvantages of using csswizardry-grids is that rather than using floats, it uses inline blocks to place the columns next to one another, so if you have a space between the columns in your HTML, you get unwanted spacing in your rendered page. There are two common ways you can use to prevent this: either by placing an HTML comment in between the elements, as shown here:

```
<div class="one-half">
        lorem ipsum
</div><!--
  --><div class="one-half">
        lorem ipsum
</div>
```

or by simply removing the spaces in between your columns, as shown here:

```
<div class="one-half">
        lorem ipsum
</div><div class="one-half">
        lorem ipsum
</div>
```

Although this is a disadvantage of using inline block, there are several advantages of using inline block over floats. It allows you to reverse the order of your content using the dir HTML attribute. This can be added to either a particular element to target a specific area of your site or it can be added to the HTML element to target the full page. The dir HTML attribute can have two possible values: ltr for left to right and rtl for right to left text. Figure 5-7 shows how using the dir attribute can affect csswizardry-grids.

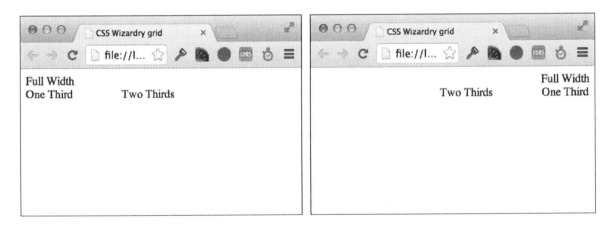

Figure 5-7. Grid default alignment on the left, the text direction set to "right to left" on the right

Using the dir attribute has its own advantages; first, you can order your content in order of importance for accessibility and search engine optimisation rather than having to structure your content simply as per the design. Second, if you are building a multilingual site where you will be supporting right to left languages, you are able to simply reverse the layout using the dir attribute.

Another benefit of using inline block for your grid is that the elements naturally have the correct height and you do not have to clear the floats.

CSS Frameworks

In addition to the open source grid systems, there are also a wide variety of open source grid frameworks. A CSS framework is an extension of a typical CSS grid system in that in addition to providing the grid layout, it also provides standard browser resets, typography, and user interface elements that you can use to build responsive sites. Although it is called a CSS framework, it is important to be aware that some of the interface elements common in these CSS frameworks often require JavaScript, which ships with the framework.

There are many different CSS frameworks available, however, there are two that really have been embraced in the web development community: Twitter Bootstrap and Zurb Foundation.

Common user interface elements that you will find in a CSS framework are:

1. Dropdowns

2. Button's and button groups

3. Forms

4. Navbar

5. Breadcrumbs

6. Pagination

7. Labels

8. Badges

9. Page header

10. Thumbnails

11. Alerts

12. Progress bars

13. Media object

14. List group

Through providing a wide selection of components, CSS framework makes the life of the developer easier as they can simply choose from existing components when they need a common element, allowing them to focus their time on the look and feel of the site along with the new custom components that are adapted to the site they are building.

Let's look at a couple of the most popular CSS frameworks.

Twitter Bootstrap

Twitter Bootstrap is a CSS framework that was initially built by Mark Otto and Jacob Thornton; however, it has since become the most popular project on GitHub with almost 600 contributors and over 25,000 forks. The framework is also quite mature, having already had 25 releases, bringing it to version 3.2.0 at the time of writing.

Clearly, Twitter Bootstrap is being used by a large number of developers, but what this does not immediately show is the scale of some of the sites using Twitter Bootstrap. Brands including Healthcare.gov, Virgin Active, and the Tumblr for Angry Birds Star Wars II are all using Twitter Bootstrap, and in very different ways, which also shows just how versatile the framework is.

Mark Otto wrote an article for A List Apart (http://alistapart.com/article/building-twitter-bootstrap) talking about the reasons behind the development of Twitter Bootstrap:

> A year and a half ago, a small group of Twitter employees set out to improve our team's internal analytical and administrative tools. After some early meetings around this one product, we set out with a higher ambition to create a toolkit for anyone to use within Twitter, and beyond. Thus, we set out to build a system that would help folks like us build new projects on top of it, and Bootstrap was conceived.[2]

This higher ambition of Mark's to try to build a toolkit for everyone to use has been very successful; Twitter Bootstrap achieved the Twitter team's objective of it being a toolkit that can be used on a wide variety of projects, and by open sourcing the project, it is providing these benefits to the wider development community.

When we start to look deeper at what Twitter Bootstrap has to offer, it is important to start with the basics, and at the base of Twitter Bootstrap is a mobile-first, responsive grid system. Out of the box the framework has a 12-column grid, with classes for extra small (mobile), small (tablet/small netbooks), medium (desktop/notebooks), and large (large screen desktop) so that you are able to completely adapt the site based on different viewport sizes.

Some of the most commonly used components that come with Twitter Bootstrap are shown in Figure 5-8.

1. **Navigation**

2. **Buttons**

3. **Forms**

4. **Typography**

---

[2]Mark Otto, A List Apart, 2012.

h1. Bootstrap heading
Semibold 36px

h2. Bootstrap heading
Semibold 30px

h3. Bootstrap heading
Semibold 24px

h4. Bootstrap heading
Semibold 18px

h5. Bootstrap heading
Semibold 14px

h6. Bootstrap heading
Semibold 12px

5. **Thumbnails**

Figure 5-8. *Twitter Bootstrap components*

This is a small sample of the components that ship with Twitter Bootstrap, and to explore them all, you should take a look at www.getbootstrap.com to get a full picture of what Twitter Bootstrap components offer.

Aside from the built-in components, the web development community has also extended Twitter Bootstrap with third-party components, which can simply be added on. Examples of some of the popular add-on components are:

1. *Fuel UX*: (http://exacttarget.github.io/fuelux/) Fuel UX extends Bootstrap by adding additional lightweight JavaScript components.

2. *Bootstrap Image Gallery*: (http://blueimp.github.io/Bootstrap-Image-Gallery) This component adds the ability to have a gallery with a light box that can navigate through a series of images.

3. *Bootstrap Application Wizard*: (http://www.panopta.com/2013/02/06/bootstrap-application-wizard/) The Bootstrap Application Wizard component allows you easily to make multipart forms with Bootstrap. These are shown inside a modal that shows above your page.

This ability to extend Twitter Bootstrap with other open source components makes it really powerful. However, unlike jQuery, which has a repository for all the custom plug-ins users have made, there isn't a repository for Bootstrap components, meaning you have to rely on a trusty search engine like Google to find these components. Although this isn't a major downside, it can make it more difficult to find the recommended components.

It is important as a developer to understand how the framework is built because often we will want to be able to remove parts we are not using so they are not bloating our site unnecessarily. With Twitter Bootstrap, the main project is built using LESS. However, there is an official SASS port so you have a choice when it comes to which version you use. I will discuss CSS preprocessors separately in chapter 7.

If you get stuck and need help with Twitter Bootstrap, there is a large community of developers you can turn to, and it's likely through a quick search that you will find someone who has probably already asked the same question, which means you can quickly resolve any issues you have.

Zurb Foundation

Zurb Foundation is a CSS framework built by the web design agency Zurb, first becoming open source as of version 2.0 in 2011. Since this initial release, there have been three subsequent releases, with 5.3.3 being the version at the time of this writing.

In looking at who is using Zurb Foundation, we can see that it is used by many large sites, including Dictionary.com, the UK HTC Online Store, and the World Wildlife Fund.

The components in Zurb Foundation are very similar to those in Twitter Bootstrap. A brief look at some of the components shows that the main ones offered by both are the same, as shown in Figure 5-9.

1. **Navigation**

2. **Buttons**

3. **Forms**

4.   **Typography**

RENDERED HTML

h1. This is a very large header.

h2. This is a large header.

h3. This is a medium header.

h4. This is a moderate header.

h5. This is a small header.

h6. This is a tiny header.

5.   **Thumbnails**

Figure 5-9. *Zurb Foundation components*

If you were to look at where Zurb Foundation really stands out from the crowd, it would be with its Interchange Responsive Content (or Interchange for short). In short, Interchange allows you to load different sections of HTML into your page for particular media queries. What this means is that when you are building HTML you do not need to include the HTML for all of the viewport widths in the main page, instead focusing on providing mobile-first HTML and then using Interchange to load the additional HTML for different viewports. Additionally, Interchange can be used to load different images based on the width of the viewport, so you can load smaller, optimized images on smaller viewports and larger images for larger viewports.

Zurb Foundation is not just an open source project that Zurb develops. It also offers paid support to help you make the most of the framework along with training and accreditation. Although this option may not be affordable for all projects, it is often seen to be beneficial to some corporate environments.

What Is Best for My Site?

Having looked at both CSS grid systems and CSS grid frameworks, you should now be familiar with the benefits and disadvantages of both. It is important to make the decision of which framework or grid system you want to use, if you use one at all, when you initially start to build a site as it can be very difficult to change once you have already progressed with your build.

The reason that it can be difficult to change framework or grid system is that you will have already committed to the code structure and naming conventions that came along with your chosen framework or grid, so changing could potentially mean a lot of refactoring would be needed. In the case of frameworks, you may have also used some of the user interface components, so changing frameworks would involve finding the alternative framework's equivalents or finding replacements elsewhere.

When it comes to making the decision between using a CSS grid and a CSS framework, it is a simple case of asking yourself whether or not you want to have prebuilt user interface components. You should also look at what else is offered alongside the interface components; things like base CSS for typography can save you significant time and you might find that this sways you to use a CSS framework rather than a CSS grid.

It is important to remember that there isn't a one-size-fits-all solution, and although you may have chosen to use a grid system or a grid framework on one web site, you may find that for another site you would make a different decision.

Where CSS frameworks often get a lot of criticism, and perhaps a reason you may have been put off in the past, is their file size. The reason behind the file size is that a CSS framework includes a lot of different components, each of which contributes to increasing the file size of the framework. To be able to get the most out of the framework you have chosen, you should be using them where possible. This isn't a reason to overlook a framework, however, as you have the option to pick and choose which parts of a framework you will use in a project and you can simply remove any unused CSS options, either manually or using automated tools such as the postprocessor uncss (which will be covered in Chapter 7).

Choosing a CSS Grid

Having decided that a grid is more your cup of tea and you want to be able to build all your own components, it is important to take a look at the options available:

When choosing a grid, there are some questions you will need to ask yourself:

1. *Do you feel comfortable working with the grid?* It is important that you feel comfortable with the grid, even small things like how classes are named can be an annoyance if it does not fit with the way you normally code, so it is important that you are 100 percent comfortable with the grid, especially because you may be maintaining the site for a number of years.

2. *Is the grid suitable for your site?* Your grid of choice should work for your site. This is especially important if you already have had the site designed without a prior discussion about grids. This means if you want to use a grid, it needs to fit the number of columns for which the site has been designed. Some grid systems will allow you to configure the number of columns they use, which can aid you in trying to get a design to fit into a grid. A better approach is to have chosen the grid before the site is designed and discuss this with the designer so you know your grid is suitable.

Choosing a CSS Framework

After deciding upon using a CSS framework, it is important to ensure you choose one that you are happy to work with—remember its unlikely you are building a site that you won't be touching again, so you need to make a choice you are happy with as you may be maintaining the site for the foreseeable future.

When choosing a framework, there are some questions you will need to ask yourself:

1. *Do you like the grid the framework is built on?* As previously discussed, the base of a CSS framework includes a grid system, so you have to be comfortable with the grid.

2. *Are you happy with the selection of components that the framework comes with?* The user interface components that the framework comes with are a core part of the framework, so it is important that you are happy with the selection. Although you can add your own, using the components that come with the framework will not only make your life easier it can also save you a significant amount of time.

3. *Does the framework suit the way you work and the tools you use?* Some frameworks might require you to use specific tools, and it is likely you already have a set of tools you know and love, so you will need to consider this when choosing a framework.

Choosing Neither a Grid Nor a Framework

There are also some instances where neither a CSS grid system nor a CSS framework is appropriate, examples of these being:

1. The design uses uneven column sizes.

2. The design has uneven margins in between the columns.

3. The width of the design is not easily divisible.

4. The site content is placed on the page in a irregular manor (an example of this could be a parallax site).

If your site falls into any of these categories, you are likely to end up spending a large amount of time trying to force your site to fit the grid and would instead be better off spending your time building your site without a grid but still following the mobile-first approach already discussed.

Prototyping a Site Using a CSS Framework

Traditionally, as part of the web site development life cycle, a user-experienced designer would put together a series of static wireframes to illustrate to the client, designers, and web developers how the web site should work. Along with the notes to explain the functionality, this would be the basis for which a web site was built. More recently, applications have been developed that have allowed interactive wireframes to be built, however, a lot of these applications are still very limited to simply tying together a series of static images with links.

This is an area outside of traditional web site development for which use of a CSS framework can offer significant improvements. CSS frameworks really shine for being able to quickly prototype a web site using the components provided as part of the framework. Without writing a single line of CSS, it is very easy to quickly mock up prototypes using the included components.

We have already explored a few different CSS frameworks, one of which, Twitter Bootstrap, we will use for mocking up a prototype for a site.

To get started, you need to set up a base template for the components to sit within. For this, you will need to include the Twitter Bootstrap CSS framework, which can be downloaded at `www.getbootstrap.com`. For the HTML for the base template, you simply need some barebones HTML, and to include jQuery, the Twitter Bootstrap CSS and JavaScript. Type in the code in Listing 5-1.

Listing 5-1. Base template HTML

```
<!DOCTYPE html>
<html>
<head>
        <title>Prototype</title>
        <meta name="viewport" content="width=device-width">
        <link rel="stylesheet" type="text/css" href="css/bootstrap.min.css">
</head>
<body>

        <script src="http://code.jquery.com/jquery-1.10.1.min.js"></script>
        <script src="js/bootstrap.min.js"></script>
</body>
</html>
```

With this in place, you can now start building the prototype out of the Twitter Bootstrap components. For this, you will be taking snippets of code for modules from the Twitter Bootstrap documentation and shortening them where appropriate.

The first element you will include is a navbar. The navbar module in the Twitter Bootstrap documentation includes drop-downs and a search form, however, in this example you will include a simplified version, as presented in Listing 5-2.

Listing 5-2. Original Source Adapted from the Documentation at `http://getbootstrap.com/components/#nav`

```
<header>
    <nav class="navbar-default" role="navigation">
        <div class="container">
            <!-- Brand and toggle get grouped for better mobile display -->
            <div class="navbar-header">
                <button type="button" class="navbar-toggle" data-toggle="collapse"
data-target="#bs-example-navbar-collapse-1">
                    <span class="sr-only">Toggle navigation</span>
                    <span class="icon-bar"></span>
                    <span class="icon-bar"></span>
                    <span class="icon-bar"></span>
                </button>
                <a class="navbar-brand" href="#">Prototype</a>
            </div>

            <!-- Collect the nav links, forms, and other content for toggling -->
            <div class="collapse navbar-collapse" id="bs-example-navbar-collapse-1">
                <ul class="nav navbar-nav">
                    <li class="active"><a href="#">Link</a></li>
                    <li><a href="#">Link</a></li>
                    <li><a href="#">Link</a></li>
                </ul>
            </div><!-- /.navbar-collapse -->
        </div>
    </nav>
</header>
```

Just as when you build responsive sites, you are building this prototype mobile first, so the first port of call is to test the navigation on an extra small device, as shown in Figure 5-10.

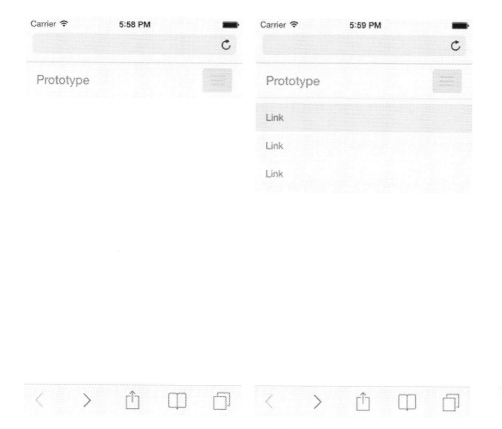

Figure 5-10. *Testing the navigation on an extra small device*

If you now test the same navigation in a desktop browser, you get a full-width navigation, as illustrated in Figure 5-11.

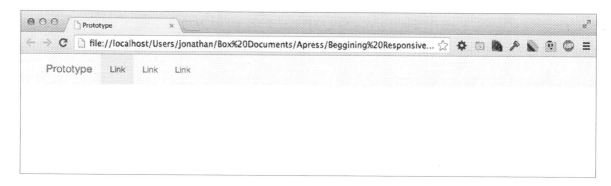

Figure 5-11. *The navigation shown on a larger viewport, showing the full-sized navigation*

Without writing any CSS or JavaScript, you now have a navigation that works responsively and collapses nicely on mobile.

Next you want to add the jumbotron component, which is essentially a big feature header area, sometimes referred to as the hero. Type in the code in Listing 5-3 to add this component.

Listing 5-3. Original Source Adapted from the Documentation at http://getbootstrap.com/components/#jumbotron

```
<section class="jumbotron">
    <div class="container">
        <h1>Prototype</h1>
        <p>This is our prototype</p>
        <p><a href="#" class="btn btn-primary btn-lg" role="button">Learn more</a></p>
    </div>
</section>
```

If you now test again on our extra small device, the header looks more complete. By simply dropping in the jumbotron component, you have added a title to the page along with a main call to action, as can be seen in Figure 5-12.

Figure 5-12. *The extra small viewport of the site featuring the jumbotron*

When you look at how the prototype now displays on desktop, you can see that the Twitter Bootstrap jumbotron component responds to the wider viewport with larger typography, as shown in Figure 5-13.

Figure 5-13. *The jumbotron viewed on a wide viewport*

Next you will add some panels to show your web site's products. For images you will use a service called lorempixel.com, which will show a random image as a placeholder. For the products, use the thumbnail component, as provided in Listing 5-4.

Listing 5-4. Original Source Adapted from the Documentation at
http://getbootstrap.com/components/#thumbnails-custom-content

```
<section class="container">
    <div class="row">
        <div class="col-sm-4">
            <div class="thumbnail">
                <img src="http://lorempixel.com/400/200/" alt="...">
                <div class="caption">
                    <h3>Product one</h3>
                    <p>...</p>
                </div>
            </div>
        </div>
        <div class="col-sm-4">
            <div class="thumbnail">
                <img src="http://lorempixel.com/400/200/" alt="...">
                <div class="caption">
                    <h3>Product two</h3>
                    <p>...</p>
                </div>
            </div>
        </div>
        <div class="col-sm-4">
            <div class="thumbnail">
                <img src="http://lorempixel.com/400/200/" alt="...">
```

```
                <div class="caption">
                    <h3>Product three</h3>
                    <p>...</p>
                </div>
            </div>
        </div>
    </div>
</section>
```

With the thumbnail components in place, you can now refresh your browser and the prototype for the home page now looks complete. So that you can see the product blocks clearly, I have included how this looks on our extra small devices in Figure 5-14.

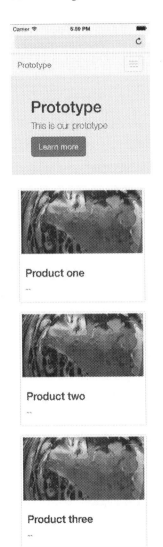

Figure 5-14. *The product panels viewed on a small device*

Again, when you look at the prototype on desktop, you can see that instead of using a single column for the products, the site now uses three columns, as illustrated in Figure 5-15.

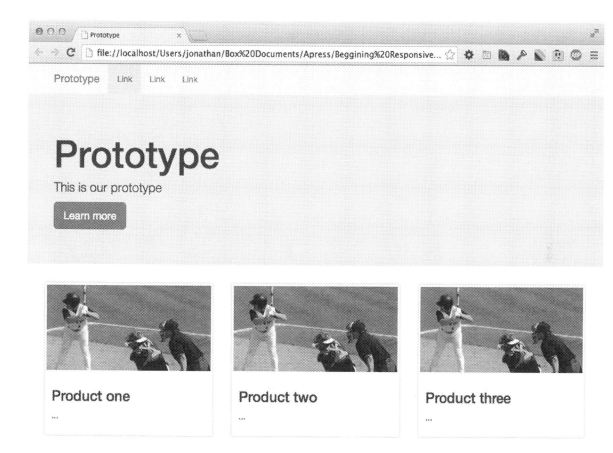

Figure 5-15. *Larger device showing the product panels alongside one another*

The reason for the three columns is because you chose to use the column class col-sm-4, which means that each column spans four of the twelve columns that make up our grid (which is a third of the width of the page). The benefit of using any of these Bootstrap components is that you can use column classes to define how they look at different browser widths. Simply changing the class to col-sm-3 and adding an extra product box will show four products side by side, as illustrated in Figure 5-16.

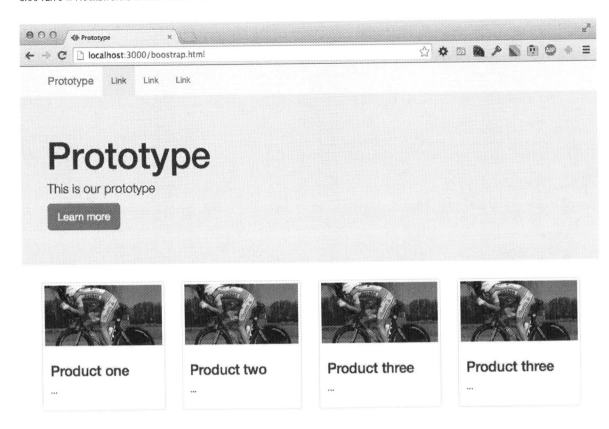

Figure 5-16. *Four product columns shown on larger device*

As just demonstrated, without writing any CSS and simply adapting the HTML found in the documentation, it is really easy to create a prototype using a CSS framework. Although this is a very simple example, it really highlights some of the benefits CSS frameworks have to offer. There are several key benefits of building a prototype rather than spending time creating wireframes:

1. Those using the prototype can get a feel for how the site will work rather than relying on the notes attached to the wireframe.

2. By using a responsive CSS framework, your prototype is by default responsive, allowing you to show how the site will function on different devices.

3. Rather than starting from scratch when building the site, you might be able to build on top of the prototype.

As per point 2 here, having built this prototype using a responsive CSS framework, you have been able to build the prototype to be fully responsive. This allows users of this prototype to quickly see how they should expect the final site to work across a variety of devices.

Summary

This chapter looked at both CSS grid systems and CSS frameworks, specifically focusing on where you might use them and the benefits each could bring to your responsive design project.

The chapter examined the importance of selecting the grid or framework best suited to your project, rather than basing it on any feelings of loyalty toward a particular framework. The most important aspect is the flexibility of the grid or framework in relation to your needs.

One area where CSS frameworks can be particularly useful is when you are looking to prototype a site, and this chapter explored how you can quickly prototype a web site by simply adapting the HTML examples taken from the Bootstrap site and putting them together to make a page. This is extremely powerful as it means that rather than build flat user experience diagrams and then have to explain the various interactions, you can build a working prototype and then the stakeholders can actually test the interactions for themselves. The prototype could then potentially form the basis for building the full site.

In the next chapter we will be looking at how we can adapt an existing site to be responsive.

CHAPTER 6

Adapt an Existing Site

Up to this point, the chapters in this book have discussed how you would build a new site from the beginning in view of the site being responsive. However, building from scratch may not always be an option, and having already dismissed building a separate site for mobile use, it is likely you will want to adapt your existing site and code base to be responsive. To achieve this, there are three options available:

1. Adapt the current styles

2. Refactor the code to be mobile first

3. Do a full reskin

Of these three options, the approach you choose is dependent on your site's individual circumstances, as each of the options has its own set of advantages and disadvantages. This chapter will look at each of these different approaches by going through an example of each so you can clearly see the steps involved in adapting an existing site to be responsive, after which you should be able to choose which approach is most appropriate for your project.

For this chapter I have put together an unresponsive site for a fictional company I will call Unresponsive design inc., which I will use to demonstrate the different approaches for converting an existing site to be responsive. It is included in the code bundle at the web site for this book (`www.apress.com`). You might want to follow along on your computer with the instruction I provide for this.

Adapt Existing Styles and Scripts

The first of the three approaches for adapting a site is to keep the existing HTML and to adapt the existing styles and JavaScript so they respond to the device viewport by adding media queries.

This approach is a desktop-first approach, and as such you would be gracefully degrading your experience for the smaller devices. There are many ways to degrade the content of a site, the first of which is to simply hide the less important content and rearrange the remaining content so it fits nicely on the smaller device's screen, both of which can be achieved using CSS alone. This approach has the benefit that it can be done relatively quickly, however, it is possible that content you deem to be less important may be important to one or more of your users. The second approach would be to adapt the content using CSS to work better on the site, and where appropriate to use JavaScript to change the way the user interacts with the content. With both approaches, the overall aim should be to provide a better experience than if the user had directly used the desktop site on the smaller device.

By taking the approach of adapting your current styles, you are keep your existing styles intact and instead using media queries to target styles that override the existing styles at the points that the site begins to break.

One of the resulting benefits of this approach is that the existing code base is likely to have already been well browser tested. This in turn will reduce the likelihood of experiencing browser-specific bugs you haven't already fixed. In browsers that do not support media queries, the site will look identical to how it did prior to adaptation. In the case of browsers that support media queries, you can focus on testing the site on the new breakpoints you have added, rather than bugs that might have been introduced during a reskin.

One of the key disadvantages of this approach is that the original desktop site that you are adapting might already have a bloated code base with inefficiencies caused by legacy or redundant code. By adapting a site that is already bloated, you are likely to make the problem worse and could face issues with performance due to loading more code on devices with a slower connection. In this situation, you would want to look at reducing these inefficiencies before embarking on making the site responsive. One of the ways you can achieve this is to look at removing any unused CSS selectors that may be left over from older iterations of the site. There are a number of tools you could use to achieve this, one of which is a Firefox plug-in called Dust-Me Selectors (`https://addons.mozilla.org/en-US/firefox/addon/dust-me-selectors/`), which will scan your web site and find any unused CSS.

Another issue with taking this approach is that in many cases the browser will still download the larger images on smaller devices. Tim Kadlec ran tests to see under what circumstances the browser would download images (`http://timkadlec.com/2012/04/media-query-asset-downloading-results/`). In nearly all the browsers he tested, he found that for images included in the page as .img elements, the browser would download the images even if the CSS specified it should not be shown. In addition, he also found that if a background image is set to an element in the CSS and a media query is specified that the element should not be shown, the image is still downloaded. There is, however, a way to prevent background images from loading. In further tests, Tim found that if you use `display: none` on the parent of the element you want to hide, the background image will not be downloaded. So if you want to hide a background image, this is the approach you will need to take.

As with simply updating a site, when adapting the existing styles, it is important to ensure you maintain the existing coding style. The reason for this is that the styles must remain consistent, including the use of the same naming convention for class names and the use of the same units for font sizes.

Having looked at the benefits and disadvantages of adapting the existing CSS and JavaScript for a web site, let's look at an example of how you might do this when building a responsive site. The first step is to take a look at the existing site and determine exactly what needs to change. I have included a screenshot of the base template for my fictional company example so you can start to see the possible ways to refine it (see Figure 6-1).

Figure 6-1. The fixed width site that will be make responsive

Defining the Breakpoints

Having looked at the original site that I want to adapt to be responsive, I need to decide on a set of breakpoints that will allow it to work across a wide variety of devices. For this site, I will add two breakpoints: the first being for small devices like tablets and the second being for extra small devices such as mobile phones.

For the first breakpoint, I want to try to scale down the existing site so it fits comfortably on small devices. I will want to add a breakpoint so that when the existing site no longer fits within the viewport, it can switch to the smaller version of the site. To achieve this, the breakpoint needs to break before a horizontal scrollbar is forced to appear due to the site being too wide. For this I need to allow for the site's width plus the width of the vertical scrollbar. Unfortunately, the width of the scrollbar can vary based on a number of factors including operating system and browser, so I will calculate the breakpoint at the site width plus 20px. This means, for this particular site, the site will have a breakpoint at 1000px. When I refer to this breakpoint later in this example, I will refer to it as the small breakpoint. The code for this breakpoint is:

```
@media screen and (max-width: 1000px){
}
```

The next breakpoint will need to target mobile devices. With the wide array of devices available, with varying dimensions and screen resolutions, it is difficult to say where a tablet size ends and where the mobile size begins. Therefore, you need to make a judgment call when it comes to determining what to classify as a mobile device using media queries. A good place to start is to look at the portrait width of some of the tablets you are looking to support. The easiest place to find this information is at www.viewportsizes.com, which allows you to find information about different viewport widths. Using this site, you can look at the viewport widths of some of the most common tablets to determine what you want to define as your mobile breakpoint. A couple you might look at are the Apple's iPad, with a portrait viewport width of 768px, and the Microsoft Surface, which also has a portrait viewport width of 768px. Therefore, if 768px is common for tablets, you can set the breakpoint for mobile devices to 767px, as this is 1px less than tablet. When I refer to this breakpoint later in this example, I will refer to it as the extra small breakpoint. The code for this breakpoint is:

```
@media screen and (max-width: 767px){
}
```

Typography

The existing typography is a good size for the majority of devices, however, on extra small devices it is a bit too big, so you will need to add some styles to your headings. To do so, you need to look at the base font size that has been used so you can calculate the font size values correctly. The code for this would be:

```
@media screen and (max-width: 767px){

    h1{
        font-size: 22px;
        font-size: 1.571em;
    }

    h2{
        font-size: 18px;
        font-size: 1.286em;
    }
}
```

Wrapper

Having adjusted the font sizes, you now need to adjust the width of the wrapper so that is does not extend farther than the bounds of the devices viewport. To do this, you need to decide how your site should work across the different breakpoints you have defined. The first breakpoint is the small breakpoint, which is defined as having a `max-width` of 1000px. As mentioned earlier, this is the breakpoint aimed at devices in between the existing desktop site and a mobile site. For this breakpoint, you would set the width of the wrapper for the site to 710px, as the site needs to work on viewports ranging from 768px to 1000px, and this includes scrollbars. You also need to take into account the 20px left and right paddings. The code for this breakpoint would be:

```
@media screen and (max-width: 1000px){
    .wrapper{
        width: 710px;
    }
}
```

When you get down to the extra small viewport, it makes sense to make the site a fluid width. There are several reasons for this, the first being that on these smaller devices, you want to try to take advantage of every pixel of the browser's viewport width to show the content, and you cannot afford to have excess spacing around the edges. The second reason is that in between 320px and 767px there is a large variation in the widths of the screens used to view a site. Therefore, you want to try to offer an optimized experience for all of these widths. To enable you to make your wrapper fluid on these extra small viewport devices, you will set the width to 100%. Upon setting this, you will notice that the wrapper is still wider than the viewport. The reason for this is that you have padding applied to the wrapper. It makes sense to keep this padding for the mobile site, so instead of removing it, you could use the `box-sizing` property to allow you to include the padding in the 100% width. In Chapter 4, I discussed applying box sizing to the universal (*) CSS selector; unfortunately, because this is an existing code base, it isn't practical to apply globally because you would likely break some of the existing styles. This is why when you are adapting existing CSS you should apply box sizing on a case-by-case basis. The final styles for the wrapper for the extra small viewport would be:

```
@media screen and (max-width: 767px){
    .wrapper{
        width: 100%;
        -moz-box-sizing: border-box;
        -webkit-box-sizing: border-box;
        box-sizing: border-box;
    }
}
```

Jumbotron

If you have been testing in your browser along with me as I have progressed, you will notice that the Jumbotron currently is expanding outside the site's wrapper. If you look at the existing CSS for the Jumbotron to see why this is happening, you will see that the Jumbotron has its width set to 940px. Clearly the media queries need to be adjusted to how the Jumbotron looks across different devices.

For the small breakpoint, you would simply need to resize the Jumbotron so it fits properly within the wrapper. Because the wrapper is 710px wide, you would need to adjust the Jumbotron to match at 710px wide using this code:

```
@media screen and (max-width: 1000px){
    .jumbotron{
        width: 710px;
    }
}
```

When it comes to the extra small breakpoint, however, you would need to make more radical changes because the Jumbotron's content will no longer sit nicely in the existing layout. You would need to adjust the layout so the content of the Jumbotron stacks when viewed on an extra small device. To enable this, the first step is to set the Jumbotron so that it fills the wrapper, leaving the wrappers padding either side:

```
@media screen and (max-width: 767px){
    .jumbotron{
        width: 100%;
        height: auto;
        text-align: center;
        padding: 20px 0;
    }
}
```

If you were to take a look at the original site for the Jumbotron, you would see the elements inside are all positioned absolutely, meaning that after changing the width and changing the height to auto, the site looks really broken. This can be fixed by resetting the positioning and the width of the elements:

```
@media screen and (max-width: 767px){
    .jumbotron img,
    .jumbotron p,
    .jumbotron h2,
    .jumbotron .roundal,
    .jumbotron .roundal span{
        position: static;
        left: auto;
        right: auto;
        bottom: auto;
        top: auto;
        width: auto;
    }
}
```

The final step to make the Jumbotron look right on these extra small devices is to adjust the heading text so that the font size is more appropriate for mobile devices. In addition, so the heading text does not approach the edges of the Jumbotron, you would add padding to the heading text:

```
@media screen and (max-width: 767px){
    .jumbotron h2{
        font-size: 22px;
        font-size: 1.375em;
        padding: 10px 20px;
    }
}
```

If you now look at the Jumbotron on the extra small device, you would see the information a lot clearer (see Figure 6-2).

Unresponsive design inc.

Figure 6-2. *Our slimmed down site for the Jumbotron*

Products

The next step is to adjust the products so they look great across the various breakpoints. First, you would start with deciding how they should look on small devices. To determine this, you need to consider whether the existing content will fit comfortably within the existing structure or whether you will need to adapt the layout. Adapting the layout could be as simple as changing from a three-column layout to a two-column layout, or it could mean changing the layout to be single columns with a fluid width. In the case of this example, however, on the small breakpoint the existing layout and content can fit comfortably within the existing three-column structure by simply changing the width of the three product elements to 223px:

```
@media screen and (max-width: 1000px){
    .product{
        width: 223px;
    }
}
```

Having adapted the small devices to continue to use three columns, albeit with a smaller width, the next step is to look at how to adjust the product elements to work on extra small devices. At this point, the viewport is getting too small to continue to show the products in three columns, and when using the extra small breakpoint, you are using a fluid width, so it makes sense to change the product elements so they are no longer in columns but instead are stacked upon one another. To achieve this, you would adjust the width of the product elements to 100%. In addition, you would want to ensure that there is a clear divider between the products, which will be achieved with padding and a border in between:

```
@media screen and (max-width: 767px){
    .product{
        width: 100%;
        padding: 20px 0px;
        border-top: 1px solid #ccc;
    }
}
```

Having added padding and borders, the first product now has an extra border at the top and extra padding, so you can use the :first-child selector to target the first product and remove the excess padding and border:

```
@media screen and (max-width: 767px){
    .product:first-child{
        border-top: 0px;
        padding-top: 0px;
    }
}
```

Similarly, there is additional unwanted padding showing beneath the last product, so this can be removed by using the :last-child selector to target the last product and remove the excess padding:

```
@media screen and (max-width: 767px){
    .product:last-child{
        padding-bottom: 0px;
    }
}
```

If you now look at how the products stack, you will notice they work quite well, as shown in Figure 6-3.

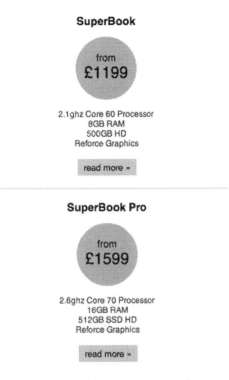

Figure 6-3. *Slimmed down product panels*

Conclusion

Having adapted the site to be responsive, you now have a site that works across a wide variety of different devices. Adapting the site in this way has both benefits and disadvantages, and I will now discuss them so when it comes to your own sites you can decide if simply adapting your existing site is suitable for your needs.

The main problem you might have noticed when you were adapting the Jumbotron is that when degrading the site to work on smaller devices, you sometimes need to override a large amount of the styles to provide a good experience to mobile. Although in this example it was relatively simple, a larger site you are adapting to be responsive may require you to do more significant overriding of styles. Whether you are working mobile first or, as in this case, desktop first, you will always be overriding some of the styles of a previous breakpoint. Usually a mobile-first site is building on top of what is already there with each breakpoint, but with a desktop-first site such as this one, sometimes having to reset values back to their browser defaults can make the code base more bloated.

The benefit from simply adapting the site in this example is that the styles of the desktop site did not need to change, which means the focus can be the new breakpoints that are being added. Not only does this save development time, it also can help make testing a lot simpler as we know that in most cases the bugs we find would have been introduced within our media queries.

Refactoring

The second approach that could be taken for adapting an existing site is refactoring the existing code base to be mobile first. The benefit here is that you are not having to start the styles from scratch. You can also make tweaks to the site design and look at removing redundant code as part of the refactoring process.

Defining the Breakpoints

As the first step of the refactoring of the site, you need to wrap the existing styles that are currently being used to style the site in a media query targeted toward the larger devices, such as desktop browsers that the site already supports. To choose a suitable media query for this, look at the site's existing styles to determine its width. If you look at the code for the example site we are making responsive, you will see that the main wrapper is 940px wide plus 20px of padding to both the left and the right, totaling 980px in width. Taking into account scrollbars, you will therefore set the media query to check for a minimum width of 1024px:

```
@media screen and (min-width: 1024px){
}
```

With this media query being used to wrap the existing styles, there are no styles being applied to any viewport with a width less than 1024px. From this point I will refer to this breakpoint as the medium breakpoint.

You will also want to be able to adapt the site to work on larger viewport sizes than the site currently supports, in this case you would need to add an additional breakpoint that targets these larger viewports:

```
@media screen and (min-width: 1200px){
}
```

In addition to the larger media queries that have already been defined, you might want to add an additional media query for small devices (like tablets). This media query will enable you to take advantage of the larger viewports offered by tablet devices, and for this you will take the smaller width of the iPad as the breaking point for these small devices:

```
@media screen and (min-width: 768px){
}
```

Refactoring the Existing Styles

Having defined the breakpoints, you can now refactor the existing styles. You have moved all the existing styles into a breakpoint, so this means that on devices smaller than 1024px, no styles will be shown, as shown in Figure 6-4.

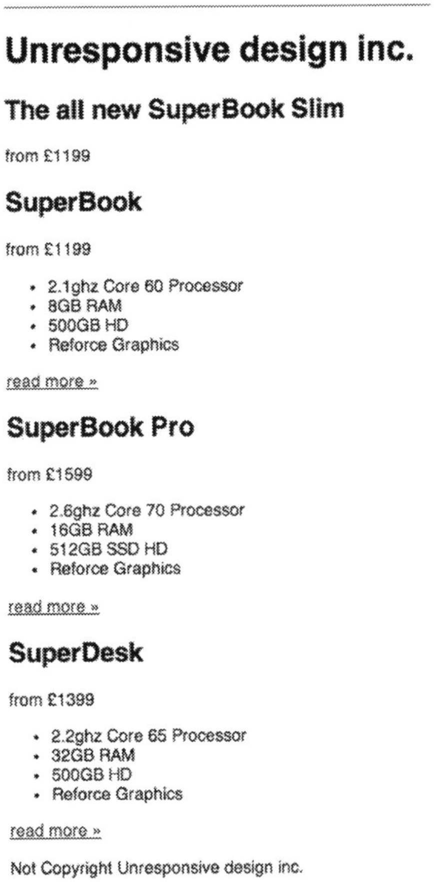

Unresponsive design inc.

The all new SuperBook Slim

from £1199

SuperBook

from £1199

- 2.1ghz Core 60 Processor
- 8GB RAM
- 500GB HD
- Reforce Graphics

read more »

SuperBook Pro

from £1599

- 2.6ghz Core 70 Processor
- 16GB RAM
- 512GB SSD HD
- Reforce Graphics

read more »

SuperDesk

from £1399

- 2.2ghz Core 65 Processor
- 32GB RAM
- 500GB HD
- Reforce Graphics

read more »

Not Copyright Unresponsive design inc.

Figure 6-4. *No styles are shown on smaller devices*

At this point you can start to migrate styles that are currently targeted at larger states so they are available globally. The kind of styles you can easily pull out to be globally available are those that apply fonts and generic spacing that would be used regardless of the breakpoint.

In the case of the example site, the site is using the default browser font, so the fonts don't need to be touched. The site doesn't apply any generic spacing to element types, but there is a clearfix helper class that is used to clear the floats. It makes sense for this to be available outside the media query as it is needed on smaller devices as well.

Having moved any of the generic styles, the next step is to look at the different sections of the site and see where you can take existing styles and apply them to the smaller viewports, refactoring them in the process.

Let's start this process of refactoring with the site's main wrapper. The padding and margins that are applied can easily be pull outside the media query. The other styles are specific to the larger viewport sizes, so let's leave them where they are:

```
.wrapper{
    padding: 0 20px 20px;
    margin: 0 auto;
}
```

Header

The next step is to look at the header styles to see which styles can be used for smaller devices. In this example, the existing styles applied to the header are simply spacing and a border bottom. It makes sense to move these out of the media query so they are accessible to the other viewport sizes. The styles that will be moved are shown here:

```
.global-header{
    margin: 0 0 20px;
    border-bottom: 1px solid #ccc;
}
```

If you look at the header in your browser, you will see that it now has some basic styling applied. However, because nothing has been done with the font sizes at this stage, the heading text appears quite large (as shown in Figure 6-5).

Unresponsive design inc.

Figure 6-5. *The site header, with no font sizes applied*

To rectify this let's add styles to the h1 element to style the font size and align the text to center:

```
h1{
    font-size: 1.4em;
    text-align: center;
}
```

Now when you look at this in the browser, the font size is more appropriate for the smaller viewport, as shown in Figure 6-6.

Unresponsive design inc.

Figure 6-6. *The site header, with the font size and alignment applied*

Jumbotron

The next element of this site that needs to be looked at is the Jumbotron. The original CSS for the Jumbotron is 35 lines long, and much of it applies to only the larger viewport widths, so it is important to look carefully at what is suitable. To this end I have included the original Jumbotron CSS below and have highlighted the lines that you might want to use as a starting point for the Jumbotron on smaller devices:

```css
.jumbotron{
        position: relative;
        background: #f4a156;
        width: 940px;
        height: 250px;
        margin-bottom: 20px;
}

.jumbotron img{
        position: absolute;
        left: 0px;
        top: 0px;
}

.jumbotron h2{
        position: absolute;
        left: 260px;
        top: 20px;
        font-size: 3em;
        width: 300px;
        margin: 0px;
}

.jumbotron .roundal{
        position: absolute;
        right: 0px;
        bottom: 0px;
}

.jumbotron .roundal span{
        position: absolute;
        right: 20px;
        bottom: 20px;
        font-size: 2em;
}
```

Taking the highlighted lines in the CSS from above, you are then left with the resulting CSS:

```css
.jumbotron{
    background: #f4a156;
    margin-bottom: 20px;
}

.jumbotron h2{
    margin: 0px;
}
```

If you now look at the Jumbotron in your browser, you will see that you have the start of the styles, as shown in Figure 6-7.

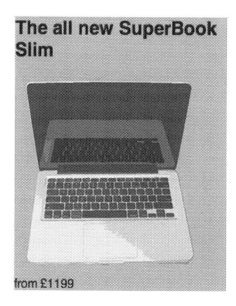

Figure 6-7. *The Jumbotron with this base CSS in place*

You will notice that the orange background for the Jumbotron does not stretch across the full viewport as you might expect. This is because of the wrapper you are using to apply consistent spacing to either side of the site. To enable you to keep this consistent spacing but extend the background to be full width, you can use a negative margin. To then add the consistent spacing within the Jumbotron, you can simply apply padding. In addition, you will want to align the text to be centered. This is shown in the following CSS:

```
.jumbotron{
    background: #f4a156;
    margin:  0 -20px 20px;
    padding:  20px;
    text-align: center;
}
```

The font sizes are also particularly large. This is because the font size for the second-level headings hasn't been set for smaller viewports, so they should now be set to an appropriate size. Since the first-level headings are set to 1.4em, the second-level headings should be set to 1.3em. You also don't want additional spacing above the second-level heading in the Jumbotron, so specifically for this Jumbotron that the margin top is set to 0px.

```
h2{
    font-size: 1.3em;
}

.jumbotron h2{
    margin-top: 0px;
}
```

147

With this in place, the Jumbotron now looks complete, as shown in Figure 6-8.

Figure 6-8. *The complete Jumbotron*

Product Panels

The next step is to build the styles for the product panels. The majority of the styles used for these panels on the larger viewports can also be used to style these panels on the smaller viewports. As before, I have highlighted the lines of the following CSS that can be used to simply move it outside the media query:

```
.product{
    float: left;
    width: 300px;
    padding-left: 20px;
    text-align: center;
}

.product:first-child{
    padding-left: 0px;
}

.product .roundal{
    width: 100px;
    height: 75px;
    margin: 0 auto;
    background: #f4a156;
    border-radius: 50px;
    padding-top: 25px;
}
```

```
.product .roundal span{
    display: block;
    font-size: 1.6rem;
}

.product ul{
    padding: 0px;
}

.product li{
    list-style: none;
    font-size: 0.8rem;
    color: #333;
}

.product a{
    font-size: 0.9rem;
    color: #000;
    text-decoration: none;
    display: inline-block;
    background: #ccc;
    padding: 5px 10px;
    border-radius: 2px;
}

.product a:hover, .product a:focus, .product a:active{
    background: #999;
    color: #eee;
}

.product *:first-child{
    margin-top: 0px;
}

.product *:last-child{
    margin-bottom: 0px;
}
```

After moving the highlighted CSS to outside the media query, you now need to add some extra padding and borders to finish off the product panels. So that there is spacing on either side of the border, add 20px padding to the top and bottom of each product panel. The border is then applied to the bottom of the product panel:

```
.product{
    text-align: center;
    padding: 20px 0px;
    border-bottom: 1px solid #ccc;
}
```

With that in place, ensure that you don't have too much spacing above the first panel. Remove the padding only for the first product panel, and this will be targeted using the :first-child selector:

```
.product:first-child{
    padding-top: 0px;
}
```

With this in place, take a look at how the product panels look in your browser, as shown in Figure 6-9.

SuperBook

2.1ghz Core 60 Processor
8GB RAM
500GB HD
Reforce Graphics

read more »

SuperBook Pro

2.6ghz Core 70 Processor
16GB RAM
512GB SSD HD
Reforce Graphics

read more »

Figure 6-9. *The product panels on a smaller device*

The final part of CSS that you need to look at is the footer. Let's start by looking at the CSS that is currently applied to the footer in the larger media query. I have highlighted the lines in the CSS that make sense in order to bring it outside the media query so it can be applied to the extra small viewports and up:

```
.global-footer{
    margin: 20px 0;
    border-top: 1px solid #ccc;
}

.global-footer p{
    text-align: center;
    font-size: 0.8rem;
}
```

There is no need to write any further CSS for the footer, and the finished footer is shown in Figure 6-10.

Not Copyright Unresponsive design inc.

Figure 6-10. *The finished footer on extra small devices*

Targeting the Different Breakpoints

At this point the site is working great on extra small devices, but we haven't yet thought about how it looks on small or large devices. It is also likely we have broken the original (medium) layout due to the new styles that have been added. Let's start by increasing the browser's width to the size of one of the small devices and see how the site looks, as shown in Figure 6-11.

Figure 6-11. *The site shown on a small device*

Now, after seeing what the site looks like on a small device, you will notice that there is a lot of space around the stacked product panels that could be better utilized by showing the products in a row next to one another. This is the same way the original nonresponsive site behaved, however, rather than set a fixed width to the product panels, you would apply a fluid width. Because you want three columns here, you would set the width to 33.33%. To get the panels to sit next to one another, apply a float and remove the padding from the top of the elements. The final code looks like this:

```
.product{
        width: 33.33%;
        padding-top: 0px;
        float: left;
}
```

If you then check this in your browser, the panels should now be side by side, as shown in Figure 6-12.

Figure 6-12. *The product panels on a small device*

If you continue to increase the viewport size until you reach the medium viewport width, you will notice that the header and Jumbotron of the site are both broken. This is because of the styles you applied to the earlier breakpoints. I have shown how the header and Jumbotron are broken in Figure 6-13.

Figure 6-13. *The medium breakpoint with the broken Jumbotron*

As part of the refactoring, you can choose to make changes to the design of the site, in this example, you will be doing this to both the header and the Jumbotron. The first step is to look at the header; currently the CSS has styles applied to the h1 making it float to the left, the CSS is:

```
.global-header h1{
    float: left;
}
```

If you don't want it to float left, you can remove this style. However, you want to increase the font size, but it makes sense that you apply the font size in the same way you did for the mobile site, which is on the h1 directly. The new styles to change the font size would look like this:

```
h1{
    font-size: 2rem;
}
```

With this in place, the next step is to look at the Jumbotron. To get started, let's look at the CSS that is currently being applied to the Jumbotron. The first part is the CSS that contains the main element for the Jumbotron, the class on this element is jumbotron. The existing CSS is:

```
.jumbotron{
    position: relative;
    width: 940px;
    height: 250px;
}
```

As you will notice, the Jumbotron has a value set defining it as 940px wide. Because we want the Jumbotron to always be as wide as the wrapper, you can simply remove the width, so the CSS now looks like:

```
.jumbotron{
    position: relative;
    height: 250px;
}
```

The next step is to position the image. Although you could refactor the HTML to use a basic grid and build the Jumbotron using that, to keep it simple, let's simply use absolute positioning to position the content of the Jumbotron. The existing styles currently position the image so it is positioned absolutely in the top left corner:

```
.jumbotron img{
    position: absolute;
    left: 0px;
    top: 0px;
}
```

But we want to place the image to the left of the center of the Jumbotron. To achieve this, you would set the left property of the selector to have a value of 50%. You can then use a negative margin equal to the width of the image to pull it to the left. You also want to bump the top down to give it an extra bit of space, so let's set the top to 20px:

```
.jumbotron img{
    position: absolute;
    left: 50%;
    top: 20px;
    margin-left: -250px;
}
```

The next step is to style the title of the Jumbotron. The way it is currently styled absolutely positions it so it sits next to the original placement of the image. Because we changed the position of the image, you also need to adjust the position of the heading so it still sits next to the image. To achieve this, position the heading so it is to the right of the center of the Jumbotron. The current CSS is:

```
.jumbotron h2{
    position: absolute;
    left: 260px;
    top: 20px;
    font-size: 3rem;
    width: 300px;
    margin: 0px;
}
```

To achieve the desired effect, simply change the left so it is at 50%:

```
.jumbotron h2{
    position: absolute;
    left: 50%;
    top: 20px;
    font-size: 3rem;
    width: 300px;
    margin: 0px;
}
```

The next step is to position the pricing in the Jumbotron. You will want it to appear below the heading text, so let's use the same technique to off-center the text. We are already using absolute positioning, so you simply need to change the position. The existing CSS is:

```
.jumbotron .roundal{
    position: absolute;
    right: 0px;
    bottom: 0px;
}
```

First, change the positioning to the left set to 50% and then the bottom set to 50px. This will position the text directly below the header. After updating the position, increase the font size so it is more prominent, in this case let's increase the font size to 2rem:

```
.jumbotron .roundal{
    position: absolute;
    left: 50%;
    bottom: 50px;
    width: 300px;
    font-size: 2rem;
}
```

Finally, you can simply remove the following styles, which originally positioned the span that was within the roundel but is no longer needed:

```
.jumbotron .roundal span{
    position: absolute;
    right: 20px;
    bottom: 20px;
    font-size: 2rem;
}
```

With both the header styles and Jumbotron styles tweaked, let's look at them in a browser, as shown in Figure 6-14.

Figure 6-14. The completed header and footer

Aside from the header and Jumbotron, there are also issues with the footer of the site, as it has an extra border showing, as shown in Figure 6-15.

Not Copyright Unresponsive design inc.

Figure 6-15. *The double border issue on the medium breakpoint*

This is because a border was added to the bottom of the products, but the larger viewport already had a border added to the top of the footer. To fix this issue, simply remove the following styles from the style sheet:

```
.global-footer{
    margin: 20px 0;
    border-top: 1px solid #ccc;
}
```

Now if you look at it in the browser again, you'll see the line has been removed, as shown in Figure 6-16.

Not Copyright Unresponsive design inc.

Figure 6-16. *The fixed footer for the medium breakpoint*

This completes the medium breakpoint, but as part of making the site responsive, you want to also take advantage of the space available on larger displays. Earlier I discussed the media query that would be used to achieve this, but now let's look at the CSS required to adapt the site.

Because everything built so far is fluid within a fixed-width wrapper, adjusting the site for a larger viewport can be achieved by simply changing the width of this wrapper. In some circumstances you might want to take advantage of the extra space by doing more than this, but for this example let's simply adjust the wrapper. As the large breakpoint breaks at 1200px, you will want to set the width of the wrapper to 1170px wide to give space for the scrollbar. To achieve this, simply place the following CSS inside the large media query:

```
.wrapper{
      width: 1170px;
}
```

Loading the finished page with a viewport equal to or greater than 1200px will show the new wider site, as shown in Figure 6-17.

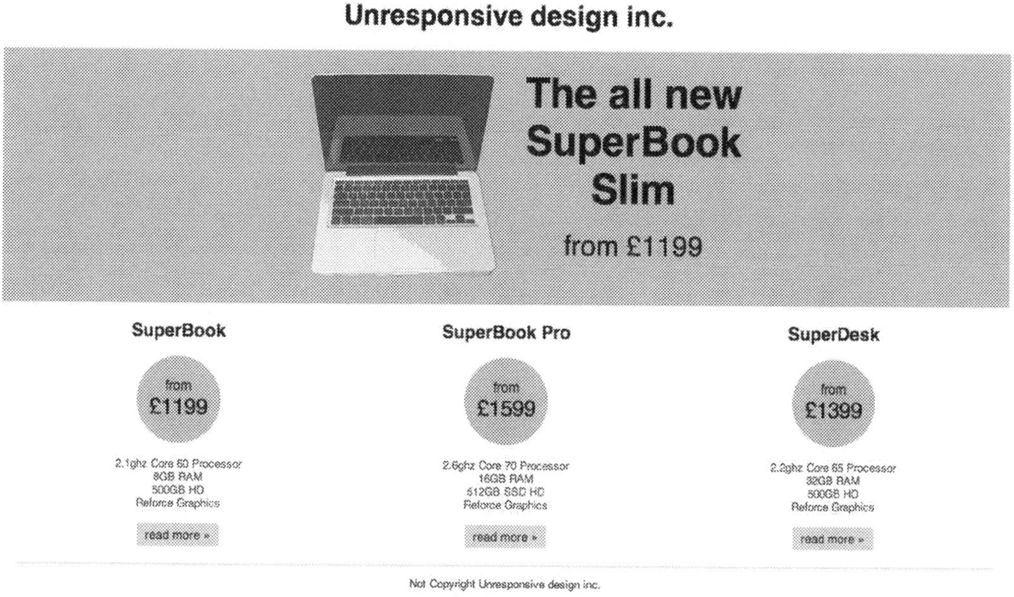

Unresponsive design inc.

The all new SuperBook Slim

from £1199

SuperBook	SuperBook Pro	SuperDesk
from £1199	from £1599	from £1399
2.1ghz Core 60 Processor 8GB RAM 500GB HD Reforce Graphics	2.6ghz Core 70 Processor 16GB RAM 512GB SSD HD Reforce Graphics	2.2ghz Core 65 Processor 32GB RAM 500GB HD Reforce Graphics
read more »	read more »	read more »

Not Copyright Unresponsive design inc.

Figure 6-17. *The completed refactored site shown on a large viewport*

Full Reskin

The third approach that could be taken for adapting an existing site is to keep the majority of the current HTML, but ditch the existing CSS and start afresh.

There are benefits and disadvantages of choosing to take the full reskin approach, with the key benefit being that by starting the CSS afresh and refactoring the HTML as necessary, you overcome any inefficiencies that may have creeped into the CSS over the life of the site. In addition, because you would be replacing the existing CSS, you can take a mobile-first, progressive-enhancement approach, building the site for the smaller, mobile devices first and then enhancing the site based on the devices feature set and viewport size.

Preparation

Being a full reskin, the first step is to clear out the original styles and see what is left. By deleting the core styles, you are left with simply the content. If you look at this in a browser, you will see that you get a very clear outline of the document, as shown in Figure 6-18.

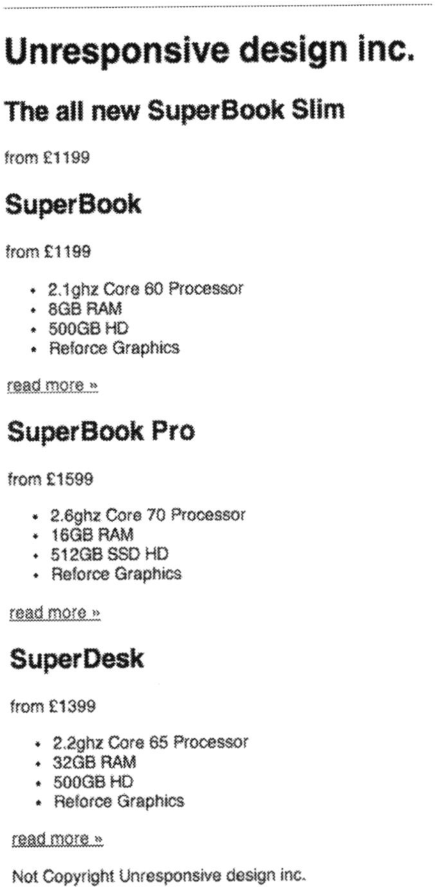

Unresponsive design inc.

The all new SuperBook Slim

from £1199

SuperBook

from £1199

- 2.1ghz Core 60 Processor
- 8GB RAM
- 500GB HD
- Reforce Graphics

read more »

SuperBook Pro

from £1599

- 2.6ghz Core 70 Processor
- 16GB RAM
- 512GB SSD HD
- Reforce Graphics

read more »

SuperDesk

from £1399

- 2.2ghz Core 65 Processor
- 32GB RAM
- 500GB HD
- Reforce Graphics

read more »

Not Copyright Unresponsive design inc.

Figure 6-18. *The initial site with the original styles removed*

Part of the reason that this remains very easy to follow is that the heading tags were used correctly, so while the site has only browser default styling, the content still has a strong, clear heading hierarchy. When looking at your own site, you might notice that some of your headings do not seem to follow a proper hierarchy. This is a good opportunity to look at refactoring your headings so they are used to provide users with a proper hierarchy to the page. As a demonstration of how an improper hierarchy might look, I put together an example as shown in Figure 6-19.

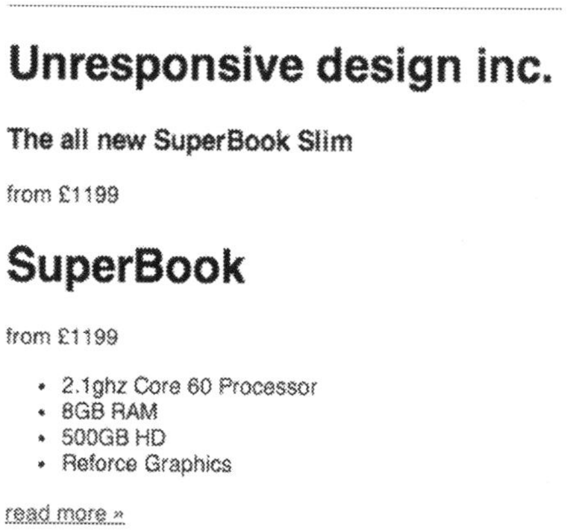

Unresponsive design inc.

The all new SuperBook Slim

from £1199

SuperBook

from £1199

- 2.1ghz Core 60 Processor
- 8GB RAM
- 500GB HD
- Reforce Graphics

read more »

Figure 6-19. *An example of a page with an improper hierarchy*

There are multiple reasons it is important that pages follow a clear hierarchy, the most important being that is makes the page much more accessible to users, especially those using screen readers that may be relying on the hierarchy of the page to navigate through the content. Another reason that heading hierarchy is important is that it enables us to easily apply styles that match up to the correct heading elements.

General Styles

Before starting the core of the coding, let's first change the default box model for the elements. This is achieved using the box-sizing CSS3 property, which was covered in Chapter 4, and applying it to all elements using the CSS universal selector (*):

```
* {
        -webkit-box-sizing: border-box; /* Safari/Chrome, other WebKit */
        -moz-box-sizing: border-box;    /* Firefox, other Gecko */
        box-sizing: border-box;         /* Opera/IE 8+ */
}
```

By setting the value to border-box, you are moving both the borders and paddings inside the elements, allowing you to use percentage values for the widths, while still using px values for the paddings. Earlier when we were adapting the CSS, we were unable to apply this technique easily to the CSS due to the potential of breaking existing styles. When reskining a site, you don't have this problem because you are able to build all the styles based on the box model you have chosen to implement.

Defining the Breakpoints

It is important to plan at what points you want to use media queries to define breakpoints. Because you are building this site mobile first, you are progressively enhancing the site at each breakpoint based on the width of the device viewport. Therefore, each of the breakpoints should try to build on top of the previous breakpoint. Building mobile first means that the base CSS that is not wrapped in any media queries is the CSS aimed at is for extra small devices. With this in mind, you will need to define three breakpoints, each using a sensible value for minimum width.

The first breakpoint to define is a minimum width of 768px. This will allow you to target devices with a viewport width starting at 768px. The reason behind this choice is that this is normally the starting point for tablets in a portrait orientation, and as tablets get bigger screens and wider viewports, you can then enhance the site to take advantage of this. When referring to this breakpoint later, I will call it the small breakpoint:

```
@media screen and (min-width: 768px){
}
```

The second breakpoint to define is a minimum width of 1000px, the purpose being to target the very popular 1024×800 screen resolution used by a large number of users. Although the previous breakpoint could assume the majority of users would be using some kind of tablet, this breakpoint is shared between landscape tablets and desktops, so it can't be used to make these kinds of assumptions. When referring to this breakpoint later, I will call it the medium breakpoint:

```
@media screen and (min-width: 1000px){
}
```

The final breakpoint to define is a minimum width of 1200px. With the growth of larger displays, as discussed earlier in the book, it makes sense to take advantage of the additional space available. When referring to this breakpoint later, I will call it the large breakpoint:

```
@media screen and (min-width: 1200px){
}
```

Typography

Once you are happy with the breakpoints, let's start by applying sensible default sizes to the typography. The first step is to set the base font size for the page. For this, a sensible default size is 14px, and this is set on the HTML tag as a percentage:

```
html{
    font-size: 87.5%;
}
```

Setting a default font size will have an effect on all the text on the site, however, you may want to set your own custom font sizes for the headings:

```
h1{
    font-size: 22px;
    font-size: 1.571rem;
}

h2{
    font-size: 18px;
    font-size: 1.286rem;
}
```

You may have noticed that for both the h1 and h2 selectors I have defined the font-size property twice, the first with a pixel value followed by a second declaration with a value in rem. The reason for this is that you want to use rem (also known as a relative em) as they are relative to the default font size. However, this is not supported by all browsers, so as a fallback I have defined the font size in pixels. The drawback to this approach is that in older browsers that do not support rem, text-size–based zooming will not work, however, full-page zooming will still work, meaning the site would still be usable to those using these older browsers.

Having defined the mobile CSS, let's increase the font size for larger devices. You will do this by adding increased font sizes to the small media query, and because you are using min-width, it will then apply to all the breakpoints greater than it:

```
@media screen and (min-width: 767px){
    h1{
        font-size: 28px;
        font-size: 2rem;
    }

    h2{
        font-size: 24px;
        font-size: 1.714rem;
    }
}
```

Wrapper

As you might already know, the HTML includes a div element with the class wrapper, which encapsulates the HTML of the site. In the site's original CSS that is being replaced, this was used to define the width of the site and center it on the page. For a mobile device, however, you would not want to set a width because you want the wrapper to be fluid. You do, however, want to apply consistent spacing to the sides of the site, so you can use a wrapper for this. This will be achieved by adding a margin to the left and right of the wrapper to space out the page:

```
.wrapper{
    margin: 0 20px;
}
```

Having added a margin to the wrapper, the content of the site will have 20px margins down the left- and right-hand sides. Although the fluid width works really well with extra small devices, you want to set a fixed width on small devices, and you also want to center the fixed width design within the viewport, which you can achieve by using margins:

```
@media screen and (min-width: 767px){
    .wrapper{
        width: 740px;
        margin: 0px auto;
    }
}
```

Having set the width for small devices, when you get to the medium breakpoint, you will find that the width you set for the small breakpoint leaves a large amount of space available. It, therefore, makes sense to make the site wider on these medium-size displays:

```
@media screen and (min-width: 1000px){
    .wrapper{
        width: 980px;
    }
}
```

Finally, you want to be able to take advantage of the extra space offered by larger displays, and as such let's increase the width of the wrapper again. In this case, I have chosen to use a breakpoint of minimum width 1200px. This is to ensure the browser does not show horizontal scrollbars. Let's set the width of the site to 1170px to allow for the browser's scrollbars:

```
@media screen and (min-width: 1200px){
    .wrapper{
        width: 1170px;
    }
}
```

Header

Having looked at both the typography of the site and the wrapper, let's move on to styling the header of the site. On extra small devices, we want to have a border on the bottom of the header spanning the width of the viewport. However, with a set margin of 20px for the wrapper, the header does not naturally span 100% of the viewport. To fix this, let's use negative margins to pull the width of the header to the full width of the viewport. You can then add this spacing onto the inside of the header using padding and then add the border to the bottom of the header:

```
.global-header{
    border-bottom: 1px solid #ccc;
    margin: 0 -20px;
    padding: 0 20px;
}
```

For larger viewports, you will want to remove this additional spacing:

```
@media screen and (min-width: 767px){
    .global-header{
        margin: 0px;
        padding: 0px;
    }

    .global-header h1{
        text-align: left;
    }
}
```

Jumbotron

Directly under the header is the Jumbotron, which is used to highlight the latest product that our fictional company Unresponsive design inc. wants to promote. This panel should stand out, so let's add a background color of orange, along with pulling out the Jumbotron so it fits the full width of the viewport:

```
.jumbotron{
    background: #f4a156;
    margin: 0 -20px;
    padding: 20px;
    text-align: center;
}
```

Next let's add some styling to the heading element shown within the Jumbotron so it does not have any margins at the top:

```
.jumbotron h2{
    margin-top: 0px;
}
```

Finally, let's style the price of this product that is highlighted in the Jumbotron. For this, let's simply increase the font size to make it stand out more:

```
.jumbotron .roundal{
    font-size: 18px;
    font-size: 1.286rem;
}
```

If you load the site in a browser now, you will be able to see the styled Jumbotron, as shown in Figure 6-20.

Figure 6-20. *The newly styled Jumbotron*

So now let's adapt this to work on larger devices. To achieve the desired effect, let's use absolute positioning. To enable this, you need to set the height and the element to position: relative:

```
.jumbotron{
    margin: 0px;
    height: 290px;
    position: relative;
}
```

The next step is to position the image. You want all the content in the Jumbotron to be central, so let's set it left to 50%, then use margin-left to add an offset. In this case, the image is 250px wide, so you'll want it to be off the center by 20 pixels—in this case the offset will be -270px:

```
.jumbotron img{
    position: absolute;
    left: 50%;
    margin-left: -270px;
}
```

Similarly, the heading needs to be central, and then off-centered using margin-left. Although the image is off-centered to the left, the text will off-center to the right. Let's also increase the font size:

```
.jumbotron h2{
    position: absolute;
    left: 50%;
    margin-left: 20px;
    width: 250px;
    font-size: 42px;
    font-size: 3rem;
    text-align: left;
}
```

Finally, let's position the price. This should be lined up with the title but nearer the bottom of the Jumbotron:

```
.jumbotron .roundal{
    position: absolute;
    left: 50%;
    margin-left: 20px;
    bottom: 40px;
    font-size: 28px;
    font-size: 2rem;
}
```

Now if you take a look at how the Jumbotron appears on larger devices, it would look like Figure 6-21.

Figure 6-21. *The Jumbotron as seen on larger devices*

Products

The products are a core part of this site, so it is important to show them in a way that tells the user about them in a clear and concise way. There is already HTML that lists the price for the name and the specification of the product, however, you would need to style this so it works well on extra small devices. It makes sense that on these devices the products would be stacked so the user can scroll up and down to see the different products. As each product is a div, which is a block-level element, each would naturally be full width and stacked. But it is also important to apply styles to space out the products. Finally, you would align the text to center to be consistent with how the header and Jumbotron are styled:

```
.product{
    text-align: center;
    margin: 20px 0;
    border-bottom: 1px solid #ccc;
    padding-bottom: 20px;
}
```

Having spaced out the products, the next step is to style the pricing of the products. For this you would use a roundal. To enable this, let's style the roundal to be 100px wide, and the height will be made up of 70px of height and 30px top padding. The circle effect will be achieved by giving it a background color of orange and a border radius of 50px. Finally, this will be aligned center using margins. To show the price in a higher font size, style the span to be display block (to force a new line) with a font size of 1.6rem:

```
.product .roundal{
    width: 100px;
    height: 100px;
    margin: 0 auto;
    background: #f4a156;
    border-radius: 50px;
    padding-top: 30px;
}
.product .roundal span{
    display: block;
    font-size: 1.6rem;
}
```

Next you would want to add styling specifications of the product. For starters, let's remove the default padding applied to the list by the browser and then remove the bullet points because they are not needed when listing the specifications:

```
.product ul{
    padding: 0px;
}

.product li{
    list-style: none;
}
```

The next step is to style the read-more link. It makes sense for this to be a button, so let's style this up:

```
.product a{
    color: #000;
    text-decoration: none;
    display: inline-block;
    background: #ccc;
    padding: 0px 10px;
    border-radius: 2px;
    line-height: 40px;
}
```

Having declared the button, you also want to add hover, focus, and active states to the button. Although your first thought might be that small touch-screen devices do not have the ability to hover as they generally have touch screens, you need to ensure you cover all bases within the CSS, because you cannot know whether users are using a touch device:

```
.product a:hover, .product a:focus, .product a:active{
    background: #999;
    color: #eee;
}
```

Finally, you will notice that there is extra spacing occurring around the product. This is caused by the margins on the first and last elements in the product elements. You can quickly remove these using the first-child and last-child selectors. The reason to do this rather than style the elements directly is that the order of the elements could change or new elements could be added, and this CSS would still apply regardless of the element:

```
.product > *:first-child{
    margin-top: 0px;
}
.product > *:last-child{
    margin-bottom: 0px;
}
```

Having built the products so they stack, you can see that they work really well regardless of the width of the browser (see Figure 6-22):

Figure 6-22. *Product stack works well regardless of browser*

Although the fluid width products work great across all viewport sizes, on the larger viewports you will notice there is a lot of space. The fluidity of the products and the elements within mean that when it comes to specifying a width on a product element, it, along with the contents within, will continue to work at the width specified. What this means is that on larger viewports you can take advantage of the extra space by placing the products into columns. To achieve this, simply set the width of the product element to 33.333% so the products take up a third of available width:

```
@media screen and (min-width: 767px){
    .product{
        float: left;
        width: 33.333%;
    }
}
```

You can then see that the columns appear side by side in the browser (see Figure 6-23).

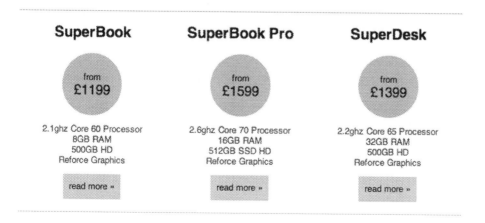

Figure 6-23. *Products line up side by side in browser*

Had you used percentages for the widths of the product elements, they would simply continue to scale up as the width of the site does.

Footer

The final thing to style for the reskin is the footer. This is really simple because the products already provide a separator between the products and the footer, so all you need to do is center align the text and add a tiny bit of spacing below:

```
.global-footer{
    text-align: center;
    padding-bottom: 10px;
}
```

These styles do not need any media queries to scale up as they will be fluid within the wrapper.

Conclusion

Having reskined the site with new CSS, you have learned how building mobile first and building upon the mobile version with each breakpoint can allow you to build a site that can be streamlined.

You have also learned that by building elements to be fluid on extra small devices, you can apply fixed width to them at different breakpoints, and then you only need to apply minimal extra styling.

It is important to remember that as you are rebuilding CSS you do not necessarily need to have an identical site as the end result. For your own site, before you embark on a reskin, it would be good to discuss with your designers and UX team whether they want to make any tweaks to the site as the reskin would be the best time to do this.

Summary

This chapter explained how to adapt an existing site to be responsive. You learned three different techniques for adapting a site to be responsive.

The first way of adapting a site to be responsive is to adapt the existing CSS. The key benefit of adapting the existing CSS is that it is a lot quicker than performing a full reskin. By adapting the existing CSS, you already have a base to start from. On the opposite side of this, this can be a disadvantage as it can lead to the code becoming a lot more bloated because you may have to override the values you have set with what would have been browser default behavior. A very simple example would be absolute positioning, where it is very unlikely that on smaller devices you wouldn't have to in some way change the way the element is positioned, often even removing the absolute positioning that has been applied.

The second way to adapt a site to be responsive was to refactor the existing code base so it was both responsive and built from a mobile-first perspective. The key benefit here is that you can get the performance and usability benefits of building a site mobile first without doing a full reskin. The key disadvantage is that on a large site you may be faced with a large code base to refactor, and it can be very difficult to isolate legacy code that is no longer needed because there might be a page embedded deep within the site that uses it.

The final way to adapt a site to be responsive was to do a full reskin the site. The key benefit of doing a full site reskin is that it enables you to build from a mobile-first perspective, building the site using progressive enhancement, which can help the code base to be much leaner. Using this mobile-first way of building a site allows you to add any additional styles as you progressively enhance the site.

Previous chapters have highlighted the benefit to building a site using a mobile-first methodology, so the preferred method to adapt an existing site is to do a full reskin, scraping the original CSS and starting using mobile-first methodologies. If, however, time is a concern, you might find that you will need to simply adapt the existing styles and, while not ideal, you will achieve a usable responsive site. Should you then find you have a bit of time left, you could look at optimizing your site to alleviate some of the disadvantages of a desktop-first build.

Although this chapter focused on the CSS side of adapting a site to be responsive, you are not limited to this. If necessary you can refactor parts of your HTML to enable you to better adapt your site. In addition, where the functionality of the site would benefit, you could write responsive JavaScript to change the way in which different elements of your site function.

The next chapter will look at how to improve the tools we use and the workflow we follow when building a responsive site.

CHAPTER 7

Tools and Workflow

With the growth of responsive design, there has also been an increase in the time it takes to develop a web site; the reason being that there are many more variables to take into account during development of a web site. With this in mind, it is increasingly important to find ways to optimize our workflow to enable us to save time in other areas of development. Alongside the growth of responsive design there has also been a growth in front-end tools, which enable us to write code more efficiently.

This chapter will look at:

1. Knowing your command line

2. Version control with Git

3. CSS preprocessors

4. Bower

5. Grunt

6. Gulp

7. Scaffolding

8. Other tools

9. Workflow

Knowing Your Command Line

The command-line interface of your operating system can be very intimidating at first, however, it can also be extremely powerful. There is a wide range of benefits that can be gained by learning how to use the command line:

1. A large number of web development tools now reside as command-line utilities.

2. It allows you to do batch file processing, such as the renaming of files, which may not be achievable using the normal graphical user interface (GUI).

3. The same interface is used when you secure shell (SSH) into servers, so the skills are transferable if you later want to manage your own hosting server.

With these benefits in mind, let's look at the command line so you can utilize it more in your web site development.

Preparing the Command Line

Before I begin this discussion of the command line, there are some basic tools you must have in place. This is slightly different between Mac OS X and Windows, so I have included separate instructions for each.

Mac OS X

In chapter 2 I discussed installing Xcode to allow you to use the iOS Simulator. Another part of Xcode that is useful to front-end developers is the command-line tools. The easiest way to install the command-line tools is to download them from the Apple developer web site at `https://developer.apple.com/downloads/index.action`. You will need to sign in using an Apple Developer account that you can register for, for free, and then download the latest "Command Line Tools" for your particular operating system. Once downloaded, you can simply run the installer to load the tools.

Once the installation is complete, you can install the Homebrew package manager, which is a command-line tool that allows you to install packages like Node.js. To install Homebrew, you need to run the command:

```
ruby -e "$(curl -fsSL https://raw.github.com/Homebrew/homebrew/go/install)"
```

The command line will then guide you through the installation of Homebrew.

Windows

To prepare the command-line tools on Windows, you will need to install both Git and Bash. These can be downloaded together from `http://msysgit.github.io/`. When downloading the msysgit package, it will advise you to download the latest version.

During the installation, you can use the default installation options. When asked which method you wish to use for installation, select "Use Git Bash only." Once the installation is complete, you can simply click Finish. Rather than use the built-in Windows command line, you will use Git Bash as the command-line interface. To open Git Bash, simply find it in the Git folder on the Start menu.

Commanding Your Command Line

Having ensured that the command line is set up correctly, you can now go through some of the basics of how to use the command line. The command line offers a simple interface to a wide range of computer functions, ranging from as simple as creating a folder to recursively changing file permissions.

Traversing Directories

One of the basic actions you might want to perform when working in the command line is navigating between and looking at the content of directories. There are two main commands you can use to achieve this: `ls` and `cd`.

ls

The `ls` command will allow you to list all the files and directories within the current directory.

cd

The `cd` command will allow you to change a directory. You can pass either an absolute path (starting with a /), for example `/Users/jonathan/`, or you can pass a path relevant to your current folder, such as `Users/jonathan`.

In addition, you can also navigate to the parent directory using `cd ..` or multiple parents using multiples, such as `../../`.

Simple File Manipulation

You also need to be able to manipulate files using the command line and be able to create, copy, move, and delete directories and files.

mkdir

The `mkdir` command allows you to make a new directory within the current directory. This is achieved by entering `mkdir dirname`. If you wanted to create a folder for a project called `project_name`, you would run the command:

```
mkdir project_name
```

touch

Sometimes when you are setting up a directory structure you might want to create placeholder files in your directories. Rather than have to open up the text editor and create each file, you can simply create them using the `touch` command. To create an empty file titled `index.html`, you would simply use the command:

```
touch index.html
```

cp

The `cp` command allows you to copy an existing file. To use the command, you simply provide the relative or absolute path to the original file, followed with the path of where you want to copy it to. The syntax of using the command looks like this:

```
cp original-file-path new-file-path
```

An example would be if you wanted to copy a file into a subdirectory of a current folder. In this case you would simply provide the path to both the original file and the location you want to copy it to:

```
cp hello.jpg images/hello.jpg
```

mv

The `mv` command is similar to the `cp` command in that you simply provide the relative or absolute path to the original file, followed by the path of where you want to move it to. The syntax of using the command looks like this:

```
mv original-file-path new-file-path
```

An example would be if you wanted to move a file into a subdirectory of a current folder. In this example, you would simply provide the path to both the original file and the location you want to move it to.

```
mv hello.jpg images/hello.jpg
```

rm

If you want to delete files that you have created, you can use the rm command. The syntax to use the rm command is:

```
rm file-to-be-removed-path
```

So if you wanted to delete the file hello.jpg from your images directory, you would use the command:

```
rm images/hello.jpg
```

■ **Note** The rm command does not place a file in the trash, but rather will permanently remove it from your system.

Other Useful Commands

Aside from the core commands already covered, there are also some additional commands that can be useful when using the command line.

sudo

The sudo command is used to run any command as the system super user (often known as root), the purpose being that if you wanted to modify files that the current user does not have permission to, you can do this by using sudo. An example of using the sudo command would be to delete a file that you do not have the rights to delete yourself, and the command line would be:

```
sudo rm protectedFile.jpg
```

cat

The cat command allows you to read the contents of a file. To use the cat command, you can run the command followed by the file you want to output:

```
cat error.log
```

Aside from allowing you to simply read a file, it can also be used to concatenate files. This is achieved through running cat followed by a list of file names you want to concatenate:

```
cat file1 file2 file3
```

In the above example, the concatenated file is simply output to the screen, however, you can choose to output it to a file by using a greater than sign (>) followed by the name of the file you want to output:

```
cat file1 file2 file3 > concatfile
```

tail

The `tail` command allows you to simply output the final few lines of a file into the command line. To use the `tail` command, you run the command followed by the file name you want to read from:

```
tail error.log
```

You can also choose how many lines you want to see using the `-n` flag followed by the number of lines you want to read:

```
tail -n 5 error.log
```

Further Documentation

Further documentation on any of these commands can be looked at directly in your terminal by using the `man` command before the command you want to learn about, for example, `man rm`.

Tool Prerequisites

Before you can start installing and using these tools, you need to install some prerequisites upon which they depend. The two prerequisites that you will need for the tools you will be exploring here are Ruby and Node.js.

Ruby

Ruby is a dynamic, object-oriented programming language that can be used for a variety of purposes. The reason for our interest in it here is that it is used by a small number of tools that you will be exploring in this chapter.

Installation
Mac OS X

Mac OS X comes with a version of Ruby. This will be the version you use in the examples in this chapter. Optionally you could update to a newer version of Ruby by installing a tool like RVM (information about this can be found at `http://rvm.io`).

Windows

To install Ruby on Windows, you can use the RubyInstaller package available at `http://rubyinstaller.org/`. This is a self-contained Windows installer that will install the Ruby language along with an execution environment and documentation.

During the installation, you will be asked for the destination of Ruby. At this stage you need to select the check box "Add Ruby executables to your PATH."

Node.js

One of the most important prerequisites is Node.js, which is a server-side implementation of JavaScript with a server-side API. This is required by many of the tools you be using in the examples in this book, including Bower, Grunt, and Serve.

Installation

Installing Node.js on Windows and Mac OS X is quite different, so I will detail the steps for each separately.

Mac OS X

To install Node.js on Mac OS X you will use a Mac OS X package manager called Homebrew. The installation is relatively straightforward, you simply need to open your terminal and run the command:

```
brew install node
```

This will then download and install Node.js for you. The benefit of using Homebrew to install Node.js in this way is that it is then easy for you to update to a newer version using the command:

```
brew update node
```

To test that Node.js is installed, simply install one of the tools below.

Windows

Node.js for Windows can easily be installed through a Windows installer, which is available from http://nodejs.org/download/.

Version Control with Git

Git (http://git-scm.com/) is version control system (VCS) that is used across a large number of open source projects to enable developers to keep track of the changes that have been made. When you initially set up the command line, you installed the Git source control management tool because it was a prerequisite for some of the other tools you would be using.

One of the core concepts to using Git is that it is a distributed VCS, which means that locally you will have a copy of the repository that you can use to perform all the main VCS actions like commit, branch, and merge. You can continue to simply use Git locally to manage code for a project, however, the power lies in being able to push your code from your local repository to a remote repository that you can use to collaborate with other developers. When you want to share code from your local repository, you can then push your local commits to the remote repository. Similarly, when you want to get the latest changes made by other developers, you can pull them down from the shared repository into your own repository.

If you have used a centralized version control system like Subversion (SVN) before, you will notice that this is very different. However, the benefit of this approach is that even when you do not have an Internet connection you can still make commits, which allows you to continue to commit in regular chunks.

To start to learn how to use the Git VCS, let's look at the basics of how to use it on the command line.

Initializing a Repository

To initialize a new repository on your local machine, you can simply run the command:

```
git init
```

What this does is create a hidden .git directory that will be used by Git to manage the versioning of the files in the directory. At this point the repository is still empty because there haven't been any files added to it.

Adding Files

When working with Git, you need to tell it what files you want it to version control. This is achieved through using the `git add` command. To add a single file, you simply run the command `git add` along with the name of the file you want to add. An example of adding a JavaScript file would be:

```
git add scripts/main.js
```

Although adding single files this way is easy, you might need to add a large number of files, especially if you are doing an initial commit. This is where `git add .` comes into play, which tells Git to add all the files under the current directory to the repository.

Making a Commit

Once you have added the files, you are ready to make the initial commit. You do this by using the `git commit` command. You can use the `-m` flag to set a commit message; therefore, the command will look like:

```
git commit -m 'initial commit'
```

After you have made this initial commit, you can continue to use `git commit` to commit any changed files.

Adding a Remote

Now that you have added some files and made your first commit, you might want to push these changes to a remote repository for sharing. To add a new repository, you need to use the `git remote add` command, providing both a name and the URL to the repository. An example of this would be:

```
git remote add origin git@github.com:jonathan-fielding/repo.git
```

Pushing a Commit

To push a commit to the remote server, you use the `git push` command. The first time you push to the remote server, you will need to set the upstream to the remote you just added, and to do this you use the `-u` flag. The command you would use to push to a remote server is:

```
git push -u origin master
```

Subsequent pushes can be achieved simply by using the `git push` command on its own.

Pull Changes

Pulling changes from the remote server can be achieved using the `git pull` command.

Cloning a Repository

So far you have been working on your own repository; however, it is likely at some point you will need to clone a remote repository. This is achieved using the git clone command followed by the URL to the repository. An example of cloning the HTML5 boilerplate repository would be:

```
git clone git@github.com:h5bp/html5-boilerplate.git
```

A cloned repository works exactly the same way as a repository you had initialized locally. You can add new files, delete files, make new commits, and if you have write access to the repository, push your changes up.

CSS Preprocessors

The core concept behind a CSS preprocessor is that it is a language that compiles down to being normal CSS. The idea being that by extending CSS by adding new features, you can write significantly less code. Some of the key features you can expect to find in a CSS preprocessor are:

1. Variables

2. Nesting

3. Import external files

4. Extend existing styles

5. Mixins

CSS preprocessors have become very popular, and with this, some of the features of preprocessors are already being adapted for submission to the W3C. The idea here is that variables, mixins, and nesting could all potentially feature in a future version of the CSS specification.

Before I discuss the individual preprocessors, let's explore the core features of them along with examples of how they work. The following examples are shown written using Sass, however, these are core concepts that apply to most CSS preprocessors.

Variables

In CSS, if you want to use a value in multiple places, you have to hard code it to those places. If you later want to update the value, you would need to go through and update the value in each of the places. This can be time consuming and it is very easy to make a mistake and miss an occurrence you want to update. CSS preprocessors alleviate this by allowing you to define values as variables that you can use throughout your code. By updating the variable, it will update all places this variable is used, making it less prone to errors. An example of how you might use a variable with a CSS preprocessor is when using the color blue. In this example, you would want to store the color as a variable, which here you will name $blue. When you need to use the variable, you would simply place the variable where you would have normally put the property value:

```
$blue: #3bbfce;

p{
        color: $blue;
}
```

Nesting

Another feature of CSS preprocessors is that they enable you to nest your CSS in a way that allows you to write less code. Take this example of an ordinary CSS:

```
.class-name{
    background: #000;
}

.class-name p{
    color: #fff;
}

.class-name p span{
    color: #eee;
}
```

If you were to rewrite this using a CSS preprocessor, you could instead choose to nest the CSS selectors in a way similar to how you would nest elements within HTML. What this means is that you are able to write less code as you no longer need to write long selectors. The example of the CSS above rewritten to use the CSS preprocessor is as follows:

```
.class-name{
    background: #000;
    p{
        color: #fff;

        span{
            color: #eee;
        }
    }
}
```

You will notice that you have nested the p selector within the class selector, and inside this you have the span. Once compiled, the CSS generated would be the same as the original CSS; however, you have written this code in a more concise way. Additionally, if you later wanted to change class-name to another-class-name you would simply have to update it in one place:

```
.another-class-name{
    background: #000;
    p{
        color: #fff;

        span{
            color: #eee;
        }
    }
}
```

Import

When writing a normal CSS document, for a large site it is normal for it to get quite lengthy even if the CSS document has been written in an optimized way. Responsive design has increased this problem as we are now adding media queries to our CSS.

Using a CSS preprocessor can help prevent you from having to work on a large file by allowing you to split the code into separate files. There are a couple of key benefits of this, the first being that it can be easier to manage smaller files, the second being that if conflicts arise in source control, they are easier to resolve.

CSS preprocessors allow you to split files by implementing a concept called *partials*, which is an individual file with a small section of your code inside. To prevent the partials from being compiled individually, you need to name your partials prefixed with an underscore (_), which tells the preprocessor that it is a partial and should only be compiled as part of another style sheet.

Normally you would have a master file used to import your partials into; inside this you can use `@import` to import a partial into the document:

```
@import "utilities/_reset.scss";
@import "utilities/_typography.scss";
```

When you compile using the CSS preprocessor, the code from the partials is moved inline in the compiled CSS document.

Extend

Having written some styles to target a particular element, you might find that you have a similar element elsewhere on your site. Rather than redeclare the CSS rule set again or adding the class name to the existing selector, what you can do is simply extend the existing styles using the preprocessor. To do this you first define the styles for your first element; in this example, you would define the styles for a simple button:

```
.button{
        display: inline-block;
        background: #ccc;
        border-radius: 10px;
        padding: 5px 50px;
}
```

Then you can define the styles for the new element; in this case you will define a small button with less padding. To extend an existing element, you can use `@extend` followed by the selector you are extending:

```
.button-sml{
        @extend .button;
        padding: 5px 20px;
}
```

Mixins

The most powerful feature of CSS preprocessors is the ability to define mixins. A mixin is a reusable block of code that, once defined, can be used anywhere in your CSS. It allows you to make a declaration of code, which you can apply variables to, to output the desired result. There are several places where using a mixin can make it easier to write your CSS. Let's look at a couple of these examples.

Prefixing

The first example shows how you can solve the problem of browser prefixing using a mixin. Earlier in the book I mentioned that as new CSS features are implemented in the browser, they are normally prefixed with the browser prefix. Because you will want to support all browsers, you need to ensure your code outputs all the correct browser prefixes, and for this purpose you can use a mixin. To write a mixin that is able to generate the prefixed code for the CSS property `border-radius` you need to write a mixin that accepts one argument (the value for the `border-radius`) and to write each of the prefixed versions of the property with the value set to the argument that has been passed to the mixin:

```
@mixin border-radius($argument) {
        -webkit-border-radius: $argument;
        -moz-border-radius: $argument;
        -o-border-radius: $argument;
        border-radius: $argument;
}
```

If you now wanted to use the `border-radius` mixin you would use `@include border-radius(value)`, where `(value)` is equal to the `border-radius` you wish to set:

```
@include border-radius(10px);
```

Shortcuts

Another area you might want to use a mixin is for writing shortcuts. An example being a mixin that takes values used to position an element and then outputs the CSS. Although this a simple example, it demonstrates how easy it is to write a mixin that handles outputting CSS you might write quite often:

```
@mixin position($top, $right, $bottom, $left) {
    top: $top;
    right: $right;
    bottom: $bottom;
    left: $left;
}
```

Functions

In some CSS preprocessors, in addition to mixins, there are also functions. Although there are similarities between mixins and functions, the key difference is that a mixin will output CSS directly, while a function will return a value that you then output yourself.

An example of where you might use a function rather than a mixin is when you want to calculate a value. In this example, you might want to return the result calculated and then use it somewhere else. You could even use the function within a mixin to perform the calculations you require.

A simple example of this kind of calculation would be where you want to convert the pixel font size to rems. An example of this is:

```
@function px-to-rem($font-size){
        $baseline-px: 16 //This is the base font size used on our HTML element
        $baseline-rem: $baseline-px / 1rem * 1;
        @return $font-size / $baseline-rem
}
```

To use this function, you would simply call it, passing the font size you want:

```
p{
        font-size: px-to-rem(12px);
}
```

Different Preprocessors Available

Having explored some of the key principles of CSS preprocessors, let's look at a couple of the popular preprocessors. I will explain why they should become part of your toolset and how they will save you time when building a responsive site.

Sass + Compass

Sass (http://sass-lang.com/) is an acronym for Syntastically Awesome Style Sheets. I previously explained some of the different features that a CSS preprocessor will typically include, and you will be happy to learn that Sass includes all of these. Sass is also the CSS preprocessor of choice of many open source projects, including Foundation, which was discussed earlier the book. Additionally, there is even a Sass version of Twitter Bootstrap.

Compass is an additional framework that sits on top of Sass, augmenting it with additional functionality. Examples of such functionality include mixins and the ability to generate sprites.

There are a wide variety of tools that can be used with Sass and Compass to compile code, so let's start by focusing on using the command-line tools.

Installation

Both Sass and Compass are installed as Ruby gems. To install them both, simply run:

```
gem update --system
gem install compass
```

When Compass is installed, it will also install Sass as it is a dependency.

Usage

The Sass syntax comes in two flavors: the first being Sassy CSS, which is a superset of the CSS3 syntax, the second being the indented syntax. I will focus on the Sassy CSS syntax because it is not only more popular than the indented syntax, but it also became the main syntax to use with Sass as of version 3 of the language.

Because you will be using Sass with Compass in the examples here, let's start by using Compass to set up this project. To do this you will use the compass create command, which will create the project directory along with basic Sass files and compiled CSS. For this example, you will tell the command that the name of the project is sass_project:

```
compass create sass_project
```

Upon running the above command, Compass will create a new folder for the project with the files inside. In addition, it will also give you instructions on how to add the compiled CSS to the HTML document (see Figure 7-1).

```
*************************************************************************
Congratulations! Your compass project has been created.

You may now add and edit sass stylesheets in the sass subdirectory of your project.

Sass files beginning with an underscore are called partials and won't be
compiled to CSS, but they can be imported into other sass stylesheets.

You can configure your project by editing the config.rb configuration file.

You must compile your sass stylesheets into CSS when they change.
This can be done in one of the following ways:
    1. To compile on demand:
       compass compile [path/to/project]
    2. To monitor your project for changes and automatically recompile:
       compass watch [path/to/project]

More Resources:
    * Website: http://compass-style.org/
    * Sass: http://sass-lang.com
    * Community: http://groups.google.com/group/compass-users/

To import your new stylesheets add the following lines of HTML (or equivalent) to your webpage:
<head>
    <link href="/stylesheets/screen.css" media="screen, projection" rel="stylesheet" type="text/css" />
    <link href="/stylesheets/print.css" media="print" rel="stylesheet" type="text/css" />
    <!--[if IE]>
        <link href="/stylesheets/ie.css" media="screen, projection" rel="stylesheet" type="text/css" />
    <![endif]-->
</head>
Jonathans-MacBook-Pro:code jonathan$ ▌
```

Figure 7-1. *Creating Sass project with Compass, with instructions to add to HTML highlighted*

At this stage you are still in the parent directory of the project you just created, so you will use the cd command to move into this project's directory:

```
cd sass_project
```

Now that you are in the directory, you can compile the Sass. To check that the compilation is working correctly, simply run the command:

```
compass compile
```

The command line will tell you that this has compiled successfully.

Having set up the project in the command line, you have yet to write any of your own code. Let's open the screen.scss file Compass generated in the text editor. Upon opening the file, you will find the following six lines of Sass:

```
/* Welcome to Compass.
 * In this file you should write your main styles. (or centralize your imports)
 * Import this file using the following HTML or equivalent:
 * <link href="/stylesheets/screen.css" media="screen, projection" rel="stylesheet" type="text/css"
/> */
```

```
@import "compass/reset";
```

What this code is doing is importing a default browser reset to the top of your style sheet. If you want to see the code that this compiles to, you can simply take a look at the screen.css file in your style sheets directory.

Being able to add a CSS browser reset using only one line of code can be very helpful for full site builds; however, for this example you will start from scratch and clear out this Sass file.

Let's start with writing some nested CSS:

```
.class-name{
    background: #000;
    p{
        color: #fff;

        span{
            color: #eee;
        }
    }
}
```

If you then compile this in your command line using compass compile and open the compiled screen.css file from your style sheet's directory, you will find your compiled code looks like this:

```
/* line 1, ../sass/screen.scss */
.class-name {
  background: #000;
}
/* line 3, ../sass/screen.scss */
.class-name p {
  color: #fff;
}
/* line 6, ../sass/screen.scss */
.class-name p span {
  color: #eee;
}
```

You will notice that along with the generated CSS you also have a comment for each selector that tells you the line number and file you can find that selector in the Sass file.

As you may have already realized, it isn't really practical to run compass compile every time you make a change. This is where the compass watch command comes in. What the compass watch command does is it watches your Sass files so if, for instance, you changed the background color of your element, it would simply recompile automatically. So that any further changes automatically compile, you would now run the command:

```
compass watch
```

Earlier I discussed how you can import several partials (part of a CSS document) into a single document. Here I will explain how this works with Sass.

First, you will create a directory for the partials, in this case let's call it partials. Inside this folder you will create two Sass files titled _layout.scss and _typography.scss. The reason that you prefix these partials with an underscore is to tell the compiler that it is a partial and it should not be compiled individually.

Inside _layout.scss you will put these basic styles:

```
.container{
        max-width: 960px;
        margin: 0 auto;
}
```

Inside _typography.scss you will put these basic styles:

```
html{
        font-size: 100%;
}

h1{
        font-size: 3rem;
}

p{
        font-size: 1.2rem;
}
```

You can then include these inside the screen.scss file by using @import. The code within the screen.scss code would therefore look like this:

```
@import "partials/typography";
@import "partials/layout";
```

You will notice that although the original file was prefixed with an underscore and had a suffix of the file extension, these are not necessary when importing the partial. Because you ran the compass watch command in the command line, Compass is watching these files for changes, so upon saving the screen.scss file, the file will be recompiled to CSS for you. If you then look at the screen.css output file, you will see the two files are now included in the same CSS file:

```
/* line 1, ../sass/partials/_typography.scss */
html {
  font-size: 100%;
}

/* line 5, ../sass/partials/_typography.scss */
h1 {
  font-size: 3rem;
}

/* line 9, ../sass/partials/_typography.scss */
p {
  font-size: 1.2rem;
}

/* line 1, ../sass/partials/_layout.scss */
.container {
  max-width: 960px;
  margin: 0 auto;
}
```

The Sass files imported are compiled and inserted in the order they are declared. Note that the comments highlight which partial each section of the code came from.

Having looked at some basic use of Sass, hopefully you have a good understanding of how to use the tools to compile to CSS. I have already covered the core functionality of CSS preprocessors, and it is important to remember that these apply to Sass too.

LESS

Another CSS preprocessor that is very popular is LESS. I previously went through some of the different features that a CSS preprocessor will typically include, and unfortunately LESS doesn't support writing your own custom functions, however, all the other features discussed are supported.

The developers at Twitter have released several open source projects that use LESS, the most popular being Bootstrap; however, they have also released a code quality tool called Recess, which is a tool for testing code quality for both LESS and CSS files.

Installation

There are several different ways to use LESS, here I will focus on using the command-line tool. The LESS command-line tool is written in Node.js, so you will need to install it using npm. The command you would use is:

```
npm install -g less
```

Usage

To get started using LESS, you need to set up a folder, which you can call less:

```
mkdir less
```

Once you have created this folder, you will create a LESS file called screen.less using the text editor. Let's start by adding some nested code to the LESS file:

```
.class-name{
    background: #000;
    p{
        color: #fff;

        span{
            color: #eee;
        }
    }
}
```

With this in place, you can now compile the LESS file to CSS using the lessc command-line tool. You need to provide the name of the file you want to compile along with the name of the compiled file:

```
lessc screen.less screen.css
```

Once the file is compiled, you can take a look at the output inside the screen.css file:

```
.class-name {
  background: #000;
}
.class-name p {
  color: #fff;
}
.class-name p span {
  color: #eee;
}
```

The output is very similar to how you would have coded without a preprocessor, however, the code you actually wrote was much simpler to write. Note that unlike Sass, LESS does not add debug comments to the source code.

I discussed the concept of imports earlier and explained how you would do this in Sass, and in LESS it is very similar. You simply use an @import statement to include several different files.

You first need to create a directory for these partials, for this example you can call it partials. Inside this folder you will create two LESS files titled _layout.less and _typography.less. So that LESS does not compile the partials, you prefix the files using an underscore.

Inside _layout.less, you will put these basic styles:

```
.container{
        max-width: 960px;
        margin: 0 auto;
}
```

Inside _typography.less, you will put these basic styles:

```
html{
        font-size: 100%;
}

h1{
        font-size: 3rem;
}

p{
        font-size: 1.2rem;
}
```

You then need to update screen.less to import both of these files using the @import statement. Unlike for Sass, you need to provide the full paths to the LESS files including the file extension:

```
@import "partials/_typography.less";
@import "partials/_layout.less";
```

To recompile the LESS file to CSS, you can simply rerun the command from earlier:

```
lessc screen.less screen.css
```

This then compiles the screen.less file into the screen.css file. If you now look inside the screen.css file, you will see that the two files are now together in the same document in the same order you declared them with the @import statements:

```
html {
  font-size: 100%;
}
h1 {
  font-size: 3rem;
}
p {
  font-size: 1.2rem;
}
.container {
  max-width: 960px;
  margin: 0 auto;
}
```

The command line isn't the only way in which you can use LESS. While you are developing you can choose to use the LESS file directly as a link similarly to how you included the CSS in the page. In addition to this, you include less.js, which is a library that will parse the LESS file in the browser. The code you would add to your head element would look like this:

```
<link rel="stylesheet/less" type="text/css" href="screen.less" />
<script src="less.js" type="text/javascript"></script>
```

This enables you to quickly test your code as you develop, however, it is advised you do not deploy live code with LESS set up this way as the browser will need to parse the file before the styles can be rendered. Also adding the less.js parser will of course add to the weight of your page as well.

Problems of Using CSS Preprocessors

As I covered earlier, using a CSS preprocessor can offer huge benefits to your development, however, they are not without their disadvantages.

The first problem you might encounter when using a CSS preprocessor is that it can lead to your CSS file becoming bloated. This is because as you write your code it is very easy to keep nesting your selectors until your selectors are extremely specific and very long. Although this is not a fault of the preprocessor, it is an easy trap to fall in to because of the temptation to keep nesting. A good example might be where you want to style a button tag. If you over nest your CSS preprocessor code, it might look something like this:

```
.main
        .container{
                .row{
                        .column{
                                p{
                                        button{
                                                color: #000
                                        }
                                }
                        }
                }
        }
}
```

This nested code would compile to CSS that looks like this:

```
.main .container .row .column p button{
        color: #000
}
```

Where it is likely, you could simply target a button within a p, as in this case the parents are likely irrelevant to targeting the anchor correctly:

```
p{
        button{
                color: #000
        }
}
```

Having seen this example, you should realize how easy it might be to accidently start to over nest. This is actually a really common mistake a lot of developers make when they first use CSS preprocessors, so don't worry if you have made this mistake before. A good rule to try to follow is to never allow your nesting to get more than three selectors deep, meaning the generated CSS will have much shorter selectors. Additionally, by not over nesting your code, it is easier to make the CSS reusable.

Another disadvantage to using CSS preprocessors is that there is a slight learning curve to using them. Although some of the simpler stuff like nesting and variables are really easy to pick up, it can take longer to learn about how you can write mixins and functions. Despite the syntax differences between some of the preprocessors I have discussed here, many of the core concepts are the same, so once you have picked one up it is easy enough to move to a different preprocessor.

A final disadvantage is that setting up using a CSS preprocessor on a project may require you to make changes to your workflow. You will not only need to compile your preprocessor code each time you save, but you might also need to add additional steps to your deploy process to handle compiling your preprocessor code in production mode.

Choosing a Preprocessor

I have discussed the two most popular CSS preprocessors, LESS and Sass, and you have seen some of the differences between the two.

Sass has a lot to offer in itself, with support for functions being a particular stand out feature. If you then add Compass into the equation, it adds a lot of value to choosing Sass as your preprocessor. For starters, Compass includes a library of mixins that allow you to generate the different versions of the prefixed code. This makes it a lot simpler than having to define all the prefixes yourself. In addition, Compass will generate your image sprites for you along with the CSS to display them on your page if you supply it a folder full of images.

LESS, however, also offers mixin libraries that try to offer similar functionality by providing mixins that will output the prefixed code. However, there isn't anything quite like Compass available to use with LESS.

Bower

Bower is a package manager from the developers at Twitter that allows you to install front-end packages. The main benefit of using a package manager is that rather than download the package manually from GitHub or the packages web site, you can simply add it to your project from your command line. In addition, alongside downloading the package, Bower will download any dependencies it might have. A simple example being that if you were to download a jQuery plug-in it will look at whether you currently have jQuery installed, and if it finds that jQuery is not installed, it will also download jQuery for you.

In addition to allowing you to install packages, Bower also enables you to update packages to newer versions, meaning it is much easier to keep your projects up to date with the latest version of libraries.

Installation

Bower is a Node package and therefore requires Node to be installed to work. It can be installed using the Node package manager using the command:

```
npm install -g bower
```

Usage

The easiest way to use Bower is to simply run `bower install <package-name>`, so if you wanted to install jQuery into this project, you would use:

```
bower install jquery
```

Sometimes, however, you might want to specify a version of a package you want to install. The most likely reason being that the latest version lacks support for the browsers you need to support. An example of this is jQuery where the 2.x branch will not work in Internet Explorer 8 and earlier, so if you wanted to support these browsers, you would need to use the 1.x branch. Installing a specific version of a package can be achieved by using `#version-number` after the name of the package. For jQuery, installing version 1.10 would require the following command:

```
bower install jquery#1.10
```

One of the benefits of using Bower is that you do not need to keep copies of the dependencies in your own source control repository. It is in fact encouraged that you simply save a list of dependencies in a bower.json file. To be able to use Bower in this way, you first need to initialize the project, and this is achieved by running the command:

```
bower init
```

What this does is initiate a series of questions regarding your project and then generate a bower.json file with this information. You can then start to add your dependencies. There are two type of dependencies:

1. *General dependencies*: These are the core dependencies used by your web site or web application in production. It is also assumed you will use these dependencies in production as well.

2. *Development dependencies*: These are the dependencies used specifically when you are developing your site, which might include unit testing, packaging scripts, and documentation generation.

If you want to save the dependency as a development dependency, you can simply append the `–save-dev` flag on to the end of the command:

```
bower install jquery#1.10 –save-dev
```

Similarly, if you want to save the dependency as a normal dependency, you can simply append the `--save` flag on to the end of the command:

```
bower install jquery#1.10 --save
```

With dependencies saved to the bower.json file, another developer who wants to set up the project can download the project from the repository and then simply run `bower install` in the root of the project to automatically download all the required dependencies.

Grunt

Grunt (`http://gruntjs.com/`) is another tool that is built using Node.js. It is sometimes called a build tool, however, this is slightly inaccurate as the sole purpose of a build tool is to convert some source code into the final product. Instead, Grunt is a task runner; the key difference being that while one of the tasks could be to build your code, it also can be used to run any series of tasks that you want to automate including unit testing, regression testing, and code quality checking. For a large project, having a task runner can be invaluable as it enables you to optimize your workflow.

There are several key benefits to using a task runner like Grunt, the most obvious is that it will save you time by automating tasks that you might have otherwise had to do manually. A further benefit is that it reduces the chance of human error—by this I mean that once the tasks are set up they run the same way every time. If this were a manual process, there would be a greater chance of making a mistake.

A large community of developers have come together around Grunt to help build an amazing ecosystem of pluggable tasks that can be added to your Grunt build. This means there are plug-ins that handle everything from building your Sass to notifying you when your build tasks are complete.

Installation

The Grunt interface is split into two components: the first is the command line interface component, which is installed globally. The second component is a local Grunt installation that is installed onto your project. Let's start by installing the command-line interface component, which is installed using npm in the command:

```
npm install -g grunt-cli
```

Usage

To get started with using Grunt, you need to first set up a package.json file if you do not already have one, achieved by simply running the command:

```
npm init
```

After running this command, you will then be asked for some information about your project, these are the questions you will be asked:

1. *Name*: This is the name of your project, which should not contain spaces or any special characters.

2. *Version*: The current version of your project.

3. *Description*: The description of your project (optional).

4. *Entry point*: This is not applicable if you are just using Grunt on a project. It is used when you are writing a Node.js package (optional).

5. *Test command*: A command used to run tests on your project, for a Grunt project you can point this to a Grunt task (e.g., grunt test --verbose) (optional).

6. *Git repository*: The URL to the repository used for your project (optional).

7. *Keywords*: The keywords about your project.

8. *Author*: Your name.

9. *License*: If you are distributing the code, what license does it fall under.

Once you have answered these questions, you will be shown the code for your package.json file. If this is okay simply press Enter. The package.json for this project looks like this:

```
{
  "name": "gruntproject",
  "version": "1.0.0",
  "description": "First Grunt Project",
  "scripts": {
    "test": "grunt test --verbose"
  },
  "author": "Jonathan Fielding",
  "license": "MIT"
}
```

You now need to perform the local Grunt installation on your project, this is done again through npm using the command:

```
npm install grunt --save-dev
```

This downloads Grunt, along with its dependencies, and will install it in the node_modules folder. In addition to this, by using the --save-dev flag you will also add this to the dependency list stored within your package.json. If you try to run the grunt command now, you would get the error message *Fatal error: Unable to find Gruntfile*. The next step is therefore to create a Gruntfile.

The Gruntfile is the file that determines the tasks you are able to run. To get started with the Gruntfile, you need to first create Gruntfile.js and inside this you need to set up the basic config, which will look like this:

```
module.exports = function(grunt) {
    //Grunt configuration goes here
    grunt.initConfig({
        pkg: grunt.file.readJSON('package.json')

    });
};
```

The Grunt configuration will load the package.json file you created earlier and store it within the configuration of Grunt, which means you can access useful information like the name of the project and the current version number without having to declare this again. With this basic file prepared, you can now find some Grunt tasks that will be useful for this project. To find plug-ins, you can simply perform a search at http://gruntjs.com/plugins. This page of the Grunt web site allows you to search through all the different Grunt plug-ins that are available. Earlier in this chapter I discussed the use of CSS preprocessors, so you could look for a task that will compile the Sass to CSS. If you were to search for *compass* on the Grunt web site, you could find a plug-in for Grunt titled contrib-compass, which is what you will use for the task in the examples that follow.

To install the contrib-compass plug-in, you again need to use npm, prefixing the name of the plug-in with grunt-. You also need to use the --save-dev flag to save it as a dependency in the package.json file. The full command to install the plug-in is:

```
npm install grunt-contrib-compass --save-dev
```

Once this has finished downloading, you can add the configuration for the Grunt compass plug-in to the Gruntfile. The first thing you need to is provide the config options, and you do this by adding to the object passed to the initConfig method. For the Compass plug-in you need to add a property called compass, and inside this you can define different targets and include different options for each. For this example, you will simply set up a development target called dev and provide some simple options telling Compass the location of the files and that you are using a development environment:

```
grunt.initConfig({
    pkg: grunt.file.readJSON('package.json'),
    compass: {
        dev: {
            options: {
                sassDir: 'sass',
                cssDir: 'css',
                imagesDir: 'images',
                environment: 'development',
```

```
            httpGeneratedImagesPath: ' images'
        }
    }
}
});
```

With this in place, you now need to set up the tasks, and you will do this by loading tasks you want to be able to use. In this case, you want to be able to use the Compass task. This is loaded using the `grunt.loadNpmTask` method. You place these commands after the configuration options, so for the Compass plug-in the command would be:

```
grunt.loadNpmTasks('grunt-contrib-compass');
```

Before you can test this, you need some files to compile. Let's use the Sass files you used earlier when learning about CSS preprocessors for this. With this in place, you can go back to the terminal and run the command `grunt compass`, which will compile the Sass to CSS. If you now check the CSS folder, you will find the Sass has compiled as you had expected.

The power in Grunt though is not to just have single tasks that you run individually, but in actually defining tasks that themselves run a series of different tasks. To do this, you use the method `grunt.registerTask`, which allows you to define a task name along with an array of tasks that will be run by the task. For this example, you only have one task in the array, which is the Compass task targeting the `dev` target you defined:

```
grunt.registerTask('default', ['compass:dev']);
```

In the above example you used the name `default` for the task, which is special in that rather than be passed as an argument to Grunt in the command line like other tasks would, the default task runs simply when you run the `grunt` command.

So far I have concentrated on using Grunt to compile the Sass code, and while you could have done this before simply by using the `compass` command-line tool, by using Grunt you can start to make it more a part of your workflow. There are already over 3000 different Grunt plug-ins available, some of the most popular ones include:

1. grunt-contrib-watch: Allows you to watch files for changes and run tasks based on what has changed.

2. grunt-contrib-uglify: Allows you to minify and concatenate your JavaScript files.

3. grunt-contrib-copy: Copies files and folders.

4. grunt-contrib-jshint: Checks your JavaScript for common errors and mistakes.

What you should take away from this is that Grunt is a really powerful and flexible tool, and that while initially it might be daunting to set up, once you have your tasks set up it will save you a significant amount of time. There is a huge community developing plug-ins and extending Grunt, so with time it will continue to grow in its usefulness.

Gulp

Gulp (`http://gulpjs.com/`) is a similar tool to Grunt in that it is a task runner that can be used to run a series of tasks. The tasks themselves are added by adding plug-ins to Gulp. Unlike the configuration-based approach that Grunt takes, Gulp takes the approach that you write the code that is run to complete your task. The way in which it does this is that it can take some files, then you are able to pipe these through different tasks that need to be run to process them. An example would be a series of JavaScript files which you might first want to concatenate and then minify, to achieve this you would simply pipe your files through a "concat" task followed by an "uglify" before saving the final file back to disk. This is very different to the way in which Grunt works.

This stream based approach taken by Gulp is really fast and this is illustrated in tests run by Zander Martineau (http://labs.tmw.co.uk/2014/01/speedtesting-gulp-and-grunt/) who found that when just compiling Sass, Gulp is more than a second faster than Grunt. Zander Martineau also suggests that there is the expectation that given time, the Sass plugin for Gulp will be optimized further resulting in the compilation being even faster.

Installing Gulp is a two-step process, the first is to install Gulp globally on your system, which is achieved with the command:

```
npm install -g gulp
```

The next step is to install Gulp into your project. To do this you need to use npm using the command:

```
npm install --save-dev gulp
```

You then need to create a file called gulpfile.js, which is the script file that determines the tasks you want to run. Inside it you will set up the basic code to begin with:

```
var gulp = require('gulp');
```

You then need to start adding plug-ins. In order to compare how Gulp works vs. Grunt, let's use the same example of using it to compile Sass. To do this, you need to install the gulp-sass plug-in into the project using npm:

```
npm install gulp-sass
```

Then you need to pull the gulp-sass plug-in into the gulpfile.js file. Because the gulpfile.js is written in Node, you simply use require to load the module into a variable:

```
var sass = require('gulp-sass');
```

The next step is to add the task for Sass so it is able to compile the Sass files into CSS. You do this by using the gulp.task method, passing a name for the task as the first parameter and a function as the second. Similarly to Grunt, if you set the name to default this task will run when you simply run the gulp command in the command line:

```
gulp.task('default', function() {
});
```

With this task set up, you can now start to add the functionality to this task. First you need to use the gulp.src method to grab the source files you want to process, which in the case of Sass is the original scss files you want to compile. You can use the pipe method to pipe the files to the Sass method, which will tell Gulp you want to compile the files. Finally, you can then use pipe to pass the compiled output to gulp.dest, which will then output the compiled source files:

```
gulp.task('default', function() {
        gulp.src('./scss/*.scss')
                .pipe(sass())
                .pipe(gulp.dest('./css/'));
});
```

This example highlights the key feature of Gulp, which is how you can pipe your files from method to method, performing tasks on them along the way. In One of the key principles of gulp plug-ins is that each plug-in handles a single thing, and its through combining these plug-ins you have the flexibility to build tasks that do exactly what you want.

There are a variety of different plug-ins available to use with Gulp. Some of the popular ones are:

1. gulp-uglify: The Uglify plug-in can be used to minify JavaScript files.

2. gulp-concat: The Concat plug-in allows you to concatenate multiple files into a single file.

3. gulp-jshint: The JSHint plug-in allows you to lint your JavaScript files for common errors.

The key weakness of Gulp is that, at the time of writing it isn't as mature as Grunt, meaning it doesn't have as many plug-ins and the community is still learning how to best use it. This doesn't mean you shouldn't use Gulp; there is a fast growing community around it and you just need to ensure that the plugins you need for your project are available.

Scaffolding

When starting a new project, it can be very time consuming to pull together the initial template, as it usually includes:

1. Putting together the base HTML

2. Pulling together any JavaScript libraries you want to use

3. Adding any CSS frameworks or CSS grids you want to use.

Thankfully, a number of different tools have been released that allow you to generate these starting templates. Let's look at a couple of these tools to see how to integrate them into your workflow.

Yeoman

Yeoman (`www.yeoman.io`) is a project scaffolding tool that allows you to quickly scaffold a project based on predefined generators. There is a wide range of generators available, although if there is not one that fits your needs, you can even write one of your own.

Some of the generators that are available include:

1. webapp

2. angular

3. ember

4. backbone

5. chromeapp

6. chrome-extension

7. bootstrap

When using these generators, Yeoman will scaffold the folder structure and some files specific to the generator. Generators will also set up any dependencies in a bower.json file and then run the Bower install to download all the required dependencies.

Installation

To get started with Yeoman, you will need to install the Node package using npm. The Node package for Yeoman is called yo and it will need to be installed globally so you can access it anywhere on the command line to get your projects started. To install Yeoman globally, you will need to use the –g flag. The full command to install Yeoman is therefore:

```
npm install -g yo
```

The installation of Yeoman can take quite some time as it needs to install a lot of dependencies. Once Yeoman is installed, you can test that it is installed correctly by simply using the command:

```
yo
```

Usage

To use Yeoman to scaffold a project, you need to create a directory for your project. This can be done either through Finder/Windows Explorer or directly from your command line. For this example let's create the folder directory directly in the command line:

```
mkdir project_directory
cd project_directory
```

Once you are in the directory, you can start to use Yeoman to scaffold out the project. When first installed, Yeoman does not come with any generators, therefore, to get started you will need to install a generator. The most common generator you will likely use is the webapp generator, so let's first install this. The first step is to run the yo command.

Then you need to select "Install a generator" using the arrow keys and press Enter. You will then be able to perform a search for the webapp generator by entering the term webapp (see Figure 7-2)

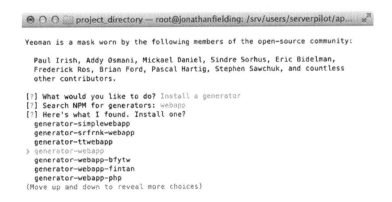

Figure 7-2. *Yeoman shows a list of generators it finds*

You then need to use the arrow keys to scroll down to "generator-webapp," and upon selecting it you would just press Enter. Yeoman will now download and install the webapp generator for you.

You should now see an additional command is now available titled "Run the Webapp generator." In the brackets it will give the version of the generator you currently have installed. If the list does not appear to have updated, simply select "Get me out of here" and run the yo command again. To run the generator, simply select it and press Enter.

Some generators allow you to additionally configure the scaffolding you are setting up by enabling you to select options before the template is set up. The webapp is one such generator and will provide you with a selection of configurable options (see Figure 7-3).

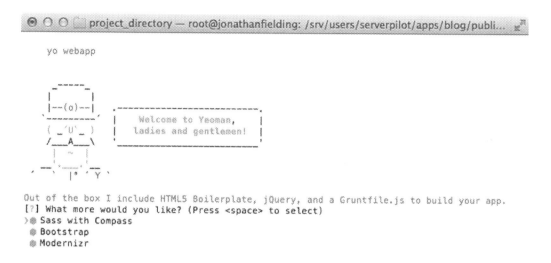

Figure 7-3. *Yeoman gives a list of configurable options*

To select/deselect these options, simply go up and down using the arrow keys and use the spacebar to select/deselect. For selected options, the circle is filled in and green, for the unselected options the circle is empty.

When you now press the Enter key, Yeoman will first scaffold your project, including preparing configuration files for both Grunt and Bower and then run the npm install and Bower install commands, which will then download all the required dependencies. This part of the process can take a while and will depend on the speed of your Internet connection.

Yeoman will then confirm that your project is all set up.

If at any point you are finding that things are not working as you expect, you might have a problem with your installation. To diagnose this, Yeoman has a command called yo doctor that will check everything is working as expected. Simply run the command and Yeoman will let you know if there are any problems you need to fix.

At this stage you will have a fully scaffolded project, so you can get on with building the site. It is important to note, however, that many of the generators will come with predefined Grunt tasks. As such, let's look at the Grunt tasks that come set up with the webapp generator:

1. grunt: Runs jshint on the JavaScript following by the test and build commands.

2. grunt build: Compiles the projects, including minifying/concatting js, building the Sass into minified CSS, and compressing and renaming images (for cache busting).

3. grunt watch: Watches the JavaScript, CoffeeScript, Sass, and style sheets to detect any changes and recompiles if they change.

4. grunt server: Creates a Node server for running the project, watches for any file changes, and refreshes browser on file change.

5. grunt test: Runs any tests set up for the project.

You have now seen how easy it is to scaffold projects using Yeoman. It is a great tool for quickly getting started with a project, and with the wide variety of generators available, it is very easy to find one that will be right for you.

If you wanted to take using Yeoman further, you could choose to write your own generator that is specific to how you want your sites to be scaffolded. Once you have written your own generator you can use it time and time again, refining it as you go. And of course, you could open source it so others can use it too.

grunt-init

The alternative command-line tool grunt-init (gruntjs.com/project-scaffolding) enables you to quickly scaffold your project.

Installation

To get started with grunt-init, run the command line:

```
npm install -g grunt-init
```

Usage

Although grunt-init shares a lot of similarities with Yeoman, the way in which you install the templates is very different. Rather than being able to simply search for generators, with grunt-init you need to add them to a folder titled .grunt-init within the user home directory.

A simple way to install them into the correct directory is to simply clone them using Git into the .grunt-init folder. An example for a webapp template that might use the webapp the grunt-init webapp template developed by Pascal Duez can be found at https://github.com/pascalduez/grunt-init-webapp. You can install this template by cloning it using the following command line:

```
git clone https://github.com/pascalduez/grunt-init-webapp.git ~/.grunt-init/webapp
```

Once the Git cloning of the template repository is complete, you can use the webapp template to scaffold new projects.

To get started you need to create the project directory, which can be done either through Finder/Windows Explorer or directly from your command line. For this example let's create the folder directory directly in the command line:

```
mkdir project_directory
cd project_directory
```

You can now generate the scaffolding for the web application using grunt-init, and this can be achieved by running the command, passing it the name of the template you downloaded earlier:

```
grunt-init webapp
```

After running this command, you will be asked the following questions:

```
Please answer the following:
[?] WebApp package and root directory. (project_directory)
[?] WebApp name. (A human-readable name for the app: Project Directory)
[?] WebApp description. (A human-readable description of the app.)
```

```
[?] Version (0.1.0)
[?] Project git repository (git://github.com/jonathan/project_directory.git)
[?] Project homepage (https://github.com/jonathan/project_directory)
[?] Author name (Jonathan Fielding)
[?] Author url (none)
[?] Licenses (MIT)
[?] Do you need to make any changes to the above before continuing? (y/N)
```

Upon answering these questions grunt-init will download and install the required components of the scaffolding.

Similar to Yeoman, grunt-init will preconfigure a Gruntfile—in the case of the webapp template, it will have the following commands:

1. grunt: Runs jshint on the JavaScript.

2. grunt server: Creates a Node server for running the project, watches for any file changes, and refreshes the browser on file change.

You have now seen how easy it is to use grunt-init. Grunt-init makes installing new templates really simple as you can simply drop them into the ~/.grunt-init/ directory. In this example you cloned a template from public Git repository, however, you could maintain your own templates in private repositories so you could also share them with friends or your coworkers. Alternatively, you can simply write your own generator and place it in the directory with no source control required.

Initializr

Initializr (`http://www.initializr.com/`) is very different from both Yeoman and grunt-init in that it is a web-based tool that will generate a scaffolding you can download as a zip archive.

Usage

To start using Initializr, simply visit the Initializr web site, after which you will be presented with three options of starting points for this template (see Figure 7-4).

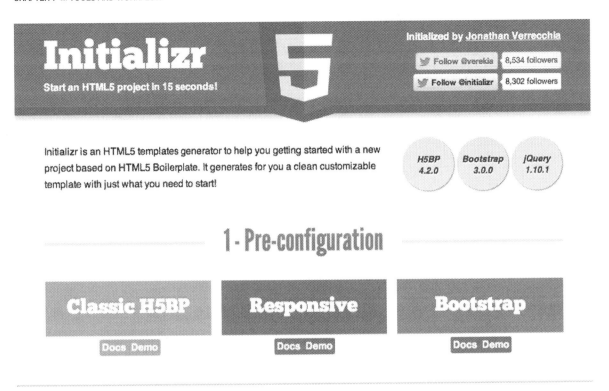

Figure 7-4. *Initializr web site allows you to choose what type of site you want*

Upon selecting an option, you are then presented with further options to configure the template. Once you are happy with your selection, you can simply click the Download it! button (see Figure 7-5).

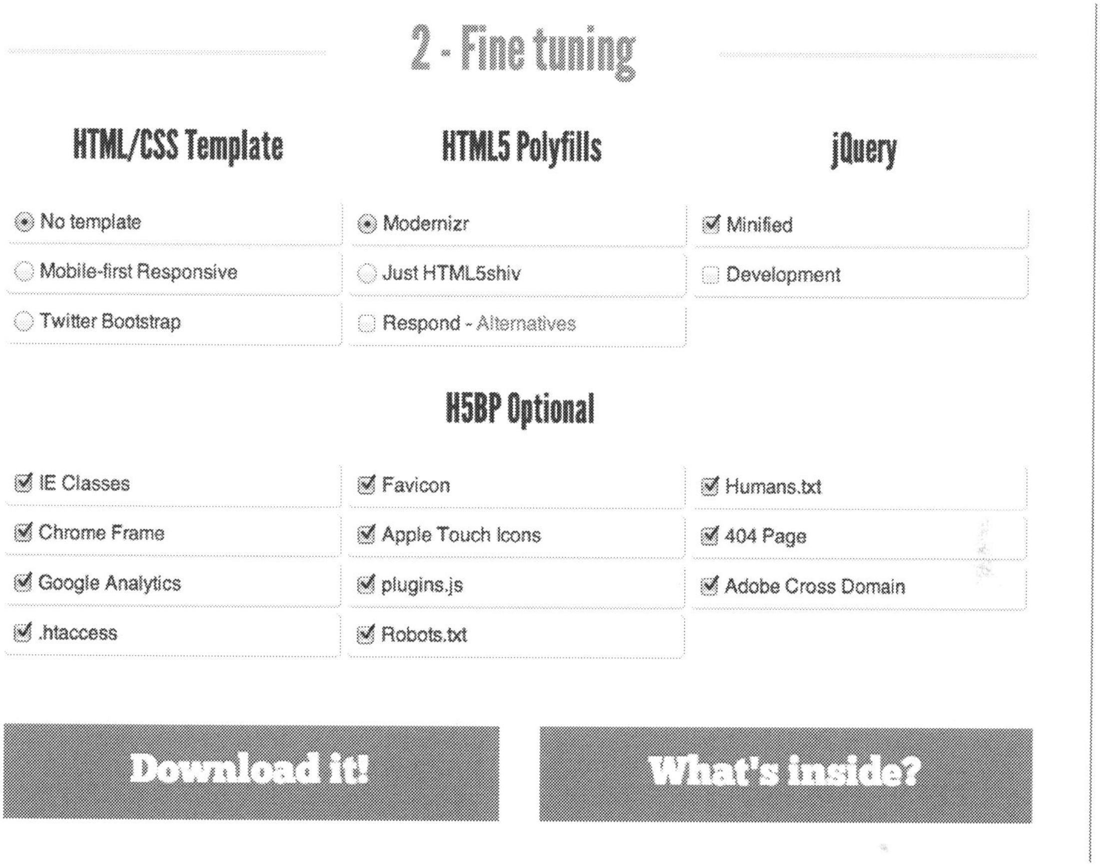

2 - Fine tuning

HTML/CSS Template

- ⦿ No template
- ○ Mobile-first Responsive
- ○ Twitter Bootstrap

HTML5 Polyfills

- ⦿ Modernizr
- ○ Just HTML5shiv
- ○ Respond - Alternatives

jQuery

- ☑ Minified
- ☐ Development

H5BP Optional

- ☑ IE Classes
- ☑ Chrome Frame
- ☑ Google Analytics
- ☑ .htaccess

- ☑ Favicon
- ☑ Apple Touch Icons
- ☑ plugins.js
- ☑ Robots.txt

- ☑ Humans.txt
- ☑ 404 Page
- ☑ Adobe Cross Domain

Download it!   **What's inside?**

Figure 7-5. Initializr provides you with the option to fine-tune your template

Once you have downloaded the scaffolded template, you can simply start coding right away.

As you can see, Initializr is really useful for quickly getting a template together for a project, however, it does have its limitations. The key limitation is that the CSS provided is just normal CSS, no set up for preprocessors is provided, so you have to do this yourself. If you're not looking to use a CSS preprocessor on your project, then you should be okay, but it is important to be aware of this.

Summary of Scaffolding Tools

I have discussed three different tools for scaffolding your projects, two of which are command-line tools and one being a web-based tool.

To start with, Initializr is a fantastic tool for generating scaffolding really quickly, but what it lacks in the ability to create custom templates it makes up in ease of use. If you want a quick, easy-to-use template, you should definitely consider using Initializr; however, if you need a more specific template then you will need to look at Yeoman or Grunt.

If you are going to be mainly using your own templates rather than downloading preset-up templates, then grunt-init is likely going to be your only choice. However, if you instead want to be able to search through a lot of different templates, then Yeoman will offer you that extra flexibility.

Other Useful Tools

jshint

The tool jslint enables you to detect errors and potential problems from within your JavaScript code. It is relied upon by developers across the world at companies including Mozilla, Facebook, and Twitter to ensure the issues it detects are not in its codebase.

The type of problems that jshint is able to detect are syntax errors, leaking variables, and bugs related to implicit type conversion and it ensures that your code follows the defined coding conventions.

The key benefits of using jshint are:

1.   Shows you any simple errors or mistakes in your JavaScript code

2.   Enables you to enforce your team's coding conventions

3.   Fully configurable so you are not forced to follow someone else's standards

I previously discussed using jshint within Grunt, however, you can also easily use it as a standalone command-line tool to quickly check the quality of your code.

Installation

The tool jshint is available as a command-line tool installable by the Node package manager. To install jshint you simply run the command:

```
npm install jshint -g
```

Usage

Using jshint is really simple—you simply pass the path to the JavaScript file you want to lint to the `jshint` command:

```
jshint jsfile.js
```

Then jshint will look for any issues in your JavaScript file, and these will be output with both the line number and the location of the character causing the problem (see Figure 7-6).

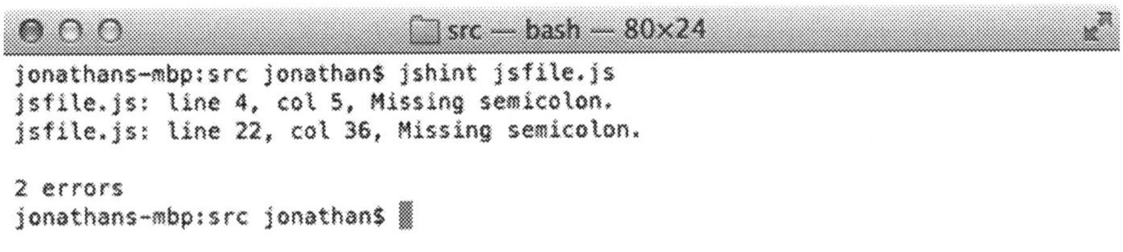

```
jonathans-mbp:src jonathan$ jshint jsfile.js
jsfile.js: line 4, col 5, Missing semicolon.
jsfile.js: line 22, col 36, Missing semicolon.

2 errors
jonathans-mbp:src jonathan$ █
```

Figure 7-6. Any issues found by jshint are output to the command line

serve

The server serve is a simple Node server that will serve the current folder you are using in terminal. This means if you need to quickly throw something up on a server on your local machine, and you can use serve and then navigate to localhost:3000 in your browser to see your site.

Installation

To install serve run the command:

```
npm install serve -g
```

Usage

The easiest way to get started with serve is to navigate to the directory you wish to serve to your browser and simply run the command:

```
serve
```

This will serve the current directory to localhost:3000, and in addition you can specify additional options:

1. `-F, --format <fmt>`: Specify the log format string
2. `-p, --port <port>`: Specify the port [3000]
3. `-H, --hidden`: Enable hidden file serving
4. `-S, --no-stylus`: Disable stylus rendering
5. `-J, --no-jade`: Disable Jade rendering
6. `--no-less`: Disable less CSS rendering
7. `-I, --no-icons`: Disable icons
8. `-L, --no-logs`: Disable request logging
9. `-D, --no-dirs`: Disable directory serving
10. `-f, --favicon <path>`: Serve the given favicon
11. `-C, --cors`: Allows cross origin access serving
12. `-compress`: Zip or deflate the response

These options are really straightforward to use. An example of how to change the port would use the command:

```
serve --port 2000
```

ios-sim

One of the main complaints about the Apple iOS Simulator is how much effort it takes to open it. First, you have to open Xcode, then go to the menu bar and select the Simulator from the developer tools. Luckily someone has developed a small tool that allows us to quickly, and easily, open the iOS Simulator from the command line, and that tool is called ios-sim.

Installation

The ios-sim is installed using *npm*, to install it you would run:

```
npm install ios-sim -g
```

Usage

To use the ios-sim command-line tool to start iOS Simulator, you can simply run:

```
ios-sim start
```

You could, however, select which device you want to use by passing the `--family` argument:

```
ios-sim start --family ipad
```

If instead you wanted to load a retina iPhone, you could append `--retina` to the command:

```
ios-sim start --retina
```

Mixture

Mixture (`http://mixture.io/`) is a tool that brings together scaffolding, preprocessors, testing, templating, building, and deploying into one interface.

When you first open Mixture, you are presented with a window where you can select the boilerplate you want to use to scaffold a project (see Figure 7-7).

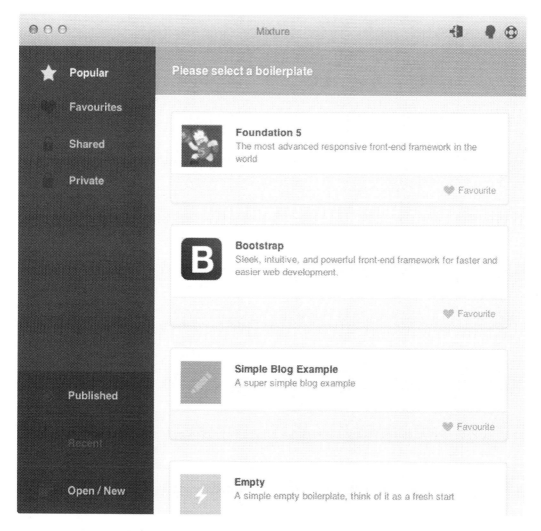

Figure 7-7. *Mixture allows you to select from a variety of popular templates*

You can select a boilerplate by clicking the one you want and you will then be asked for a directory for the project. Upon selecting the directory, Mixture will download the required files for your boilerplate from GitHub.

Once set up, you are ready to go, you can now click View Locally (see Figure 7-8) to see your project directly in your browser.

Figure 7-8. A project shown in Mixture

Mixture will watch your files and if you make any changes, it will process the compilation of the CSS from the CSS preprocessor and automatically reload the page for you. This means that you can use your text editor side by side and quickly see the changes you are making as you make them.

Mixture is a really powerful tool, and while it lacks some of the flexibility of using Yeoman, Grunt, and Bower, it can be a lot simpler to use as within a few clicks you can have a project configured and ready to work on. When your project is finished, you can then easily deploy it to a live server.

Workflow

So far I have discussed some fantastic tools, however, in themselves they are only part of the solution when you are building a web site. It is when you start integrating them into a workflow that they can become really powerful and help you build your web sites more efficiently.

When you start to look at development workflow, you can separate it out into five separate distinct steps, which is illustrated in Figure 7-9.

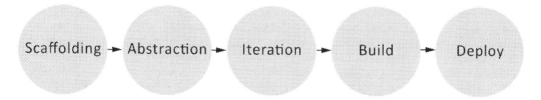

Figure 7-9. *The five steps of the development workflow*

A look at each of these steps in greater detail will help you understand exactly what each involves.

Scaffolding

When you first start a new project, you will usually take time to set up the project directories and base files and download the standard libraries like jQuery and respond.js. This process is called *scaffolding* and is normally the first step in the development process.

Earlier in the chapter I discussed three tools that could be used to scaffold a project: Initializr, Yeoman, and grunt-init. These tools essentially allow you to complete this initial step of your build faster by automating it so you simply have to tell them what you need.

Abstractions

When developing, an *abstraction* is a way in which you write code that will ultimately be compiled down to another form. In this chapter I discussed CSS preprocessors, which are abstractions of the CSS you would have written previously. However, CSS preprocessors are not the only abstraction tools you might be using on your project. There are abstraction tools for JavaScript including CoffeeScript, Dart, and Typekit, and there are also abstraction tools available for HTML including HAML, Markdown, and Emmet.

What all these abstractions aim to do is make your development more efficient. They do this in multiple ways, including adding functionality and sometimes even simplifying the original form. The reason this is part of the workflow is because you are developing in the abstraction rather than the original form.

Iteration

As you build a site, you iterate by regularly switching between your text editor and your browser, checking the changes you have made. This typically involves switching to the browser, refreshing, checking the changes, going back to the text editor, making changes, and then repeating. In addition, if you are using some kind of abstraction, you need to build the abstraction so that it can be displayed in the browser.

This is where iteration tools set out to make our lives easier; they are tools that allow us to automate the building of abstractions, automatically refresh our browser when we have made changes, and much, much more.

In this chapter I covered several different iteration tools, the first being the `compass watch` command, which will rebuild the CSS whenever the Sass files are changed. This is really important as you don't want to have to manually rebuild in between every page refresh of your browser. This is, however, a single-purpose iteration tool, and often you might be using multiple abstractions or want to automate more while you are iterating through your project. The problem with this is that you don't want to have to run multiple single purpose tools because not only can this be hard to manage, but there could also be potential conflicts of tools trying to use the same files simultaneously.

Another tool I discussed earlier is the task runner Grunt, and as you learned, it is great for running multiple tasks, so using it as an iteration tool makes sense because with each iteration you can use it to run a list of tasks. Grunt in itself doesn't watch files, however, you are able to add this functionality using the grunt-contib-watch plug-in, which you can use and configure in a similar way you would for the Grunt plug-ins. What this means, though, is that you can tell Grunt to watch a directory, and when you make changes to the files you can have it automatically run a series of tasks that you have defined. This means you can compile multiple abstractions within a single tool, and in addition there are plug-ins that allow you to run tasks like reloading the browser and running unit tests to check you haven't broken anything.

Other than Grunt, I also discussed Mixture, which is a GUI tool that allow you to set up an iterative workflow for your site. Mixture allows you to compile a list of abstractions, and it can minify your CSS/JS so both will reload the browser for you when you have made a file change. The tool's weakness is that you cannot add any custom tasks, so if you find there is a feature you want that this application does not support, you are unable to add it.

The iteration stage of the build is where you spend a lot of your time, so getting the tooling right here is really important. There are many tools out there that will help you improve how you can handle your iterations, and investing time in setting this up correctly can save you more time later on. One thing to remember is that your iteration workflow can evolve as you see fit, so if you find parts are not really working well for your project, you can adapt it to better suit your needs.

Build

After you have built your site, you will want to be able to build your code ready for a live deployment. This might include running unit tests, building your abstractions, minifying your CSS and JS, and compressing your images.

It can be time consuming to perform these build tasks manually, so this is where it is important to have build tools set up. As I explained earlier, you can use Grunt to define tasks that in themselves perform multiple tasks, meaning that you can define a build task for Grunt that will run a series of tasks you have defined. When I discussed using Grunt to compile Sass, I mentioned how you can define targets for your tasks and different options for each. When working on writing a build task you should look at using these targets within your tasks to allow you to tell tasks like Compass that that you are deploying to production.

Aside from using Grunt to build your site, you can also use Mixture. However, similar to the limitations of how you can use this in the iteration stage, you are unable to easily add extra functionality to the build process on top of what they already support, meaning you are limited to the build functionality that Mixture supports.

Having looked at how you can optimize your build workflow, it is easy to see how simple it is to automate the build process. As it is likely you will use this build process time and time again, it is important to get it right. Therefore, ensure that you are able to spend adequate time on this, and similar to your iteration workflow, don't be afraid to make changes to your process and continue to evolve it to suit your needs going forward.

Deploy

The final step with site development is to deploy it to the production environment; historically, this could be a very manual process especially on servers that you could only access through FTP.

How you deploy is likely to be very specific to your server set up, so rather than changing how you work to suit a tool, your tool needs to allow you to customize it to your set up. This is why a task runner like Grunt can be a great addition to your deploy workflow, as you can define your own deploy task that will carry out the steps required by your specific set up to deploy a site. The Grunt deploy task can be built from pluggable tasks, which means that it is very easy to build a workflow that works for you.

Another tool that is also able to automate the deployment process is Mixture. Mixture is able to deploy sites to both FTP servers and, in the case of open source sites, it is able to deploy to GitHub pages. This means that once configured you are able to quickly deploy the built site with the click of a button. The main problem is that Mixture is limited to only deploying to Mixture.io, FTP servers, and GitHub pages, so if your deployment process needs to involve anything else, you are out of luck.

Workflow Summary

Having looked at the different steps involved in a developer workflow, you should take a look at how each of the tools discussed in this chapter fits within these steps (see Figure 7-10).

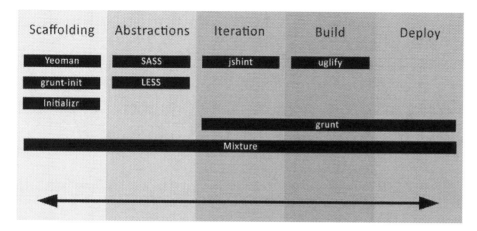

Figure 7-10. *How tools fit into the different parts of your workflow*

It is important to note that some tools encompass a workflow within themselves, an example being Mixture. As you can see, Mixture will take you straight from scaffolding to deployment. What this means is that if you choose, you can use a single tool (aside from your code editor) throughout your project workflow. The limitation of this is that you do not have as much flexibility to work the way you want to work.

Alternatively, tools like Grunt can be used to help you manage a significant part of your workflow; it can encompass other tools as tasks, offering you a common interface to use while you are iterating through code, building, and finally deploying. Using Grunt in this way does take time to set up correctly, so you need to be able to invest this time to be able to get the most out of using Grunt. Some of the tools are simply single-purpose tools, and they all serve a specific purpose, but for most of these there is a Grunt plug-in that wraps the functionality and makes it available as a Grunt task. This makes them much easier to use and allows you to integrate them better with your workflow.

In general though, you need to ensure that your workflow is what works best for you. This chapter has tried to present various tools that you can use to improve your workflow, but just how helpful they will be depends on how you work. I recommend that you look at each of the tools and give them a try—some you might love, some you might hate, but the most important thing is being aware of tools that might benefit you.

Summary

The tools that we use can make a huge difference to our development workflow in that they can enable us to work in a more productive way, allowing us to deliver a better site when it is finished.

Early in this chapter I explained how to use the command line. Understanding how to use the command line is really important, so I explained some of the basic commands to get you started. With an understanding of the command line, I then explored how to use version control to mange the source code of your web sites. Although this is particularly important when working within a team, it can also be useful when working on a personal project as it allows you to see what changes you have made over time, and if a bug has been introduced, it would allow you to see what changes were made that introduced it.

When styling your site, there are also tools you can use to make your life easier. I explained the CSS preprocessors that allow you to write styles using an abstraction of CSS and then compile the abstraction into CSS, allowing you to write styles faster and in a more flexible way.

Managing, installing, and upgrading dependencies into your site can be a tedious process, although having discussed the use of Bower, you can see there are easier ways to achieve these goals. I also explored the benefits and disadvantages of popular task runners, so you should now be aware of how to utilize them when it comes to typically laborious tasks.

Ultimately, your workflow is really important, and it can be a very individual thing, so it's important that you choose what is right for you. Don't be afraid to evolve your workflow over time, however, as new tools are always being developed and your needs may change over time.

In the next chapter we will look at how we can optimize the user experience of our responsive site through managing the user journey.

CHAPTER 8

Making the User Journey Responsive

The user's journey is a series of steps that are taken through a web site, and as such it is a large contributing factor to the experience of using it. The user's journey can vary from site to site dependent on who the target audience is, what they need to get from the site, and how they will be using the site.

There are two major factors that contribute to the user journey of a website: the needs of the business and the needs of the user. When it comes to the business needs, this is where the aims of the site to the business are determined; these might be to drive sales, increase engagement, or develop brand awareness. When it comes to the users' needs, this is what users are trying to achieve when they visit the site, including both their goals and their motivations.

With this in mind, let's look at an example user's journey featuring a health club web site. In this case, the user's need is to find information about the health club so they can determine if they are interested in signing up. For the business, their need is to sell health club memberships. The user journey should therefore try to meet both of these needs through looking at how they can be aligned. This is achieved by having a clear user's journey that first provides the user with the information they need about the health club but ultimately encourages them to sign up by driving them to the sign up page.

Although the example here isn't very complex, not all user's journeys are this simple or would work well across all devices. In the case where the journey doesn't make sense on one or more of the devices that you are supporting, you should look at how you can adapt the journey to provide the users a better experience.

This chapter will teach you how to adapt the journey the user takes through your site in a way that optimizes their user experience, regardless of the device they are using. To achieve this, I'll cover:

1. Adapting your content

2. Adapting the user's journey

3. User testing your responsive site

4. Using web analytics tools

Adapting Your Content

If you are building a web site, the HTML, CSS, and JavaScript that make up the site allow you to present the content to the user.

If you were to open an HTML page alone in your browser without any CSS or JavaScript applied, you would simply see the site with the browser's default styling applied, and, if structured correctly, it should still have a meaningful flow.

If you were to think of the HTML as the skeleton of the site, the CSS would be the flesh of the site, the padding and the detailing that makes the site more complete. By adding the CSS, you have begun to add the visuals that help make the content easier to read and provide structure. In keeping with this analogy, the JavaScript would therefore be like the nervous system of the site, coordinating the functionality that has been added to the site.

As this analogy highlights, the content is at the heart of the site, and as such, when building a responsive site, you want to ensure it is presented in the best possible way. The way in which you do this is by adapting the content dependent on the device it will be viewed upon.

When choosing to adapt the content of your responsive site, there are a variety of different things you will need to consider. We will now look at the key considerations we will need to make when adapting our content.

The Size of the Viewport

With the devices used to view the site coming in such a wide variety of different shapes and sizes, it can have a major impact on how you choose to adapt your content, as you will need to consider the user's experience across a wide range of different viewport sizes.

When responsive design first started to become popular, two methods for adapting content based on the size of the viewport became popular, the first being hiding content that is deemed less important and the second being to stack the content on top of each other.

Let's start by looking at the first method, and you will quickly see the problems that can arise from using it. In his book *Responsive Web Design*, Ethan Marcotte talks about how fragmenting content across different experiences is not sustainable. Although he is specifically talking about having separate mobile and desktop sites, when you are taking the approach of simply hiding content to make a responsive site sit well on mobile, you are fragmenting the content that the user sees. The key difference here is that the users don't have the option to simply switch to the desktop site to see the full content, making this content completely inaccessible on the devices they are using.

Although simply hiding some of the content might lead to the page being a more pleasant length, the problem is that, by completely hiding it from the user, you run the risk that it might actually be the content that the user was looking for and potentially brought them to the page when searching on Google. What really needs consideration is whether the content is unimportant enough to be shown on mobile, and whether it is of any real benefit to the users on larger viewports. If it offers no real benefit to the user, it would be better to remove it completely from the site rather than just hiding it on mobile.

The second method is to stack the content that would otherwise be side by side on larger devices. The problem with this is that if the web site in question has a large amount of content, when stacked, this could potentially lead to a very long page, and this in turn can lead to the content the user is looking for being fairly far down the page.

Although both methods were very popular, especially on sites built from a desktop first perspective, as I have covered earlier, they both have disadvantages. To overcome the disadvantages of these methods, you can instead choose to combine the methods. The solution here would be to adapt the content on the responsive design so that content you feel is less important is collapsible, meaning that the user has the option to expand the section if they are interested in reading it without having to resort to having a really long page.

Certain types of content lend themselves to being adapted better than others, an example would be a series of FAQs. You could display these differently across different viewport sizes without completely hiding the content from the user. On smaller devices, you could look at collapsing the FAQs so only the questions are visible, until clicking the question to expand with the answer. This benefits the user, as they can quickly find the question for which they need an answer. On larger devices, you could have this open by default, as space and length are less of an issue.

Features that the Device Supports

Some content is specific to a device that supports a given feature. You'll need to consider the devices you are targeting and whether or not they have features you can incorporate into your web site, but it is also important to remember that other devices in the same state size may not have these capabilities. When it comes to targeting features that only some of the devices using a site support, you need to ensure that wherever possible, those who use devices that do not support a feature do not get a worse experience.

An example of content that is specific to a feature of a device would be "Find my nearest store," where you would be using the geolocation API to determine the location of the user and then finding the stores closest to them. In this situation, not all devices will support the geolocation API, so by default you could show an input field that the user would then use to enter their location. In the case of devices that support the geolocation API, you could then progressively enhance the site by detecting the API (using the feature detection techniques discussed in Chapter 9) and then adding the functionality required to detect the user's location using the API.

User Input Methods

The way in which a user interacts with web content can have a significant effect on the way you should display it. There are a wide range of input methods you need to think about when considering how to adapt your content, some of the most common being keyboard, mouse, and touch screen.

Unlike when targeting content based on features, here you are unable to reliably detect the input method the user is using. The best you can do is display the content in a way that works well across the different input methods you are supporting. Where you can offer a better experience, however, is through adding different interactions based on the input method the user has used to interact with the page.

An example of where you might use different interactions dependent on the input method used would be for a carousel. In the case of the user using a keyboard to navigate through the carousel panels, they would be able to traverse the content using the left and right keys. When using a mouse, they could instead use buttons to navigate forward and backward. For touch input, you might instead choose to allow the users to use a swipe gesture between the different panels.

A second example would be a user navigating with a touch device having the ability to swipe between panels of content, and similarly a user navigating with a mouse who could see different content when hovering over an element. These are just two examples of user interactions that make sense for certain input methods. Because these input methods directly control how the content is shown, you need to consider how this can be adapted across different responsive states.

Having looked at these two examples, you have seen that different interaction methods can provide a very different experience to the users and as such you need to understand the different ways to utilize them to provide the best experience you can.

Although you are unable to reliably detect which input method the users are using, you can instead add support for different kinds of events such as touch events and keyboard events (such as keydown and keyup).

It is important to remember when building a web site that there is the potential that new input methods will be developed, and in the event that a new input method becomes popular, you might need to adapt your site to support it.

The Content Itself

When building a responsive site, your content will fall into one of two situations: you will be starting with existing content that will need adaptation in order to work responsively, or you will be fortunate enough to be able to start from scratch with your content.

Adapting Existing Content

When starting a new responsive build or adapting an existing site to be responsive, it is likely you might already have existing content to use, possibly from an older version of the site. It is therefore important that you consider this existing content when thinking about adapting it.

One of the first things you need to consider when working with existing content is what value it adds to the users. If you feel that there are parts of the content that don't really help your user, you could potentially discuss this with your stakeholders and with their permission strip it out.

Building Content for a Responsive Site

If you are in the situation where you are building new content for a responsive site, you are at an advantage as you can build your content specifically for your smaller devices first and then, instead of adapting it to work on smaller devices, adapt the content to work better on larger viewports. This means rather than trying to take away from the content, you would instead look at what value you can add to the larger experience by adapting the content to suit it.

When adapting a site's content for these larger devices, however, you shouldn't simply start by trying to fit extra content into the page. You should first start by spacing out the content you were using on your smaller devices and then look at how you can use increased spacing and imagery to enhance the experience.

Prioritizing Content

Having decided on whether to adapt existing content or build new content for the responsive site, it is important to consider how to prioritize the content. You also need to consider how to ensure that the most relevant content for each device is shown in a visible way. Let's take, for example, a restaurant. When users are using a desktop computer, they are likely wanting to find out information about the restaurant, perhaps browse menus, see what kind of atmosphere the restaurant has, and view information about the area the restaurant is in, like local theaters and other things to do. On a mobile device, the aims of users might be quite different; they may only want the opening times of the restaurant or to make a reservation and find directions from their current location to the restaurant. These differences in goals of the users can have a deep impact on how you would adapt the content of your site.

To prioritize the content in this way, you can use the order property of the CSS Flexbox specification. To start, let's put together some HTML with a simple wrapper div containing three blocks that will show in a different order at different viewport sizes. As there is no polyfill available for flexbox, in order to correctly order the flex items on browsers that do not support flex box, we should order the child elements in the order we want them to be shown in unsupported browsers. The code for this would be:

```
<div class="wrapper">
    <div class="block block1">
        <p>This is the first block</p>
    </div>
    <div class="block block2">
        <p>This is the second block</p>
    </div>
    <div class="block block3">
        <p>This is the third block</p>
    </div>
</div>
```

Having put together the HTML, the next step is to tell the browser to display the wrapper as a flex container, and you would do this by setting the display property to have a value of flex. This enables the flex context for the child elements of our flex container, these child elements are known as flex items.

Upon setting up our flex container we can also specify the direction of the elements it contains. This can be achieved by setting a value for the flex-direction property. The default value for the flex-direction property is row, which shows the flex items side by side, ordered left to right. The alternative values we can use are: column, which stacks the flex items on top of one another, row-reverse which will reverse the order of items and column-reverse which will stack the items on top of one another in reverse order.

For this example, let's order the elements stacked on top of one another. To achieve this we will need to apply the flex styles to our wrapper, the first step is to set the display property to have a value of flex, then set the property flex-direction to have a value of column. The CSS we have applied to our wrapper is shown below:

```
.wrapper {
    display: flex;
    flex-direction: column;
}
```

Having told the browser that the child elements of the wrapper are flex items, you can now set the order in which they are shown. Earlier we chose the order of the flex items so that by default the items are shown in the way we want our content to be ordered in browsers that do not support flexbox. While this means that in this case our HTML is not mobile-first, it does mean that for browsers that support flexbox we are progressively enhancing the site. This means if we want to have a different order on our smaller devices we will need to define the order we want the items to appear. We do this by setting a value to the order property with the value of the position it should appear in.

```
.block1 {
    order: 2;
}

.block2 {
    order: 1;
}

.block3 {
    order: 3;
}
```

For larger devices, you might want to change the order of the blocks again, so you can simply use a media query, changing the value for order for each of the blocks as shown in this section of code:

```
@media only screen and (min-width: 1200px){
    .block1 {
        order: 3;
    }

    .block2 {
        order: 2;
    }

    .block3 {
        order: 1;
    }
}
```

The flexibility that is offered by the new Flexbox specification can be really helpful when building a site, and although here I am discussing how you could use it to prioritize different content by setting the order based on the viewport size, the specification itself is a lot more broad, providing new, efficient ways in which you can lay out your sites.

There are currently a few limitations to using the Flexbox specification. First, it is not supported across all the web browsers you will likely have to support, with the earliest version of Internet Explorer to support Flexbox being Internet Explorer 10.

There are also two separate specifications, the old specification, which are in some of the first browsers to implement Flexbox, and the new specification implemented in the newer browsers. Internet Explorer 10, for example, uses the older specification, but Internet Explorer 11 uses the new specification. What this means is that when writing your code, you need to consider supporting both specifications to support the widest number of browsers.

Although it's not supported across the board, you don't need all browsers to support Flexbox to start taking advantage of it to prioritize your content. You can default to a common content order in your HTML and then use Flexbox to reorder the content at different viewport sizes where appropriate for browsers that support it.

Full details of up-to-date browser support can be found on the "Can I Use" site at `http://caniuse.com/flexbox`, where partial support is indicated, it is likely that the implementation is using the older specification.

Adapting the User's Journey

It is important that before you embark on building a site, you ensure that you have properly planned the journey that users can take though the site. As part of this, you need to consider how you might adapt the user's journey to work well across a variety of different devices with different viewport sizes, different input methods, and different feature support.

Before responsive design, it was easy to map out the different journeys a user could take through a site, often having a start point and an end point you wanted to get them to and having a limited number of ways in which they would get between them. Although there are situations where you could maintain this approach with responsive design, it often makes sense to build in additional user journeys based on the device the user is using.

Common Site Interactions

There are a wide variety of site interactions that make up the parts of a user's journey, and when building a responsive site, is important to examine each of them to determine if they will work well responsively. As you do this, you may need to consider any adaptations that are needed to improve the user's experience. Let's look at some examples of user interactions you might implement on your site and explore how you might want to adapt them to provide a better experience across the variety of devices your site supports.

Modal Windows

The first common site interaction is the modal window. A *modal window* is a method in which you can show new content in a container on top of the content on the page the user is currently viewing. Originally intended to show larger versions of images, its use has since expanded and is used across a large number of web sites for a number of different purposes. With this flexibility to show content on top of the page the user is currently viewing, it can allow you to show content related to the current page without navigating the user to a new page.

As mentioned, the original and still common use of a modal window is to show a larger version of an image thumbnail. On larger viewports, this can work really well, however, often on smaller devices the "zoomed-in" image actually appears really small in the lightbox. This is particularly true with images of different aspect ratios: when the device is portrait, a tall image might appear okay, but with a wide but short image, the image would appear small.

Another use of a modal window is to collect information about the user by allowing them to input data into a form. A reason this might be put into a modal window rather than another page is that you want to make it more convenient to the user. Such data collection could simply be a contact form or it could be the login form for the web site.

With both these examples, a modal window isn't really the right answer on smaller devices because it provides a subpar experience for the user. However, it still makes sense to use one on larger devices. This is a really good example of where you could easily provide a slightly different journey to users with smaller devices rather than larger devices, with the aim to provide the best experience for each individual device.

There are a couple of key reasons why modal windows offer a worse experience on smaller devices. The first is that the techniques used to position a modal window (the CSS property position set to the value fixed) do not work reliably across all mobile browsers. In fact Brad Frost[1] decided to look into how well fixed positioning actually works in mobile browsers. In his results, he found that the support was inconsistent across browsers; even mobile browsers that appear to support position fixed can sometimes be quirky in their implementation.

---

[1]`http://bradfrostweb.com/blog/mobile/fixed-position/.`

The second reason is that on a smaller viewport, even if it is displayed correctly, the whole experience of having a modal window can be clunky or awkward for a mobile user. Depending on the length of content you are showing inside a modal, it could potentially extend beyond the height of the browser viewport. In this case, the user would need to scroll the content inside the modal window. Unfortunately, in some mobile browsers, scroll bars are only shown when you are scrolling content, so it might not be clear to the user that they can scroll the content. In addition to this, when the user wants to go back to the main content of the page, it might not be immediately obvious how to do this. On a larger viewport, the user has multiple ways in which they can exit a modal; usually they can be exited by clicking a close button, clicking outside the modal window, or pressing the Esc key on the keyboard. On a smaller viewport, there isn't any space around the modal window to allow the user to click or touch to exit the viewport, and on a touch device, the user might not have a keyboard. Although you can implement a close button in a similar way you would with other viewport sizes, being a full-screen modal window may give the users the perception they are on a new page. In this situation, they might use the browser navigation buttons instead, which could take them to the wrong page.

A solution to this would be that on smaller viewports the user would open the content on a new page but on larger viewports it would continue to be shown in a modal window. The benefit here being that the user on a smaller device would be able to view the content like any other page, along with having access to things like the navigation and other information that a modal window would have hidden.

To illustrate how this might work, let's look at the example of an image gallery. On larger viewports when the user taps on a gallery image, it will show the larger image in a lightbox. This journey does not take the user away from the gallery, and they can simply close the lightbox to continue looking at the galleries images. I have illustrated this in Figure 8-1.

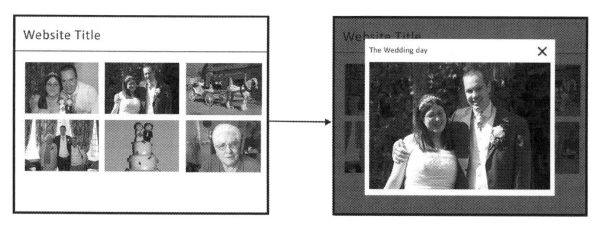

Figure 8-1. *The journey the user takes on larger viewports*

If you look at how this would work on smaller viewports, you can then adapt the journey the user takes through the site so that upon tapping an image it opens a new page to show the larger image. In addition, on the new page, you need to ensure that you include a link back to the original gallery. The steps the user would take through the site are illustrated in Figure 8-2.

Figure 8-2. *The journey the user takes on smaller devices*

The way you achieve this is by setting an anchor link around the image to link to the new page, and in the case of the larger viewports, you simply use JavaScript to load the image in a modal window instead. I will explain how this can be achieved in Chapter 9.

Product Search

Typically, if your site is dedicated to one product, it would be easy for your users to quickly find information about your product; however, for larger retail sites that sell a variety of different products, it is incredibly important that the users can quickly and easily find the product and information about it they are looking for.

A typical journey for a user searching for a product on a large retail site would be to enter the product name in the search box and then be taken to a search results page, as shown in Figure 8-3.

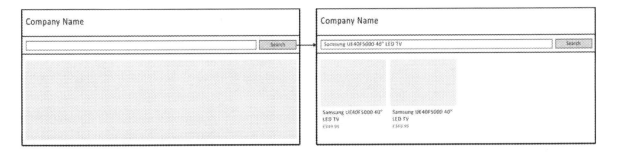

Figure 8-3. *Path to the results page after entering a search term*

This journey works well on a responsive site, however, it doesn't take into account the situation of the users, in this case the combination of both the current location of the user combined with the purpose of the actual search.

A traditional situation you would expect users to be in would be at home on their desktop computer searching for products, comparing features and the price. This traditional situation is how most users would have used the site in the past. With the popularity of smartphones, however, new situations have arisen where someone might be out shopping and see a product they are interested in and want to ensure they are getting the best price. To do this, the user pulls out their phone and searches for the product online, perhaps by visiting your site, and searching for the product.

This situational behavior was not something that would have been take into account previously, but with a responsive site, developers now need to start assuming that a site could be used anywhere, and therefore this needs to be considered when designing web sites. Part of the problem is that the situational behavior of the visitors is not easy to detect. The developer will not know whether the user will be in a store or whether they are at home, and while you could try to determine their location using the geolocation API, this is impractical for a few reasons. You would have to know the location of all the different stores your customers might be in and you would also need to ask the user for their permission to use their current location.

It makes sense then that rather than try to detect the user's situation, you should instead take an educated guess about the expected user situation. To do this, you should examine the typical situation where a user would choose to use a particular device, and then consider what functionality they would benefit most from in that particular situation. Additionally, if you already have a version of the site online and you have access to analytics data, you could look at what your users are already using your site for to inform how you would optimize your site for a situation.

If you again look at the example of product search, you might expect that users are likely to use the site to look up prices when they are in a store. Naturally, you would want to ensure they can do this in as few steps as possible. The first step in doing this would be to prioritize the content used for product discovery; in the case of a site that sells a variety of products, this would be by ensuring that when the page loads, the product search box is immediately visible to the user. If your site instead focuses on selling a few of your own products, you should aim to show some basic information, including the price, so the user doesn't even have to leave the page they land on to find the information they want.

On larger viewports, although search is still a big feature of the site, users are much more likely to simply be browsing the site, not entirely sure what they are looking for (perhaps looking for a gift for a friend but unsure of what to buy). Therefore, you will want to ensure that product discovery is a big part of the site by showing things like categories and suggestions based on previous purchases.

Aside from how you prioritize content, you should also consider how you can use progressive enhancement to take advantage of new features that devices offer. An example for a product search would be to enable the user to take the photo of either a product or a barcode to search for a product. The benefit to the user would be that rather than type a complicated product name like "Samsung UE40F5000 40" LED TV," they would instead simply snap a photo.

To achieve this, you would determine if the device supported the camera API, and then for those devices with support, provide the user with an additional button they can activate to load the camera. If only one product was found, the web site could then take the user directly to the product, otherwise they would just be taken to a search results page. The user journey for this example is shown in Figure 8-4.

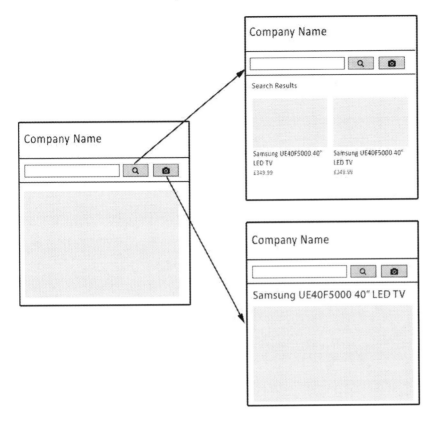

Figure 8-4. *User journey for devices that support the camera API*

Tabbed Containers

One way to organize content on a web site is to separate it into containers toggled with tabs. These enable you to divide your content into meaningful sections, allowing the users of the site to directly find the content they are looking for by displaying a clear title for the content on the tab. They work fantastic on larger displays, however, on smaller devices, the tabs can become cramped, often without enough room to properly show the titles. In this situation, it makes sense to adapt the functionality so it is more suitable for smaller viewports.

One way you could change the functionality on smaller viewports would be to adapt it so that on smaller viewports the tab panels show like an accordion. By doing this, the titles would have more room to be visible and the user could still click through the different containers of content.

Menu Drop-Downs

It is common for web sites to include drop-downs as part of the main navigation, and usually these are activated by the user hovering the mouse cursor over the drop-down. Unfortunately, this functionality doesn't translate well to mobile devices where users are using a touch screen instead of a mouse. Some mobile browsers have attempted to fix this by triggering CSS hovers when the user taps on the item, however, usually it is then difficult for the user to disable what they have hovered. Therefore, you need to look at how to adapt these drop-downs to work better across devices. One suggestion, used by Twitter Bootstrap drop-downs, is to lose the hover functionality all together and simply allow the user to click or tap to toggle the drop-down being open or closed.

Parallax

Parallax is a technique that scrolls the elements of the page at different speeds as the user scrolls up and down. This technique allows you to show animations as the user scrolls down in order to add more depth to the page.

Where the technique excels is on larger viewports where there is space for over-the-top animations. It can be a really good technique for telling a story, whether about a product, a service, or a company. The problems begin when you start looking at how this would work on smaller viewports, where there is less space to tell the story.

A problem developers face when trying to get parallax to work on small devices is that typically parallax uses fixed positioning to position elements as the user scrolls. Unfortunately, fixed positioning cannot be relied on for smaller devices, as many mobile browsers have an incomplete or buggy implementation.

Another problem is related to the way in which the browser fires the onscroll event. On desktop browsers, it is fired continuously as the user scrolls, but on smaller devices the onscroll event is not fired until the scrolling action stops. This means that you can't use the onscroll event for animating elements as the user scrolls because the elements wouldn't be updated until after the user has stopped scrolling.

By building a site mobile first, you can consider this from the start, building a linear page that the user can scroll up and down with ease, and then for larger viewports, you can progressively enhance the page. By progressively adding parallax effects, it enables you to build a responsive parallax site.

Social

With the increased popularity of social networks, there has been a trend toward including buttons that enable users to share content with their friends and followers at a click or touch of a button. There are a large number of these different buttons for sharing content available. Notable ones include the Facebook "Like" button, the Twitter "Tweet" button, the Google+ "Plus one button," and the Pinterest "Pin" button.

Sharing your content is just a small part of the possible user journeys through your site, however, it is worth considering that how your user interacts with them is likely to be different depending on the devices they are using. In fact, a recent post on Marketing Land[2] talks about how almost twice as many social shares come from mobile devices. The implication of this is that developers need to ensure that buttons are in a clear location and of a suitable size (Apple's guidelines suggest that a button on a mobile device has a minimum size of 40×40px). This can be difficult on a small device due to the limited space available, especially with the number of different share buttons, so it is important you select the social networks that are most relevant to your users and the subject of your site.

Aside from knowing that two-thirds of the social network shares could come from mobile devices, it is important to look at how effective the social share buttons are in general, because two-thirds of none is still none. Recently, the United Kingdom government web site ran a trial of including social sharing links within their pages.[3] They found that after ten weeks, only 0.2 percent of page views resulted in the user sharing the page on their social network. If you then look at the breakdown of the data from the trial, there was a noticeable link between the type of content and how often it was shared, with the most popular content being shared on world location pages (0.58 percent) and the least popular being information on consultations (0.06 percent).

Summary of Adapting the User's Journey

Having looked at examples of some common user interactions, you should now have an understanding of the kind of user interactions that might not work well across all viewport sizes. With this in mind, you should now be able to adapt these interactions where needed to work better on accommodating different viewport sizes.

---

[2] http://marketingland.com/when-it-comes-to-social-media-sharing-mobile-rules-52750.
[3] https://insidegovuk.blog.gov.uk/2014/02/20/gov-uk-social-sharing-buttons-the-first-10-weeks/.

User Testing Your Responsive Site

Often, developers have to make a lot of informed assumptions about our users, however, it isn't possible to always be right, and it's through learning about our users that we can continuously improve our web sites. The best way to learn about web users is through user testing, where you have real users use your site to see how they interact with it.

Waiting until the end of the development process of your site to start thinking about or even doing user testing is too late; it is important that from an early stage you know what kind of testing you are able to use with your site. You might have heard the term "minimum viable product"; this is essentially your bare-bones site, without the frills, but it is functional and has the user journey in place. Essentially the site should be at the stage where if you went live with it, it would still work for the users. It is when you have this minimum viable product that you are able to start getting users to test the site so you can start getting some feedback on how all the different parts of your user's journey work.

There are several important things you can learn from user testing:

1. The different journeys the user takes through the site, so you can then compare this against how you originally thought the user would go through the site and learn from it.

2. Where the user faces difficulties using the site.

3. What the user likes about the site, which can guide how you develop the site going forward as you continue to use similar ways of displaying content.

You might have used user testing on previous sites, however, it can become much more difficult when you start to use user testing with a responsive site because of the way it is built to work across a large variety of different viewports. What this means is that in reality, testing a responsive site is more like testing several sites, each directed at a different device, rather than simply testing a single site. This is especially true where you have offered different user's journeys to different users.

Carrying Out User Testing

There are many different ways to carry out user testing, however, all have different advantages and disadvantages that come with them, so it is important you weigh the pros and cons of each before you make your decision.

Focus Groups

A *focus group* is where you gather a group of individuals, preferably no more than ten, who are part of your target market and have them test the site. After testing the site, you then bring them together as a group with a moderator and have them discuss their thoughts about the site. The aim of the focus group is to gather a variety of different people's thoughts on the way in which a web site works.

There are many benefits of running focus groups, the key benefit being that they enable you to get a picture of what users think about your site. The people chosen for the focus group are from the target market, so this will give you an idea about the users you are targeting, including what they find easy and what they find difficult.

In addition, during a focus group, with the direction of the moderator, the users can discuss their thoughts about the site. This allows the users to build on one another's answers, explaining where they both agree and disagree with others in the group. With this format, it enables you to balance any extreme views of individual users about the site that might otherwise skew the results of the focus group. As part of the focus group, it is the moderator's responsibility to prevent unwanted bias, and as part of this they would need to be responsible for ensuring that one or more members of the focus group do not lead the responses. Instead, you want to ensure that the responses you get are balanced across the group.

When it comes to running focus groups with a responsive site, it is important that your users are all discussing the same thing. This is why for each of your site breakpoints you would need to run an individual focus group. In this way, you might have a focus group for your mobile experience, a focus group for your tablet experience, and focus group running on your desktop experience. In addition to this, you might want your focus group to concentrate on a particular user journey that is critical to your site, and if that is the case, you should ask the members of your focus group to direct their attention there.

There are a number of disadvantages associated with using focus groups to test a site, the primary being the cost associated with running a focus group. Not only do you need to reimburse the focus group members for their time, you also need to employ an independent moderator for the duration of your focus groups to conduct the sessions. You also need to consider that a focus group is not in a natural setting; by this I mean that the users are typically being observed while using the site, potentially making them feel uneasy and less likely to be forthright with their feelings about the site.

There is also the potential that in asking the focus group members question, the moderator could introduce bias by asking questions in a way that influences the answers. It is therefore incredibly important that questions are vetted before the session to ensure the wording does not skew the answers.

Usability Testing

Usability testing is a one-on-one session between a member of the target market and a facilitator. The role of the facilitator is to run the user through tasks you want them to perform and then analyses how the user performs on each of the tasks.

In a similar way to focus groups, you need to run usability testing across all the different responsive breakpoints you have set. Unfortunately, having each user test all the different states of the site might introduce unwanted bias, so you would need to run through each state with different users.

The key advantage to using usability testing is that with this one user, one moderator approach, the moderator watching the user using the site can pick up on difficulties the user is experiencing when using the site that might not have come up in a focus group environment. Similar to this, difficulties the user faces that might be embarrassing to bring up in the focus group might be more easily discussed with the moderator without others present to hear.

In addition to the moderator watching the user as they use the site, it is also worthwhile recording the sessions so you can later go back and review the difficulties the users faced in more detail. This ability to rewatch sessions means that issues that might have otherwise gone unnoticed can also be fixed.

Similar to running a focus group, there is a cost associated with running usability tests. For each usability testing session you run, you will need to reimburse both the user and facilitator for their time. With the added nature that usability testing is a one-on-one session, it can be more expensive than running focus groups simply because you have to pay for a facilitator for each of the users you run a session with.

Friends, Family, and Work Colleagues

If both focus groups and usability testing are not suitable options due to the cost involved, it is likely that you know friends, family, and even work colleagues who would be happy to give your site a run through and give you their thoughts.

The process you would take with testing with these users would be to sit them in front of a device and get them to use your site, potentially by giving them a simple task to achieve during the use of the site. During the testing, you should note how long they take to complete the given task, as this will help you to determine if the journey is too complicated.

In addition to taking notes, if you have access to a video camera, you could film the person testing the site, in particular ensuring the camera can see the screen. This means that you can play the video back later in case you missed anything when taking notes.

Friends and family can be valuable resources to use to test your site, however, it is important to consider whether they are the target audience of your site or even the product your site is trying to sell as you may end up getting false results with how the site would naturally function. You may also find that they are over- or undercritical because of their relationship with you. These problems could potentially skew the results gained by asking them for their help.

Work colleagues are likely to know your product and potentially be the target audience, but this could mean that they have an invested interest that clouds their judgment when testing the site.

These problems aside, friends, family, and work colleagues are the cheapest option when it comes to user testing, and although you may find that some results might need taking with a pinch of salt, you will also hopefully get some feedback you can use to improve the user experience of your site.

Web Analytics Tools

When it comes to building a responsive user journey, it is important to be able to measure how the journey affects users so you can look to improve this. After any improvement you make, you can measure whether it has had a positive or negative impact on the users' experience.

The main way to measure the user's journey is by tracking the effectiveness of a site. By this I mean by looking at the length of time the user is using the site, how likely they are to leave the site after looking at only one page, and the flow they take through the site. Measuring the effectiveness can be really important, for example, in the case of a business, where they will want to ensure that the site is fulfilling its purpose of converting the users of the site into customers. You also need to be able to measure whether changes that have made to the site to improve it are having a positive or negative impact on the site. The best way to do this is through the use of web analytics tools.

Web analytics tools are tools that can be installed on web sites that enable you to measure the web traffic with the aim to assess and improve the effectiveness of a site. They do this by tracking how users are using the site, with the kind of tracking depending on the individual analytics tool used.

There are a number of web analytics tools available, some of which are available completely free of charge and some that charge for their services. The two analytics solutions I will focus on here are Google Analytics and ClickTale, both of which offer a very different feature set and can be used simultaneously to help you learn more about your users.

Google Analytics

Google Analytics is a free analytics web site available from Google that allows you to track information about the users of your site. The information is completely anonymized, but it can give you a clear indication of the type of users who are visiting your site. It is likely you have used Google Analytics before on your site or some of your clients sites, however, what you might not have done is drilled down into the statistics to look at the types of devices visiting your site or used it to look at the journey your users are taking through your site.

One thing that is really important to developers is knowing which browsers and devices the visitors of our sites are using. Although global statistics like those provided by StatCounter (http://gs.statcounter.com/) present a good picture of what users in general are using, this can vary significantly from what you experience with your own site. The primary reason for this is that the target audience of your site can have a major impact on which browsers and devices they are using. For example, companies supporting government organizations may have a large number of users coming from one particular browser, because that is the browser chosen by the government to use. This is where an analytics tool like Google Analytics can add value for developers, because they are able to keep record of the technologies that the users are using.

When it comes to providing information about browsers, Google Analytics can offer a lot. To access the browser section of Google Analytics, you would click on the Audience menu item, then you should click Technology, and then Browser & OS. This will then present a table of all the browsers used to visit the site, sorted by the most popular. Included is information about the number of users visiting from that browser along with information about their behavior. If you look at the screenshot of the Google Analytics tool I have shown in Figure 8-6, you will notice there is also the additional option to filter this information further by adding a second dimension, or you can choose to click the name of the browser to find out more information about the specific versions of the browser being used to visit your site. The view used to see the breakdown of the browsers and operating systems that were used to view my site can be seen in Figure 8-5.

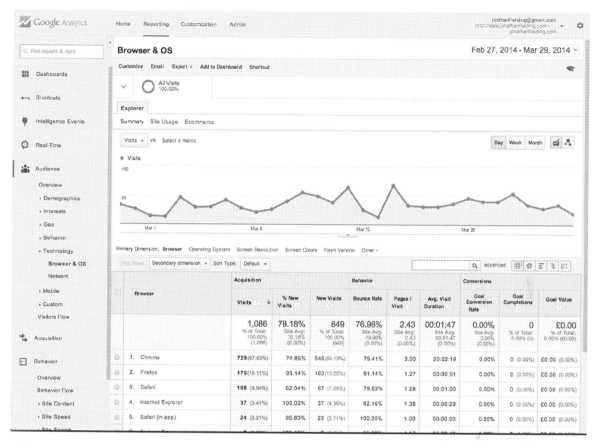

Figure 8-5. *Breakdown of different browsers being used to access my site in Google Analytics*

Being aware of which browsers are being used to visit your site is really important because you will want to know which browsers you need to support and to test your web site with. However, because you are developing a responsive site, it is also important to see which devices are being used to access a site because this will enable you to ensure that your site is tested on the devices used most often when visiting your site.

There are two parts to Google Analytics' device information; first, there is the overview page. To access the browser section of Google Analytics, you would click the Audience menu item, then click Mobile, and then Overview. In this section, you will find a breakdown of devices by device category, currently these are desktop, mobile, and tablet. This allows you to get a good understanding of the types of devices your users are utilizing. It is important to check these figures regularly, as with the current rate of adoption for new device types, these are likely to change on a frequent basis.

The second part of the device information part of Google Analytics allows you to determine which devices your users are using to access your site. To look at this information, it is located in the Audience section under Mobile within the Devices page. Within this page, you can easily see the different devices visiting your site, including statistics regarding the percentage of users coming from each device. The screenshot in Figure 8-6 shows you the device view, which by default shows the devices sorted by the number of visits per device, with the most common devices shown first. A little Easter egg that Google has included in this view is if you click the little camera icon next to the device name, you will be shown an image of the device. The device list view from Google Analytics for my web site is shown in Figure 8-6.

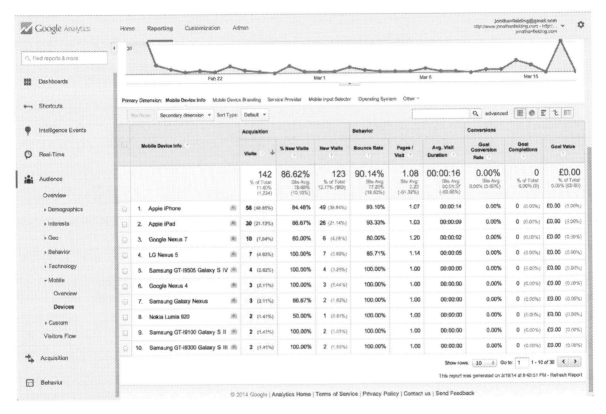

Figure 8-6. *Breakdown of the devices used to access my site as shown in Google Analytics*

Knowing about the browsers and devices the users are using is really important to developers, but as this chapter has highlighted, developers also need to be thinking about the user journey taken through a web site. Planning how you think users will travel through a site is important, but you also need to be able to measure this to see if your expectations match the reality. This is where Google Analytics Behavior Flow tool can be especially helpful.

As shown in Figure 8-7, the Behavior Flow tool starts on the left showing the page that users landed on when they arrived on my site. Moving left it shows where users have continued on with their journey though the site, and the drop off is the number of users who have left the site at that point.

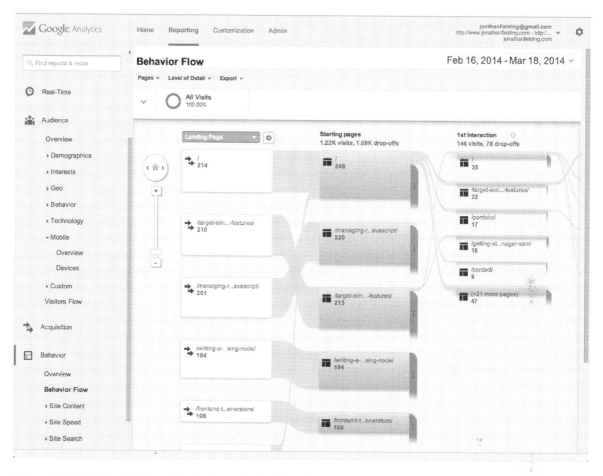

Figure 8-7. *The Behavior Flow of a site shown in Google Analytics*

Having looked at how your users are using your site, you might want to experiment with changes you could make to improve it. It is difficult to be sure that improvements that were make to a site will provide users with a better experience; however, what Google Analytics enables you to do is create an experiment where one of multiple versions of a page will be shown to a user. This works in a similar way to how social networks like Facebook and Twitter roll out new features to a small subset of their users to experiment with how users interact with them. Successful experiments are then rolled out across the site and the less successful experiments are thrown away or looked at to see why they went wrong and rerun after changes have been made.

When using Experiments within Google Analytics, you would click Create experiment, which would take you to the Experiment Creation screen. The experiments listing page for my web site is shown in Figure 8-8.

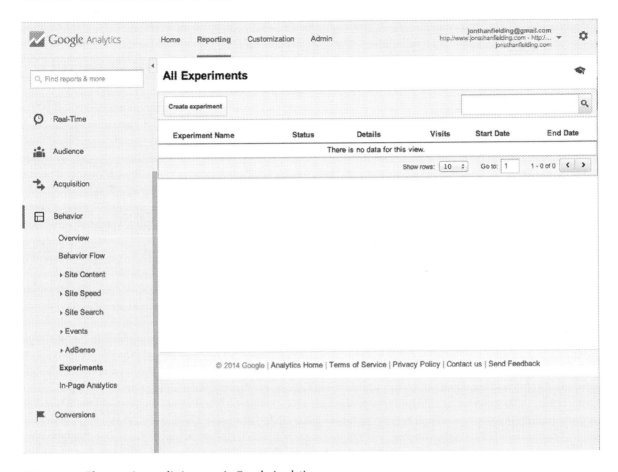

Figure 8-8. *The experiments listing page in Google Analytics*

You will then be prompted to enter a name for the experiment, define an objective, and then select the percentage of traffic you want to use for the experiment. It is important to note that the percentage of traffic you select is completely dependent on the number of visitors you expect your site to get while you are running the experiment. You want to guarantee that you get a good enough sample size from the experiment, however, you also want to ensure you minimize the risk of the experiment. The lower the percentage, the lower the risk. There are also some additional advanced options that will allow you to define how long the experiment will last and how the traffic will be distributed during your experiment. Figure 8-9 shows how to create an experiment.

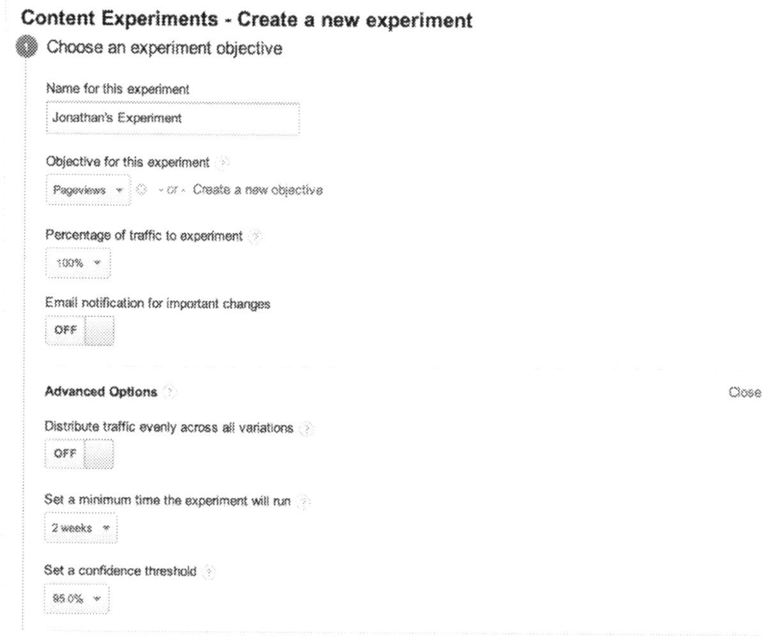

Content Experiments - Create a new experiment

① Choose an experiment objective

Name for this experiment

Jonathan's Experiment

Objective for this experiment

Pageviews ▾ ⊙ - or - Create a new objective

Percentage of traffic to experiment

100% ▾

Email notification for important changes

OFF

Advanced Options   Close

Distribute traffic evenly across all variations

OFF

Set a minimum time the experiment will run

2 weeks ▾

Set a confidence threshold

95.0% ▾

Figure 8-9. *Creating an experiment in Google Analytics*

After you have set up the objectives of the experiment, you can click the next step button and you will be able to start configuring it. To configure the experiment, enter the URL to the original page you want to experiment with and then you are able to add up to nine variations of the page (Figure 8-10). You can name each of your variations, and you need to include a link directly to each variation.

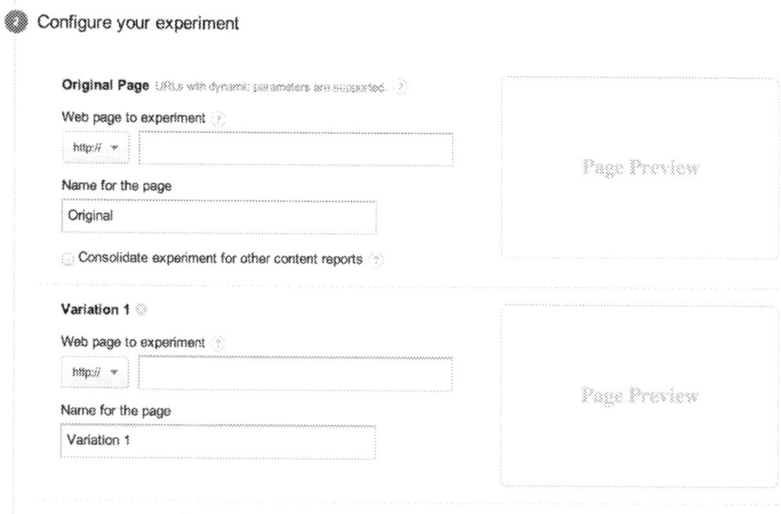

② Configure your experiment

Original Page URLs with dynamic parameters are supported.

Web page to experiment

http:// ▾

Name for the page

Original

○ Consolidate experiment for other content reports

Page Preview

Variation 1 ⊙

Web page to experiment

http:// ▾

Name for the page

Variation 1

Page Preview

Figure 8-10. *You can configure multiple variations for your experiment*

Having set up the variations and clicked the next step button, you will be given the option to either manually insert the required code for the experiment into your web page or to e-mail it to the webmaster. Because you are the developer, you will simply want to copy the code from the text box (as shown in Figure 8-11) and paste it into your page.

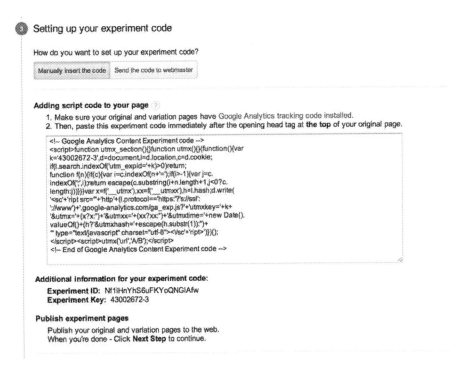

Figure 8-11. *The final step of creating an experiment outputs the script to add to your page*

Having added the code to your web page, you can now click the next step button, which will validate the code is in place and allow you to start the experiment. You can then check back periodically to see how the different variations of your page are performing.

Using Experiments in Google Analytics can be really powerful for allowing you to test new ideas on how to improve your users' journey. If used correctly, these tools allow you to continue to improve your site and enable you to learn which improvements the users like and which they don't.

ClickTale

ClickTale is a different type of analytics tool that focuses on measuring information about how many visitors are visiting a site, looking instead at the behavior of the visitors.

One of the core features of ClickTale is its ability to record how a user interacts with a web site, which it does by tracking the actions the user performs on the page and recording them. What this means to developers is that we can easily see where users are struggling when they are navigating through a site.

In Figure 8-12, a ClickTale session is being played. There is full control of how you play the user's session, with the ability to play, scroll through the video, and playback at different speeds.

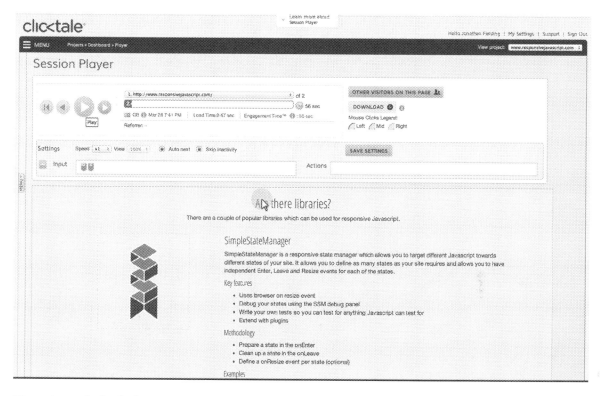

Figure 8-12. *Playback of a ClickTale user session*

In addition to recording the users viewing the web site, ClickTale can use these data to generate heatmaps. Heatmaps are graphical representations of data that show the correlations in the data, which in this case is how the users interact with a site. ClickTale allows you to look at a series of different heatmaps, each focusing on a different metric: mouse movement, where users click, where users place their attention, and where users typically scroll to on the page.

To view a heatmap in ClickTale, simply select the heatmap you want to view from the main dashboard. In Figure 8-13, I have selected the mouse move heatmap, and as expected, you can see that the main area the users have been moving their mouse to is along the main navigation. You will also notice that around the links on the nav is a small box with a percentage underneath it. This is the percentage of users who clicked on those links.

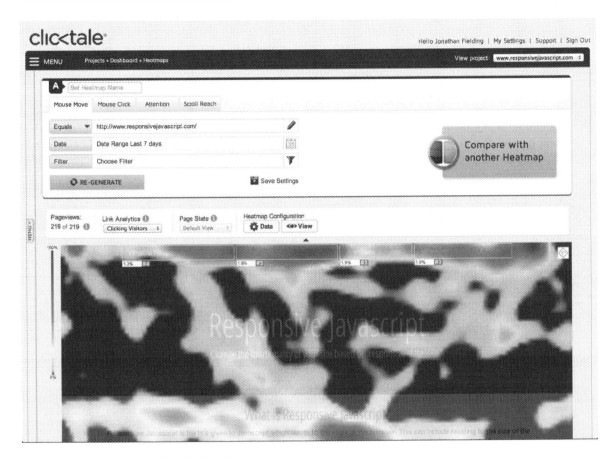

Figure 8-13. *The heatmap view of ClickTale*

Similar to Google Analytics, ClickTale allows you to look at how users progress through a site, which is achieved using their Conversion Funnel. The benefit of ClickTale's implementation over that of Google Analytics is that it allows you to filter much more easily without having to do a lot of configuration, and it is focused on looking at where users drop out of your site before reaching the end goal. The interface is also a lot cleaner and easier to use.

To get started using the Conversion Funnel (as shown in Figure 8-14), either go to the dashboard and scroll down to the Conversion Funnel section, clicking the View/edit funnel link, or use the sidebar menu and select Conversion Funnel.

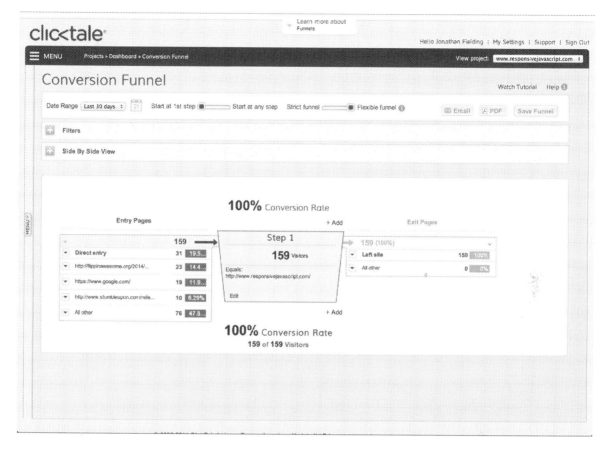

Figure 8-14. *The ClickTale conversion funnel*

Although ClickTale is a commercial service, it offers a free account that is able to record 5,000 pageviews. Although this is only a small sample, you can make it fairer by providing ClickTale with estimates of how many pageviews you expect to receive, so it can record a random sample. For example, if you expect 50,000 pageviews, ClickTale can be set up to record one in ten of those users.

Summary

I believe that managing user experience isn't a science but more of an art form—as such there isn't a strict right or wrong way to do things. This chapter has simply aimed to guide you in getting started with shaping the journey of your responsive site. It is important to note that while a lot of the things discussed work well as starting points for how you build your responsive journey, the best experience for your users is tailored around what they are trying to achieve with your site.

The content of your site is the heart of your site, and you shouldn't be afraid to adapt it as you learn what your users are interested in. You can do this by using both user testing and the analytics tools discussed here to measure what users are interested in, and then adapting and measuring again to see if you have made any improvements.

When developing your user journey, it is important to remember that you might not necessarily get it 100 percent right the first time, and that is okay; that is the nature of building a good user experience. What you need to ensure, however, is that you take what you learn onboard and feed it back into improving and evolving your site.

Responsive design is a relatively new technique that can be incredibly powerful, but as with everything new in web site development, there are a lot of unknowns to how it will affect the user experience. This is why it is really important to properly measure how well your site accomplishes the goals laid out for it so that you can iterate and improve it.

As part of this chapter, I explained ways in which you can analyze the user journey of your site, specifically looking at how you can use user testing and analytics tools to further improve your site. Both of the methods of testing your user journey explained in this chapter have a place within your site, and they can complement each other nicely.

The next chapter will look at how to apply some of the techniques discussed in this chapter to a site using responsive JavaScript techniques.

■ ■ ■

## CHAPTER 9

JavaScript Across Responsive States

The most common way to make web sites responsive is by using media queries in the style sheets. The media query defines the rules the browser much meet to show those particular styles. The main limitation of using media queries, however, is that they can only be used to change the look and feel of a site as they only have a limited use for changing the way a web site functions. To properly respond to the differences between the different types of devices a web site supports and to provide a truly responsive experience, other technologies must be used in conjunction with the media queries in the style sheet.

The potential need for a change in functionality will be determined by both the differences in the features available on the device and the size of the viewport that it offers. The disparity between devices can mean that users on different devices could potentially be interacting with your site in completely different ways. In particular, the varying input methods, such as touch screens, TV remotes, keyboards, and mouse interactions, all need to be incorporated in different ways to allow for the broad spectrum of devices to access the highest level of site functionality.

To cater to this requirement to change the functionality across responsive states, you'll need to learn how to use JavaScript to respond to the browser. Even as I sit here writing this chapter, I realize that both user experience designers and developers are thinking of new interactions that could be add to a site. Upon trying them out, you might find that these interactions do not work well across the variety of devices you are aiming to support and you might want to be able to adapt the functionality. Because it is impossible to cover every interaction you might find yourself implementing, this chapter focuses on arming you with the tools necessary to allow you to handle changes through the use of progressive enhancement techniques.

This chapter will explore:

1. Different functionality across responsive states

2. Techniques for changing functionality

3. Implementing responsive JavaScript techniques

Different Functionality Across Responsive States

Prior to responsive design, when building a web site, the developer aimed to provide the same functionality of a site across the wide variety of browsers they wanted to support. Where this wasn't possible, they would likely try to provide a degraded experience to the older browsers. What developers could rely on, however, was that users would likely be interacting with the web site with a keyboard and mouse, because the number of input methods used to control web sites was much more limited. Knowing that users would only interact with the site with their keyboard and mouse meant developers could optimize for this experience, an example being adding functionality for when a user hovered over a particular element of the page.

With new devices (smartphones in particular) entering the main stream, developers have seen a growing number of input methods in which users have started to interact with a web site. New input methods such as touch screens and simplistic remote controls for smart televisions have broadened the old input spectrum substantially. Developers therefore now need to consider these new input methods when adding functionality to a site. With this, developers need to consider that some user interactions they have come to rely on like hover, mouse enter, and mouse leave won't work on a touch screen.

Aside from the different user input methods, there are also a growing number of features that are available on the devices for which a web site built. Among these features, it is becoming more common to find devices that have support features like camera, geolocation, motion, and different device orientations.

If we look out onto the horizon, there are many new features coming for devices. One such new API is the vibration API that notifies the user of a change within an application, or alternatively provides feedback similar to how game consoles provide feedback through vibration.

With all these new capabilities, it gives developers the ability to add new kinds of functionality that couldn't have been achieved in a desktop browser. These technologies need to be implemented using progressive enhancement, because not all devices are created equal. So although you might already be progressively enhancing your site using media queries, you also need to start doing this in JavaScript.

Chapter 8 looked at different, common user interactions with the aim of exploring ways to adapt them to work better responsively. Chapter 8 provided several examples of common user interactions, and five of these required making changes to the functionality that is built with JavaScript:

- Modal windows

- Product search

- Tabbed containers

- Menu drop-downs

- Parallax

Techniques for Changing Functionality

Having explored why you would want to change functionality on different devices based on their capabilities in Chapter 8, let's look at how to perform these changes in functionality.

The techniques that can be used for changing functionality can be separated into two categories: feature detection and state management. It is important that you have a good understanding of both of these techniques so you know when it is appropriate to use either individually or together to achieve the desired result.

Feature Detection

One of the main areas that media queries are extremely limited is for detecting the features of the browser. Although the media types can be used to a small extent to determine the type of device the user is on, there are a variety of devices with a huge range of different features available, all of which respond to the media type "screen." The implication of this is that you can't rely on media types to give you any idea as to which features a device might have. Similarly, although media queries can detect the size of the viewport or the device pixel density, they can't detect JavaScript APIs or the majority of the HTML5 features. With this in mind, you need to find other ways to detect these features, and this can be done within JavaScript.

Using JavaScript, you can programmatically detect if a feature is supported and a web site can be built to respond appropriately. Depending on the type of feature you want to detect, there are different techniques that can be employed to determine whether it is supported. It is important to understand the different ways to detect features, so let's look at the different methods that can be used.

Part of Global Object

The easiest method to detect if a feature is supported is if it is exposed on the global object (e.g., the window object). If it belongs to the window object, then the feature is supported.

An example of where this technique can be applied is to test whether the browser supports the localStorage API. You can simply check for the existence of localStorage on the window object, as shown in the following code:

```
var hasLocalStorage = function(){
        return 'localStorage' in window;
}
```

Part of an Element

If instead you wanted to test for support of a particular element that was added as part of the HTML5 specification, you would need to create an element and test for a specific feature of that element.

An example of an element that you can test using this approach is the Canvas element. You first need to create a dummy element. In this example, you will store it in a variable named elem. You can then test the element for support of the canvas API by attempting to call a Canvas-specific method on the element; in this case you will use getContext. Usually when you call getContext, if Canvas is supported, you will get back a Canvas Rendering Context, otherwise you will get back undefined. To turn this into a Boolean value, you can simply use two exclamation marks (!!) before the elem.getContext, resulting in the method returning true if Canvas is supported and otherwise returning false, as shown in the following code:

```
var hasCanvas = function(){
        var elem = document.createElement('canvas');
        return !!(elem.getContext)
}
```

Simply knowing an element is supported is not always enough; one example is the HTML5 video element, which supports different video formats in different browsers. If you are dynamically adding videos, it doesn't make sense to add all the different formats into the page, therefore, you would need to be able to determine which video formats the browser supports. An example of this is the H264 video format that is supported by Webkit browsers including Safari on the iPad and iPhone. To test for H264 support, you would first want to test for the method canPlayType, and if it is supported, you can then use the method to test for support for the H264 codec.

It is important to note that the value from canPlayType will return a string with three possible values: probably, maybe, or an empty string. With this in mind, you need to typecast the variable (change the variable type) to Boolean so it can return true or false. To achieve this, you would use double exclamation marks (!!) before returning the value. The first exclamation mark will typecast the value based on whether its truthy or falsy and then inverse its value. The second exclamation mark will then inverse the value again so it is as expected. The following code shows this:

```
var hasVideoH264 = function(){
        var elem = document.createElement('video');

        if(!!elem.canPlayType){
                return !!(elem.canPlayType('video/mp4; codecs="avc1.42E01E, mp4a.40.2"'));
        }
        return false
};
```

237

Checking if Values Are Kept

Sometimes you want to test for new features of older elements, and you can do this by adding a value to a property and testing if the browser keeps the value or falls back to something else that is supported.

An example of where you would use this is for testing if the browser supports new input types. You would do this by setting the attribute type to have a value of email and then testing whether the browser ignores the new value. In the case of the value being ignored, the browser will have defaulted the input type to be set to text. The following code shows this:

```
var hasInputEmail = function(){
        var elem = document.createElement('input');
        elem.setAttribute("type","email");
        return elem.type === "email";
}
```

Using a Library

Having looked at writing tests, you can easily see that it is relatively simple to test for support for a particular feature. The problem comes when you need to test for a large number of features because it can be time-consuming to write and test for each of the features across different browsers. Rather than write your own tests, you can instead choose to use a library that contains a variety of different tests that can be used in your code. One such library is Modernizr.

Modernizr is a feature detection library created by Faruk Ateş and developed by a community of developers. The aim of Modernizr is to allow you to test for a large variety of features. The feature detection can be used in two distinct ways: first, it can be used in CSS, and second, it can be used within your JavaScript.

You can use Modernizr very easily in your JavaScript by checking against values stored on the Modernizr object. What this means is that you can easily wrap code related to a specific browser feature in a conditional statement to check for support before you run your JavaScript. An example of checking for support of the geolocation API using Modernizr is:

```
if(Modernizr.geolocation){
        //JavaScript specific to the geolocation API
}
```

Modernizr also allows you to react to the availability of different features in your CSS; it does this by adding classes to the HTML element that you can use from within your CSS to add styles to your site for use with a particular feature:

```
.geolocation .local-search{
        background: #666 url('geosearch.png') center center no-repeat;
        width: 40px;
        height: 40px;
}
```

Alongside adding classes for features that the browser supports, Modernizr also adds classes for features it doesn't support, these classes have the prefix no-. You can use these prefixed classes to hide parts or provide alternatives or fallbacks for any unsupported features you have chosen to use on your site. An example would be:

```
.no-geolocation .local-search{
        display: none;
}
```

This enables you to progressively enhance your site, taking advantage of the features your users' browsers offer, while providing fallbacks for users whose browsers do not support the features.

Dynamically Loading Based on Features

I have already explained that you can respond to a feature by simply checking it using a conditional statement, and then if it is true you can add or remove specific functionality. There may, however, be some instances where you want to load additional JavaScript libraries or polyfills when a feature is available or unavailable. An example would be for devices that don't support the window.matchMedia API, where you could conditionally load a polyfill. To handle this conditional loading of JavaScript, you can use a JavaScript library called yepnope.js. This library allows you to provide a test and then provide an array of JavaScript files that you want to load depending on the pass or fail of that test.

To use yepnope, simply pass an object with your parameters to the yepnope method. The parameters the yepnope.js method supports are:

1. `test`: The test you want to use, this should be either true or false, however you can use a method if you immediately run it.

2. `yep`: An array of JavaScript files to load if the test passes.

3. `nope`: An array of JavaScript files to load if the test fails.

4. `both`: An array of JavaScript files to always load for both yep and nope.

5. `load`: An array of JavaScript files to always load (similar to "both").

6. `callback`: A callback for after the file has loaded.

7. `complete`: A callback for after all files have loaded.

If you wanted to take a look at how you would use yepnope.js to test whether the matchMedia API is supported and to load a polyfill in the case that it is not, you would need to provide a test and add the polyfill to an array passed to the nope parameter:

```
yepnope({
    test : function(){
        if(typeof window.matchMedia === "function"){
            return true
        }
        else{
            return false;
        }

    }(),
    nope : ['matchMedia.js']
});
```

With this in place, you are now conditionally loading the polyfill if the window.matchMedia API is unavailable.

State Management

Although being able to conditionally run code and apply CSS based on a browser's feature set is really powerful, sometimes you need to manage the code that runs based on the state of the browser.

When you first think of a browser state, you might think about it in terms of key viewport sizes. By thinking this way, you might surmise that there are four different states: extra small, small, medium, and large. The definition of a browser state can, however, be simplified further to being the size of the viewport at any given point. This means that when talking about states, rather than thinking about them in terms of key viewport sizes or devices, you should think about them in terms of a range of dimensions that your code targets.

Understanding what a state is allows you to properly think about what you need to be able to do to manage your states. The key things you need to do when managing your states are how to activate, deactivate, and manage the transition between different states. When a state is activated, for example, you might want to add a piece of functionality, and later when the state is deactivated, you might want to remove the functionality.

There are many ways you can use the APIs offered by the browsers to manage the browser states. The first of the two APIs that I will explain is the window.matchMedia API, which is a new API brought in alongside media queries to allow you to test a media query from within JavaScript. The second API I will explain is the window.onresize API, which, although not originally intended for responsive design, as I will explain, can be applied to manage responsive states.

To properly understand how to use each of these APIs, let's explore each individually, looking at the benefits of each approach.

window.matchMedia

Using the window.matchMedia API, you are able to test an individual media query to check whether it matches the current browser state. The media queries you use with the API are the same as those you have already learned about using within the CSS.

The simplest way to use this API is for checking whether a media query currently matches. This can be achieved by calling `window.matchMedia` and passing the media query you want to test as the parameter. The API will then return a MediaQueryList, which is an object containing several properties, one of which is `matches`, which when queried will have a value of either true or false. If you put this together as a simple conditional statement to check if a media query matches, it would look like the following code:

```
if (window.matchMedia("(max-width: 767px)").matches) {
    // the viewport is a small device
} else {
    // the viewport is a larger device
}
```

Although being able to test if a media query currently matches is really useful, where the true power of the window.matchMedia API lies is in its ability to add listeners to the MediaQueryList you created using your media query. If you add listeners to the MediaQueryList, it allows the browser to notify you when the media query becomes matched or unmatched, allowing you to respond appropriately.

I have already explained that passing a media query as a parameter will return a MediaQueryList object that has a number of properties. To enable you to use these properties as necessary, rather than calling them directly off the API call, you can store your MediaQueryList in a variable:

```
//Create match media list
var mql = window.matchMedia("(max-width:767px)");
```

It is easy to see what this MediaQueryList object looks like in the browser console, you would simply run this code in the browser and then check the value of the variable you defined (see Figure 9-1).

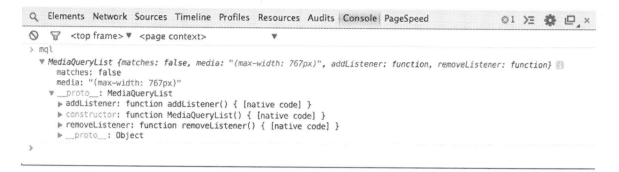

Figure 9-1. *The media query list object as shown in the browser console*

As you can see from looking at the object in the console, the MediaQueryList provides the ability to see immediately if the media query matches by looking at the `matches` property and to both add and remove listeners.

To add a listener to the MediaQueryList, you can use addListener by passing a `listener` method. The listener you define will pass the MediaQueryList back as the first parameter, which you can then use to check whether the media query the user has defined currently matches. This is achieved by using the `matches` property discussed earlier and checking if the value is equal to true or false. If you use a conditional statement, you can easily separate the entering the state (matches will be equal to true) from the exiting the state (matches will be equal to false). Put together, the `listener` method will look like this:

```
//Create an the listener for mobile
var mobileListener = function(mqlObj){
    if(mqlObj.matches){
        console.log('enter mobile');
    }
    else{
        console.log('exit mobile');
    }
};
```

It is important to note that although you could pass an anonymous function to the addListener method, there is a disadvantage to this when it comes to adding listeners. This is because when you pass an anonymous function, you do not have a reference point to use when you want to later remove the listener.

With both the MediaQueryList and the `listener` method complete, you can now attach the `listener` method to the MediaQueryList. This is achieved by simply using `mql.addListener`, passing the listener method as a parameter:

```
mql.addListener(mobileListener);
```

If you look at this all together, you get the following:

```
//Create match media list
var mql = window.matchMedia("(max-width:767px)");

//Create an the listener for mobile
var mobileListener = function(e){
    if(e.matches){
        console.log('enter mobile');
    }
```

```
        else{
            console.log('exit mobile');
        }
};

//Add the listener to the MediaQueryList
mql.addListener(mobileListener);
```

The second method that the MediaQueryList object has for managing listeners is the removeListener method. The purpose of this method is to allow you to easily remove a listener you previously added. Prior to adding a listener, you assigned the listener to a variable; so to remove a listener, you will need to pass this variable to removeListener, which will remove the listener from the MediaQueryList:

```
mql.removeListener(mobileListener);
```

So far I have explained how to both add and remove a listener to a single media query. More often than not, this will not be enough as you will most likely need to manage a variety of different states. You can therefore choose to set up multiple MediaQueryLists, attaching state-specific listeners to each:

```
//Create match media list
var smallMediaQuery = window.matchMedia("(max-width:767px)"),
    mediumMediaQuery = window.matchMedia("(min-width:768px) and (max-width:991px)"),
    largeMediaQuery = window.matchMedia("(min-width:992px)");

//Create an the listener for small devices
var smallListener = function(e){
        if(e.matches){
                console.log('enter small device');
        }
};

//Create an the listener for medium devices
var mediumListener = function(e){
        if(e.matches){
                console.log('enter medium device');
        }
};

//Create an the listener for large devices
var largeListener = function(e){
        if(e.matches){
                console.log('enter large device');
        }
};

//Add the listener to the MediaQueryList
smallMediaQuery.addListener(smallListener);
mediumMediaQuery.addListener(mediumListener);
largeMediaQuery.addListener(largeListener);
```

In the above example, I have created a MediaQueryList for each of the media queries, attaching a different listener to each. Optionally, I could have created a shared listener method, which would have been added to each of the MediaQueryLists, however, in this case, I would have had to additionally query the MediaQueryList passed to the listener to determine which state was being managed.

As you have now learned, you can easily manage your states using the window.matchMedia API, with the key benefit being that you can reuse the same media queries you used within the CSS from within the JavaScript.

It is important to note that the browser support for the matchMedia API is limited to newer browsers, therefore, if you want to use the matchMedia API in browsers older than Internet Explorer 10, you will need to use a polyfill.

window.onresize

Having already looked at the window.matchMedia API, let's look at how to use the window.onresize API to manage a responsive state. This API was around long before responsive design, so it was not originally intended for managing responsive states, however, it is perfectly suited for doing so as it fires as the browser is resized, much like how you would want to switch responsive states when users resize the browser.

With this in mind, let's look at how to use the window.onresize API in a responsive manner. The examples here will look at how to respond to the browser's viewport width.

For this example, I will be using the revealing module pattern developed by Christian Heilmann as an adaptation of Richard Cornford's module pattern. This makes sense because it encapsulates the code. I won' be going into the pattern I am using in depth, however, if you want to read more about it, Christian wrote a useful post about it on his blog.[1] The example begins with the simple code:

```
var stateManager = (function(){
    return {
    }
}());
```

Because you need to know which state you are in at any given moment, you will need to create a variable at the top of the module, which you will use to store the name of the current state:

```
var stateManager = (function(){
    var state = "";

    return {

    }
}());
```

As the resize method fires, you need to check the browser width to determine whether the current state has changed. With this in mind, you need to write a method that will determine the width of the browser. Unfortuantely this is not as simple as you might expect as the way in which we can find the width of the browsers is inconsistent across different browsers.

```
var getWidth = function () {
        var x = 0;

        if (typeof(document.body.clientWidth) == 'number') {
                // Newer generation of browsers
                x = document.body.clientWidth;
        }
```

---

[1]http://christianheilmann.com/2007/08/22/again-with-the-module-pattern-reveal-something-to-the-world/.

```
        else if( typeof( window.innerWidth ) == 'number' ) {
                //None Internet Explorer
                x = window.innerWidth;
        }
        else if( document.documentElement && document.documentElement.clientWidth ) {
                //Internet Explorer 6 and above in 'standards compliant mode'
                x = document.documentElement.clientWidth;
        }

        return x;
};
```

With this method for checking the width of the browser in place, you now need to write the method to handle the resize event. The methodology for the resize event can be broken down as follows:

1. Check the width against different values to determine which state the browser is currently in.

2. Determine if that state is currently active.

3. If the state is not active, fire the relevant method and set the state to the name of the new state.

With this methodology in mind, the code for the method looks like this:

```
var onResizePage = function () {
        if (getWidth() < 768) {
            if (state !== "small") {
                //Enter mobile method goes here
                state = "small";
            }
        }
        else if (getWidth() >= 768 && getWidth() < 992 && state !== "medium") {
            if (state !== "medium") {
                //Enter tablet method goes here
                state = "medium";
            }
        }
        else if (getWidth() < 992) {
            if (state !== "large") {
                //Enter desktop method goes here
                state = "large";
            }
        }
};
```

The next step is to define the methods that will be called when you enter each of the states. Because you have defined three states, you will create three methods: enableSmall, enableMedium, and enableLarge. For this example, simply log to the console the name of the state:

```
var enableSmall = function(){
    console.log('enter small);
};
```

```
var enableMedium = function(){
    console.log('enter medium);
};

var enableLarge = function(){
    console.log('enter large);
};
```

Having defined the methods for when you enter a state, you will now want to add the calls to these methods into the onResizePage method already created:

```
var onResizePage = function () {
        if (getWidth() < 768) {
            if (state !== "small") {
                enableSmall();
                state = "small";
            }
        }
        else if (getWidth() >= 768 && getWidth() < 992 && state !== "medium") {
            if (state !== "medium") {
                enableMedium();
                state = "medium";
            }
        }
        else if (getWidth() < 992) {
            if (state !== "large") {
                enableLarge();
                state = "large";
            }
        }
};
```

Earlier when you defined a module, you defined a return value as an object; now you will want to add a key value pair to this object, setting the key to init and its value to a method. Inside this method, you will define and run the onResizePage method and then add a resize event listener, which will run the onResizePage method whenever the browser is resized:

```
var stateManager = (function() {
        var state = "";

        var getWidth = function () {
                var x = 0;

                if (typeof(document.body.clientWidth) == 'number') {
                        // Newer generation of browsers
                        x = document.body.clientWidth;
                }
                else if( typeof( window.innerWidth ) == 'number' ) {
                        //None Internet Explorer
                        x = window.innerWidth;
                }
```

```
                else if( document.documentElement && document.documentElement.clientWidth ) {
                        //Internet Explorer 6 and above in 'standards compliant mode'
                        x = document.documentElement.clientWidth;
                }

                return x;
        };

        var onResizePage = function() {
                if (getWidth() < 768 && state !== "small") {
                        enableSmall();
                        state = "small";
                }
                else if (getWidth() >= 768 && getWidth() < 992 && state !== "medium") {
                        enableMedium();
                        state = "medium";
                }
                else if (getWidth() < 992 && state !== "large") {
                        enableLarge();
                        state = "large";
                }
        };

        var enableSmall = function() {
                console.log('enter small');
        };

        var enableMedium = function() {
                console.log('enter medium');
        };

        var enableLarge = function() {
                console.log('enter large');
        };

        return {
                init: function() {
                        onResizePage();
                        window.addEventListener("resize", onResizePage, true);
                }
        };
}());
```

Having completed the state manager, the final step is to run it, this can be achieved by simply running the returned init method:

```
stateManager.init();
```

The key problem with implementing responsive states using the window.onresize method is that you have to do a lot of the work yourself. The purpose of the window.onresize event in the browser is to simply fire some JavaScript when the browser is resized by the user so it has no concept of responsiveness or states. This means, in this simple example, that you would have had to check if a state is valid and keep track of when the states are enabled yourself.

Although being able to write a responsive state manager using the `window.onresize` method is a good solution to targeting JavaScript toward different responsive states, to get it right, it can take more time to implement than the window.matchMedia API does. With this in mind, don't let this extra work involved put you off to using this method. With support for the window.onresize API in all the major browsers out of the box, this method offers the best browser support.

It is also worth being aware that if you are using a window.matchMedia polyfill, the listener events will use the window.onresize API to polyfill the window.matchMedia API. The implication of this is that you may have to do additional testing across different browsers because your code will be working in different ways depending on whether or not the window.matchMedia API is supported.

Libraries

Having looked at the two core APIs that can be used when writing responsive JavaScript, you now have a good understanding of the differences and capabilities of both. One of the things you might have noticed is that both require you to write a fair amount of code to manage your states. Thankfully, there are a number of libraries available that enable you to write less code and offer additional functionalities over what the browser APIs provide.

I will focus here on two JavaScript libraries: SimpleStateManager and enquire.js. Both of these libraries take a different approach to responsive JavaScript but aim to solve the same fundamental problems developers face when trying to target different functionality toward different responsive states.

SimpleStateManager

The first JavaScript library I will explain is SimpleStateManager, which is a responsive state manager built on top of the window.onresize API.

Before you can use SimpleStateManager, you need to download the library and add it to your site. There are two ways you can add the library to your project: the first, and easiest, way is to use Bower, which as you'll remember is the package manager discussed in Chapter 7. You can use Bower to add SimpleStateManager to the project with the following command:

```
bower install SimpleStateManager
```

Once you have downloaded the package using Bower, simply include the JavaScript file in the page:

```
<script src="bower_components/SimpleStateManager/dist/ssm.min.js"></script>
```

■ **Note**   It is important to note that the path to SimpleStateManager may be different depending on the way in which you have configured Bower.

If you are not using Bower on your project, an alternative way to add SimpleStateManager to your project is to simply download the library directly from `www.simplestatemanager.com` and include it in your page.

Having set up SimpleStateManager within your project, you can now add your responsive states. A state in SimpleStateManager is defined by setting a number of configuration options, including defining any callbacks to be run when entering, leaving, and resizing a state. To add a state in SimpleStateManager, use the `ssm.addState` method, which allows you to define the state with a series of different options. The supported options for a state in SimpleStateManager are:

1. `id` (optional): The ID is the unique identifier, if provided, you can use this ID to query the state and later remove the state if necessary.

2. `minWidth` (optional): Allows you to define the minimum width that the state is active.

3. maxWidth (optional): Allows you to define the maximum width that the state is active.

4. onEnter (optional): Allows you to define a callback for when you enter the state.

5. onResize (optional): Allows you to define a method for when the browser is resized while the state is active.

6. onLeave (optional): Allows you to define a method for when you leave the state. This potentially could be used to clean up your state when you leave it.

It is important to understand that all the options in SimpleStateManager are optional, allowing you to use the library in a way that best suits your project. Now that you have seen what options are available when creating a state, let's add the first state. The first state will be aimed at mobile devices, applying a maxWidth of 767, and for the onEnter, onResize, and onLeave methods, you will simply log what the state is currently doing to the console.

When you have set up all the states, you then need to tell SimpleStateManager that you are ready for it to apply the states. This is achieved using the ssm.ready method, which does not take any parameters and simply tests each of the states to see if they are valid. For any valid states, the onEnter method will be run. The use of ssm.ready is simply as follows:

```
ssm.ready();
```

Now that the states are all set up, you may find that later in the JavaScript, perhaps as part of handling a user action, you want to determine whether a particular state is currently active. This can be achieved using the ssm.isActive method, which takes one parameter, which is the ID of the state you want to check for active status. If you were to test if the mobile device state is active, you would likely want to use a conditional statement. In this example, you would log to the console if the mobile state is currently active:

```
if(ssm.isActive('mobile')){
    console.log('mobile is active');
}
```

Sometimes the states might become redundant, so you would need to remove them; this is achieved using the ssm.removeState method. Similar to the ssm.isActive method, this method takes one parameter, which is the ID of the state you want to remove:

```
ssm.removeState('mobile');
```

The important thing to note is that the removeState method simply removes the state from SimpleStateManager and does not handle any tidying up that may be required. This is intentional, as the library doesn't know your intent when you are removing your states. In some cases you may find you need to fire the onLeave event if you remove the state. Although SimpleStateManager does not do this for you, it is very easy to use the ssm.getStates method to get the state you are removing and fire the onLeave method yourself.

When adding states to SimpleStateManager, you are not limited to adding a single state at a time. You can use the ssm.addStates method to add multiple states by passing an array of the objects defining the options for each state:

```
ssm.addStates([
    {
        id: 'mobile',
        maxWidth: 767,
        onEnter: function(){
            console.log('enter mobile');
        }
    },
```

```
    {
        id: 'tablet',
        minWidth: 768,
        maxWidth: 991,
        onEnter: function(){
            console.log('enter tablet');
        }
    },
    {
        id: 'desktop',
        minWidth: 992,
        onEnter: function(){
            console.log('enter desktop');
        }
    }
]);
```

With SimpleStateManager, you can add an infinite number of states, which are able to overlap one another. It is important to note that although it is possible to add a large number of states, there are potential performance implications, so it is important to be sensible with the number of states you add.

Where SimpleStateManager really stands out is in its ability to add your own custom configuration options to your states. What this means is that you can define a test and then within a state's options you are able to set a value that you can test against.

To add a custom config option, you would simply pass an object containing the name of the test (this will become the option you pass to the state so it is suggested you use camel-cased lettering), and you then pass the test method. The test method is then able to read the values set in the state's options and test whether the conditions have been met. The method should then return true or false. If you look at an example of how to implement a new config option, it would look like this:

```
ssm.addConfigOption({name:"maxHeight", test: function(){
    if(typeof this.state.maxHeight === "number" && this.state.maxHeight
>=document.documentElement.clientHeight){
            return true;
    }

    return false;
}});
```

For this config option, you would be defining a rule that allows you to target the maximum height of the viewport within the viewport. If your browser's viewport exceeds the height defined by maxHeight in the state options, that particular state will not be applied or will be deactivated.

To test the new config option, simply add it to the state and use it in the same way you used the default config options that come with SimpleStateManager:

```
ssm.addState({
        id: 'mobile',
        maxWidth: 767,
        maxHeight: 320,
        onEnter: function(){
            console.log('enter mobile');
        }
}).ready();
```

Having tested the custom config option, you can now see how easy it is to set up custom tests to run against your state. The real power with this is that anything you can test in JavaScript that is able to return a true or false value will work as a config option, meaning that this can be taken further than simply querying the viewport, but also could be used to test if a particular feature is supported by the browser. An example of this would be to test if the device supports `localStorage`:

```
ssm.addConfigOption({name:"localStorage", test: function(){
    if('localStorage' in window){
        return true;
    }

    return false;
}});
```

You can then simply add it as a config option on your state:

```
ssm.addState({
        id: "localStorage",
        localStorage: true,
        onEnter: function(){
            console.log('supports local storage');
        }
}).ready();
```

You don't even need to provide any width config options if they are not necessary and could have a set of browser-supported features be a state within themselves.

Aside from adding custom config options, there is another way you can add functionality to SimpleStateManager—by using or writing your own plug-ins. Similar to how jQuery allows you to write your own plug-ins, SimpleStateManager allows you to write plug-ins that extend its functionality. An example of a plug-in you might use with SimpleStateManager is SSM with Colorbox (`http://colorbox.simplestatemanager.com/`), which is one of the official plug-ins developed by the SimpleStateManager team. This plug-in wraps the jQuery plug-in Colorbox with a wrapper that allows you to enable and disable the plug-in within your states.

When considering whether SimpleStateManager is right for your project, it is important to look at the benefits it will bring to the project. The key benefits of using SimpleStateManager are:

1. It removes the need to manage your responsive states manually, you simply add a state and the library manages the activation and deactivation.

2. You can define enter, resize, and leave events for each of your states.

3. You are able to extend SimpleStateManager with custom config options, allowing you to add custom tests to your states.

4. There are a growing number of plug-ins for SimpleStateManager, allowing you to extend the library further.

5. Through using the window.onresize API, the library does not require a polyfill to work in older browsers such as Internet Explorer 7, 8, or 9.

On the opposite side of the equation, there is one main disadvantage of using SimpleStateManager. SimpleStateManager uses configuration options to define a state, and you cannot use the same media query you are using in your CSS or JavaScript but instead have to provide values to the options.This is just a short example of what you can do with SimpleStateManager. There is full documentation on the SimpleStateManager web site at `www.simplestatemanager.com`.

enquire.js

Another library you can use is enquire.js, which in this case is built on top of the window.matchMedia API and allows you to write responsive JavaScript. It is built as a wrapper for the API, extending the functionality and making it simpler to use and adding the flexibility to degrade in browsers that do not support the API.

The first step to start using enquire.js on a project is to download the library and add it to your site; this can be achieved in two ways. The first, and simplest, way to add the library to your project is to use the Bower package manager discussed in Chapter 7. You can simply use Bower to add enquire.js to the project with the following command:

```
bower install enquire
```

Once you have downloaded the package using Bower, simply include the JavaScript file in your page:

```
<script src="bower_components/enquire/dist/enquire.min.js"></script>
```

It is important to note that the path to the enquire.js library may be different depending on the way in which you have configured Bower.

If you are not using Bower on your project, an alternative way to add enquire.js to your project is to simply download the library directly from http://wicky.nillia.ms/enquire.js/ and include it in your page.

The way you add states with enquire.js is through registering them with the enquire.register method. This method takes two parameters, the first being the media query that defines when a state is applied. The second parameter can take two forms, one being a callback, which it simply fires when the media query is matched, and the other is an object containing different events for the state. The options that you can pass to enquire.register are:

1. match: Provides a method that will fire when the media query is matched.

2. unmatch: Provides a method that will fire when the media query is unmatched.

3. setup: Provides a method that will fire when the state is first registered.

4. deferSetup: Provides a method that will fire when the media query first matches.

5. destroy: Provides a method that will fire when the state is unregistered.

It is optional to provide callbacks to these events, which allows you to choose the callbacks most appropriate to use for your state changes. Let's look at how to create the first state. You will do this by taking what you have learned earlier about writing media queries and write a media query that targets mobile devices. For this example you will use the media type screen and the media expression max-width: 767px, which when put together is coded screen and (max-width: 767px). You will pass this as the first parameter, and for the options let's pass a match and unmatch method, both logging to the console. Put together, it looks like this:

```
enquire.register("screen and (max-width: 767px)", {
    match : function() {
        console.log('enter mobile');
    },
    unmatch : function() {
        console.log('leave mobile');
    }
});
```

When tested in your browser, after you enter the state, the console will output *enter mobile*, and when you leave the state the console will output *leave mobile*. As you can see, adding a single state with enquire.js is really simple, but adding multiple states is just as simple because enquire.js is a chainable library, meaning you can chain commands just like you chain commands in jQuery. With this in mind, let's try to add multiple states by chaining the .register method. For this example, rather than pass an object of different methods as the second parameter, let's simply pass a single method that will be used when the state is matched:

```
enquire.register("screen and (max-width: 767px)", function() {
    console.log("enter mobile");
})
.register("screen and (min-width:768px) and (max-width:991px)", function() {
    console.log("enter tablet");
})
.register("screen and (min-width:992px)", function() {
    console.log("enter desktop");
});
```

So far you have added states, however, sometimes you may find that you want to remove states. This can be achieved by simply passing the original media query to the enquire.unregister method:

```
enquire.unregister("screen and (max-width: 767px)");
```

Having successfully removed a state, let's look at how enquire.js handles browser support. As discussed previously, the window.matchMedia API that enquire.js is based on is only supported by newer browsers. This means that Internet Explorer 7, 8, and 9 will not support the API. But enquire.js takes this into account and enables you to degrade your experience to a desktop-only experience. This is achieved by passing true as the third parameter to the register method for the desktop state, telling enquire.js that if the window.matchMedia API is not supported, this stage should always be matched:

```
enquire.register("screen and (min-width:992px)", function() {
    console.log("enter desktop");
}, true);
```

If you want to have your tests work in these older browsers rather than degrade, you can use a polyfill for the window.matchMedia API to add support for the API to older browsers. I discussed one such polyfill earlier when I explained the window.matchMedia API.

When considering whether enquire.js is right for your project, it is important to look at the benefits it will bring to the project. The key benefits of using enquire.js are:

1.   It takes away the need to manage your responsive states manually, simply add a media query and relevant listeners.

2.   You are able to use the same media queries in your JavaScript as you are using within your CSS

On the opposite side of the equation, there are some disadvantages of using enquire.js:

1.   It does not provide a built-in plug-in API.

2.   It requires the use of a matchMedia polyfill in order to support older browsers such as Internet Explorer 7, 8, and 9.

This is just a short example of what you can do with enquire.js. There is full documentation on the enquire.js web site at http://wicky.nillia.ms/enquire.js/.

Using Feature Detection for Advanced States

So far I've explained how to use feature detection to respond to the features of a browser; however, I have stopped short of explaining how to build states that take into account the features of a browsers. What this means is that states are limited to simply responding to the viewport width; while for many sites this might be enough, it is important to understand why and how you can take into account features from within your states.

As developers, we are often forced to make assumptions about our users when we build responsive sites. It is common for us to compartmentalize devices by their viewport; an example being that all small devices are smartphones. This sort of assumption can damage our users' experience, as users on small devices that are not smartphones could potentially get a worse experience. This is because we have assumed they are using a smartphone, when in reality they may have simply resized their browser window. This is where it becomes important that when targeting features like touch screens, it becomes part of the way we progressively enhance a web site.

If you are progressively enhancing your site to use device-specific features, you might need to test for these from within your states. This is because a change to functionality may only be required in the circumstance of a pairing between a specific viewport state and a device-specific feature. This adds an extra level of complexity to your states, because not only are you targeting functionality based on the browser state, but you are also separating that functionality based on the features available.

To continue on with the smartphone example, let's look at how to target a small device with a touch screen. For this example, let's use the Modernizr feature detection library discussed previously. To determine whether the device is a touch screen, you can check the value of `Modernizr.touch` from within your state:

```javascript
var smallState = function(){
    if(Modernizr.touch){
        console.log('small device with a touch screen');
    }
    else{
        console.log('small device without a touch screen');
    }
}
```

From this example it is easy to see how simple it is to combine using states with feature detection. However, by just adding one conditional statement to determine whether or not it's a touch device has doubled the type of devices being testing for. Instead or just testing for "small devices," you are now testing for "small devices with support for touch events" and "small devices without support for touch events."

This adds more complexity to what otherwise would have been a simple state. An example of where this might get more complex would be if you wanted to test for the geolocation API alongside the touch API but requiring a different response based on whether it's a touch device or not:

```javascript
var smallState = function(){
    if(Modernizr.touch){
        if(Modernizr.geolocation){
            console.log('small device with a touch screen and geolocation');
        }
        else{
            console.log('small device with a touch screen');
        }
    }
    else{
        if(Modernizr.geolocation){
            console.log('small device without a touch screen but with geolocation');
        }
```

```
        else{
            console.log('small device without a touch screen');
        }
    }
}
```

As you can see, by adding the geolocation API, you have now doubled the number of different use cases that could happen. Although this is manageable, it's important to highlight that while combining feature detection within state management can offer huge benefits, you need to be aware that it can add complexity to the code you will need to manage.

One option to manage this code is, as discussed previously, using the SimpleStateManager library, which allows you to add custom configuration options and allows you to add feature detection. This also allows you to configure your feature detection on a state level, however, the disadvantage here would be that you would need to define a new state for each different combination of features you are supporting.

Implementing Responsive JavaScript Techniques

So far I have focused on the theory behind why you would want to change functionality and how you would achieve this, but once you understand this theory, it is important to understand how you can apply responsive JavaScript techniques to your web site.

For this example, let's look at how to implement a login prompt on a site that will appear on a new page on smaller devices and on larger devices will appear in a modal window. For simplicity of these examples, I will be using jQuery to handle some of the DOM manipulations. If you would prefer to use native JavaScript or an alternative library, feel free to replace the usage of jQuery.

As a starting point, let's take the code built in Chapter 5 using Twitter Bootstrap. This is included in the code bundle for chapter 5. Having set up the project with this as a starting point, you can start by adding a new hyperlink to the navigation to link to the login page. To achieve this, simply add a second navigation to the navbar. Because you want this navigation to be on the right-hand side of the navbar, let's add the class navbar-right:

```
<div class="collapse navbar-collapse" id="bs-example-navbar-collapse-1">
    <ul class="nav navbar-nav">
        <li><a href="#">Link</a></li>
        <li><a href="#">Link</a></li>
        <li><a href="#">Link</a></li>
    </ul>
    <ul class="nav navbar-nav navbar-right">
        <li><a href="login.html" class="login-link">Login</a></li>
    </ul>
</div>
```

Once you have added this link, it will then appear on the navigation bar. The medium viewport is shown in Figure 9-2.

Figure 9-2. *The navigation on the medium viewport*

To enable you to add functionality, add a new JavaScript file, which you will name main.js, to the bottom of the page just before the closing body tag. You will also be using SimpleStateManager to manage the responsive states, so let's also add this to the page:

```
<script src="js/ssm.min.js"></script>
<script src="js/main.js"></script>
```

Having linked to the login page and added a new JavaScript file, let's create the login page you just linked to. The easiest thing to do is to duplicate the index.html file, naming it login.html.

Having created the login.html page, you can now start to create the login page. To start with, you will want to update the Jumbotron with information telling the user to log in:

```
<section class="jumbotron">
    <div class="container">
        <h1>Login</h1>
        <p>Login to your account</p>
    </div>
</section>
```

Next you want to replace the current product panels with your login form. As this site is built using Bootstrap, you can simply implement the forms using the classes indicated in the Bootstrap documentation (http://getbootstrap.com/css/#forms). Please note that I have added the id content to the section element, this will be used later when you pull the content into the modal window on larger devices:

```
<section class="container" id="content">
    <div class="row">
        <div class="col-sm-12">
            <form role="form">
                <div class="form-group">
                    <label for="email">Email address</label>
                    <input type="email" class="form-control" id="email">
                </div>
                <div class="form-group">
                    <label for="password">Password</label>
                    <input type="password" class="form-control" id="password">
                </div>
```

```
                <button type="submit" class="btn btn-default">Submit</button>
            </form>
        </div>
    </div>
</section>
```

Having implemented the form, build the user journey that you intended to implement for smaller viewports, which upon clicking the login link in the header will take the user to the login page, as shown in Figure 9-3.

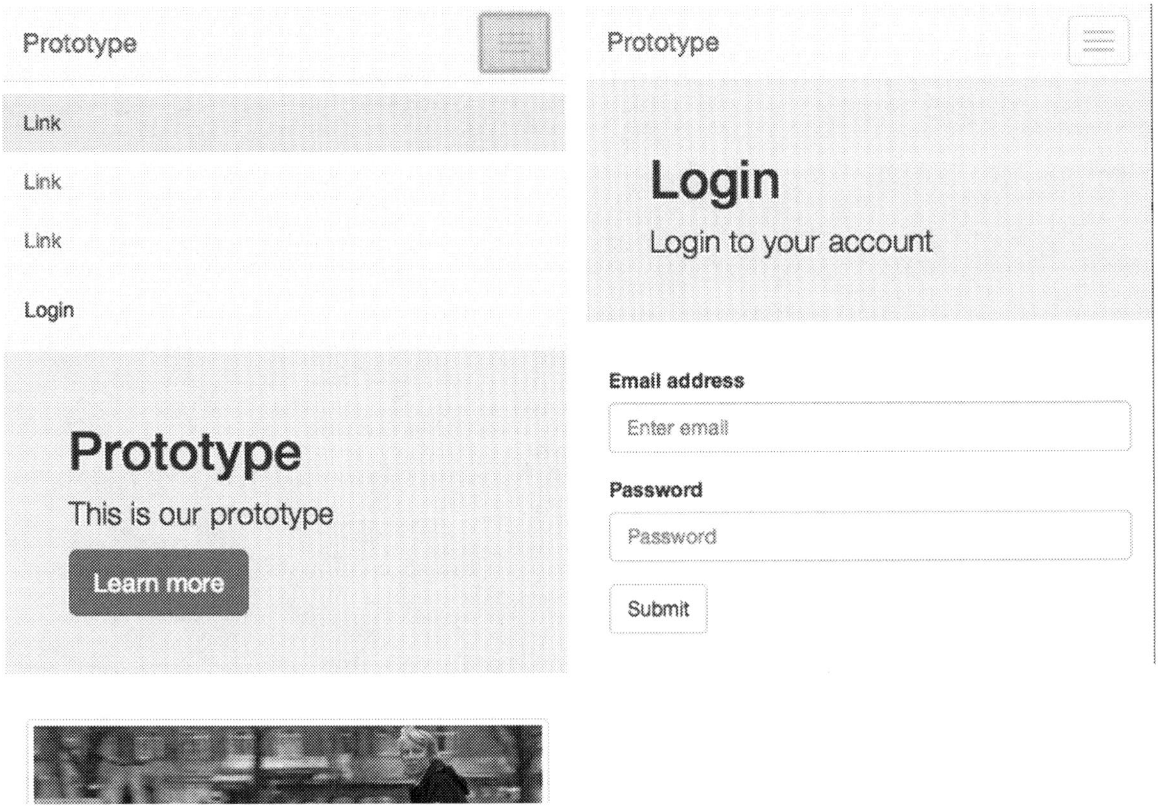

Figure 9-3. *The home page with navigation open (left), and the login page the user clicks through to (right)*

The next step is to look at how to progressively enhance the site by instead loading the login form into a modal window on larger viewports. Let's use the default modal styles that come with Twitter Bootstrap, but you will then add JavaScript to show and hide the modal on medium and large viewports. To start with, add the modal HTML to the index.html file (this is taken from http://getbootstrap.com/javascript/#modals). You will notice in the code I have left the modal-body empty, this is because I will be dynamically pulling this content in from the login page so that when updating the form I only have to update the HTML once:

```
<div class="modal fade">
  <div class="modal-dialog">
    <div class="modal-content">
        <div class="modal-header">
            <button type="button" class="close"><span aria-hidden="true">&times;</span>
            <span class="sr-only">Close</span></button>
            <h1 class="modal-title">Login</h1>
        </div>
        <div class="modal-body">
        </div>
    </div><!-- /.modal-content -->
  </div><!-- /.modal-dialog -->
</div><!-- /.modal -->
```

Having set up the HTML for the modal window, open the main.js file and start to write the functionality. Let's start by creating an immediately invoked function expression, which is essentially an anonymous function that is invoked as soon as it is read by the JavaScript engine. In this case, it allows you to scope the variables privately to the codebase:

```
(function(){
}());
```

The next step is to cache the modal window in a variable so you can access it later. You will also at this point create the site overlay, which appears behind the modal window in a variable so that you can add it to the page when the modal window is shown:

```
var $modal = $('.modal');
var $modalBackdrop = $('<div class="modal-backdrop fade"></div>');
```

The next step is to put together the method that will open the modal window when activated. To begin with, declare the method as a variable called loginClick:

```
var loginClick = function(e){
};
```

I mentioned earlier that the form included on the login.html page would be pulled into the modal window. To achieve this, use jQuery's ajax method, passing the URL to the login page and an object containing the success method:

```
$.ajax('/login.html',{ success: function(data){
}});
```

Having retrieved the HTML for the login page, filter it to extract the login form from the page. To do this, use jQuery's filter method, passing the id specified earlier in the section containing the login form. Having filtered the returned HTML, use the html method to get the final HTML from the filtered data and to output it into the variable:

```
var html = $(data).filter('#content').html();
```

Having filtered the HTML, add it to the body of the modal window. Because you already have the modal cached in a variable, you can simply use the jQuery find method to find the modal body and then use the html method to update the modal bodies content with the HTML from the login panel:

```
$modal.find('.modal-body').html(html);
```

Having updated the modal body, you can now show the modal window. First, use jQuery's show method to show the element, then use the removeClass method to remove the class out (which the element might have from previously fading out the content), and finally use the addClass method to add the in class, which will cause the element to fade in using CSS3 transitions:

```
$modal.show().removeClass('out').addClass('in');
```

Next you will show the backdrop by inserting it after the modal window using insertAfter, show it using the show method, and then add the class in, which will perform the CSS animation:

```
$modalBackdrop.insertAfter($modal).show().addClass('in');
```

After putting all this together, the code for the final method looks like this:

```
var loginClick = function(e){
        $.ajax('/login.html',{ success: function(data){
                var html = $(data).filter('#content').html();

                $modal.find('.modal-body').html(html);
                $modal.show().removeClass('out').addClass('in');
                $modalBackdrop.insertAfter($modal).show().addClass('in');
        }});

        e.preventDefault();
};
```

At this stage, you have written the method to show the modal window, but you haven't had to write any CSS because you simply used the styles that come with Twitter Bootstrap. Having done this, write the method used to hide the modal.

First, define the method as a variable called modalClose:

```
var modalClose = function(e){
};
```

Next, remove the in class you added to the modal when you showed it using the removeClass method:

```
$modal.removeClass('in');
```

Then do the same thing to the backdrop:

```
$modalBackdrop.removeClass('in');
```

Removing these classes will cause the modal and its backdrop to fade out. Once this animation is completed, hide the modal and remove the backdrop, and to do this, you will need to set a timeout. The animation specified by Twitter Bootstrap is 300ms, so let's set timeout to run after 300ms. Inside the timeout, use the jQuery hide method to hide the modal and then use the remove method to remove the backdrop:

```
setTimeout(function(){
        $modal.hide();
        $modalBackdrop.remove();
}, 300);
```

Finally, at the end of the modalClose method, use the preventDefault method of the event to prevent the button from firing the default browser action:

```
e.preventDefault();
```

After putting together this close method, the code looks like this:

```
var modalClose = function(e){
        $modal.removeClass('in');
        $modalBackdrop.removeClass('in');

        setTimeout(function(){
                $modal.hide();
                $modalBackdrop.removeClass('in').remove();
        }, 300);

        e.preventDefault();
};
```

So far I have discussed both the open and close methods, but I have not attached them to any events yet. You only want the modal window to be shown on larger viewports, so you will only add these event listeners when you are on these larger viewports. To achieve this, use SimpleStateManager to create a state where when you enter the state, the event listeners are added, and if you leave the state, the event listeners are removed.

To add a state, use SimpleStateManagers' addState method, as discussed previously. Set the minimum width of the state to 768px so that on extra small devices the user will simply go to the new page. For the onEnter callback, use jQuery's on method to add a click event to the login link in the header and to the close button on the modal. In the situation where the user resizes the browser and leaves the state, simply use jQuery's off method to remove these event listeners:

```
ssm.addState({
        id: "mediumUp",
        minWidth: 768,
        onEnter: function(){
                $('.login-link').on('click', loginClick);
                $modal.on('click','.close', modalClose);
        },
        onLeave: function(){
                $('.login-link, .modal').off('click');
        }
});
```

Having added the state, now simply run SimpleStateManagers' ready method to tell the library to set up the states:

```
ssm.ready();
```

With this in place, open the page in a browser with a larger viewport and click the login link. This will now show the lightbox, as illustrated in Figure 9-4.

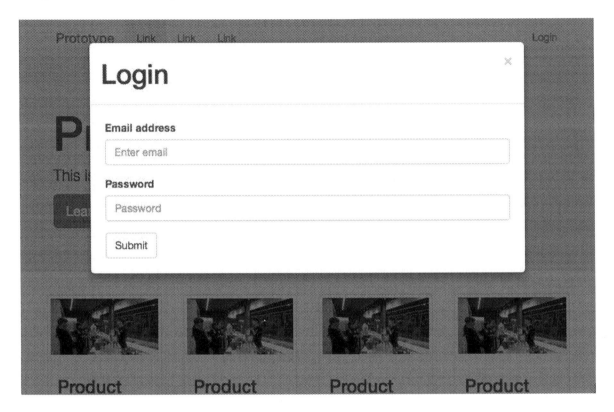

Figure 9-4. *The modal window shown on larger viewports*

After following this example, you will have now implemented your first piece of responsive JavaScript. As you can see, it isn't difficult to offer users different functionality based on their responsive states, however, it does allow users to have a better experience overall when using a web site. The aim therefore should be to identify areas of a web site that don't work particularly well on specific devices and then look to optimize them using these techniques.

Summary

Having looked at both feature detection and state management separately and then looked at how to use them together, you should now have a good understanding about how to use JavaScript to improve your users' experience by changing your site's functionality to best suit the user's device.

There are some key points you should take away from this:

1. Providing the same functionality to all users, regardless of device, can cause a bad user experience.

2. Functionality can be targeted based on both the state of the browser and the features it supports.

3. You can use feature detection alongside the state of the browser to enable you to progressively enhance your site.

Having looked at how you can respond to the device and change the functionality based on the viewport size and the features the devices support, the next chapter will look more in depth at the user experience decisions you have to make when building a responsive site.

CHAPTER 10

Optimizing Your Responsive Site

Whether you have already built your site or you are about to embark on building a responsive project, you need to ensure you take time to optimize your site for performance. Performance is not a nice-to-have feature, but rather a necessity of the multidevice modern web, as it is a key part of the user experience. Web site performance, however, is a very large subject area. In fact, there are books dedicated to only parts of it, so I am going to focus in this chapter on areas of web site performance and site optimization that can make the biggest difference to a responsive site.

In the past few years, both home and office Internet connections have increased significantly in speed, allowing the content of the Web to become more rich, interactive, and diverse, taking advantage of the increase in available bandwidth. The problem is that this has led to the average size of a web site ballooning, with both images and JavaScript in particular increasing in weight.

During this same period of time, users have been changing their browsing habits, moving to mobile devices, which at best have a 4G connection, but its more likely they will have a slower 3G or sometimes even 2G connection. This means that more than ever we need to look at ways to slim down our web sites while offering the users the best experiences.

This chapter will look at ways in which you can optimize the performance of your site. Specifically, you will learn about:

1. Improving network performance

2. The critical rendering path

3. Server-side optimization techniques

4. Measuring your site performance

Why You Should Care About Site Performance

Web site performance has become a big issue over the past couple of years, and web pages are getting bigger, with statistics from HTTP Archive indicating that in March 2013 the average web page was 1,311KB and in March 2014 the average web page was 1,703KB.[1] This is an increase of 392KB over the period of a single year.

---

[1] http://httparchive.org/.

If we look further into this at the breakdown of the assets of an average web page in March 2014 (taken from HTTP Archive), you would find the following sizes of the various forms of display:

1. Images: 1,063KB

2. Scripts: 276KB

3. Other: 207KB

4. HTML: 56K

5. Style sheets: 48KB

While the average web page is increasing in size, the user expectation of load times is decreasing, with *Web Performance Today* highlighting that the time users will wait for a site to load before giving up is decreasing every year.[2] Another article highlights the fact that slower web pages lead to users engaging less with the web sites, which means that it makes the site less effective.[3]

Sometimes it is hard to justify the need for performance to the business because optimizing a site has a time cost. There is, however, a relationship between web performance and converting users to sales of the products offered. In April 2014, *Web Performance Today* posted an article about this relationship, highlighting that Wal-Mart's web site found that for every second of improvement in load time, there was a 2 percent increase in conversions.[4] Similarly, the article highlighted improvements found by Mozilla when they decreased the load time by 2.2 seconds, which resulted in a 15.4 percent increase in the number of downloads and translates to an additional 10 million downloads per year. This relationship highlights a business's need for better web performance.

Improving Network Performance

The network can have a major impact on the speed at which web sites load for the users. The effect that the network can have on the performance of a web site can be split into two areas: bandwidth and latency.

Bandwidth is the speed at which data can travel from point A to point B across the Internet, which is usually the measure by which an ISP will sell an Internet package to the end user. Usually bandwidth will be measured in bits per second, so an Internet package is usually sold as X Mbs. The bandwidth primarily affects the users of the site through the rate at which it allows them to download the site's assets.

Latency is the round trip time that occurs in between the time when a data packet is sent to the server until a packet is received by the sender. However, improving the bandwidth does not have a direct correlation to improved latency. This is evident in that although bandwidth has continued to rapidly improve, the same hasn't been seen for latency. This is further illustrated by Ilya Grigorik in his blog post illustrating how latency is becoming the new web performance bottleneck.[5]

In his book *High Performance Browser Networking*,[6] Ilya Grigorik discusses the latencies involved across the different types of mobile networks before the user reaches the Internet, in particular he notes that on a 3G connection the user typically has a latency of between 100 and 500ms. On a 4G connection, this is improved to about 100ms, however, Ilya highlights that the lines between both 3G and 4G are blurred because of the way in which the standards have evolved. This is because 4G in itself is not a technology, it is in fact a list of requirements a technology must meet to classify itself as being 4G. This has lead to two different technologies being developed—LTE and HSPA+—and each is different from the other, meaning it is expected that there will also be differences in both the latency and the bandwidth.

---

[2]http://www.webperformancetoday.com/2011/07/20/new-findings-mobile-web-users-are-more-disappointed-than-ever/.
[3]http://www.webperformancetoday.com/2013/12/11/slower-web-pages-user-frustration/.
[4]http://www.webperformancetoday.com/2011/07/20/new-findings-mobile-web-users-are-more-disappointed-than-ever/.
[5]http://www.igvita.com/2012/07/19/latency-the-new-web-performance-bottleneck/.
[6]http://chimera.labs.oreilly.com/books/1230000000545.

Natasha Rooney spoke at the London Web Standards meeting in February 2014 about how the mobile phone networks affect web sites, and in particular she spoke about how they add latency to the network connections.

The reason for the added latency is that in between a mobile phone and the Internet there is the mobile phone network (shown in Figure 10-1), which introduces latency at several points along the way.

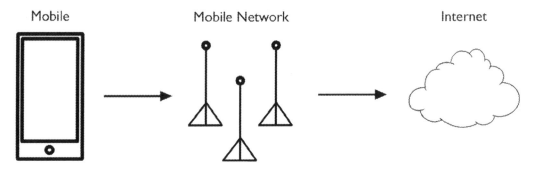

Figure 10-1. *Illustration explaining how a mobile phone connects to Internet*

When talking about the latency, Natasha mentioned the different latencies that are involved:

1. *Control plane latency* (approximately 100ms latency): To establish the radio connection, a one-time latency is introduced due to the process of the device's radio transitioning from being in a standby state to an active state.

2. *User plane latency* (approximately 5ms latency): The latency incurred by each packet of data being transferred between the device and the carrier's radio tower.

3. *Core network latency* (approximately 30-100ms): The latency caused by transferring packets between the radio tower to the carrier gateway, which is variable dependent on the mobile phone network.

4. *Internet routing latency* (variable latency): The latency between the carriers gateway and the requested destination address.

These latencies have negative implications to loading a web site, and each additional HTTP request that the site makes will incur additional latency. This is why if you look at techniques to improve network performance you will notice there is a recurring theme; the aim is to reduce the number of HTTP requests and to reduce the data that are being transferred to the users.

Now with an understanding of the problems developers face when it comes to network performance, let's go through the different techniques that can be use to enable improvement in the performance that can be achieved through the network.

Concatenate Files

One of the problems of network performance is that when you attempt to load a large number of files, it adds overhead to your web site. This is because the web site needs to perform a large number of HTTP requests. To overcome this problem, you need to determine how you can reduce the number of HTTP requests, and to do this you need to reduce the number of files you are including in your web site.

One way to reduce the number of files is to concatenate them, by this I mean you merge them together. One example would be taking several style sheets and merging them into a single file in the order they are referenced on the page.

Concatenating files manually can be a time-consuming task, however, in Chapter 7 I explained the use of the tool Grunt, which can be used to automate this task. In particular you can use the grunt-contrib-concat task to concatenate your files.

Optimize Images

On the majority of web sites, images account for most of the page's weight, so it is important to optimize them. There are many ways in which you can optimize the images that are used on your web site, and by combining the following techniques you can reduce the page weight and reduce the latency experienced by a user loading your site.

Sprites

When using images within the CSS for backgrounds, it is possible to end up having a large number of images, and loading each of these images adds additional HTTP requests.

One way to reduce the number of HTTP requests used for loading background images is to use sprites. This is where you combine multiple images into one image and then use background positioning to select the part of the image you want to use.

To create a sprite, simply merge the image assets into one master image. This can be achieved in a graphics package like Photoshop or by using a sprite-generation tool like SpritePad (http://wearekiss.com/spritepad). Generally you won't need any space in between the images, and the resulting sprite should look like the image shown in Figure 10-2.

Figure 10-2. *An example of a sprite showing four icons*

Having put together the sprite sheet, you now need to write the CSS to display this to your users. This is achieved by setting a shared background image and then simply changing the background position based on the image you want to show. The resulting CSS looks like this:

```
.orange-smile-icon,
.green-smile-icon,
.blue-smile-icon,
.pink-smile-icon {
        width: 25px;
        height: 25px;
        background: url('sprite.png') 0 0 no-repeat;
}

.orange-smile-icon{
        background-position: 0 0;
}

.green-smile-icon{
        background-position: -25px 0;
}

.blue-smile-icon{
        background-position: -50px 0;
}
```

```
.pink-smile-icon{
        background-position: -75px 0;
}
```

Aside from the number of HTTP requests, sprites can also offer a small savings to the size of your assets, an example being that the sprite you just used was only 2.6KB whereas the combined file size of the individual images would have been 5.6KB. The reason for this savings is a result of the way the file has to include the descriptors to define the file format, so because you only have one file vs. four files, you only have one set of the descriptors adding to your file size.

In Chapter 7 I discussed CSS preprocessors, one of which was Sass, which can be extended with a framework called Compass. One of the popular features of Compass is that it allows you to generate a CSS sprite along with the corresponding code from a folder of images. The benefit here is that you do not have to manually create the sprite sheet, and adding a new sprite is as easy as dropping a new image into the folder containing the image.

Inlining Images

A data URI (Uniform resource identifier) is a way in which you can include data inline within your web site's files in a similar way to which you would include an external resource. They enable you to reduce the number of HTTP requests by opting to include the data for the asset within your HTML or CSS rather than perform an additional request to get an external file.

As a simple example of what a data URI might look like, you can use the Base64 File Encoder found at http://jpillora.com/base64-encoder/. You will encode a simply smiley face (shown in Figure 10-3), which is sized at 25px × 25px.

Figure 10-3. *Individual icon before Base64 encoding*

By converting it from the image to a Base64 encoded image, it can then be used as a data URI, you end up with the following:

data:image/png;base64,iVBORw0KGgoAAAANSUhEUgAAABkAAAAZCAMAAADzN3VRAAAAGXRFWHRTb2Z0d2FyZQBBZG9iZS
BJbWFnZVJlYWR5ccllPAAAAyRpVFh0WE1MOmNvbS5hZG9iZS54bXAAAAAAADw/eHBhY2tldCBiZWdpbj0i77u/IiBp
ZDOiVzVNME1wQ2VoaUh6cmVTek5UY3prYzlkIj8+IDx4OnhtcG1ldGGegG1sbnM6eDOiYWRvYmU6bnM6bWV0YS8iIHg6eG1w
dGs9IkFkb2JlIFhNUCBDb3JlIDUuMy1jMDExIDY2LjE0NTY2MSWgGMjAxMi8wMi8wNi0xNDo1NjoyNyAgICAgICAgIj4gPHJkZ
jpSREYgeG1sbnM6cmRmPSJodHRwOi8vd3d3LnczLm9yZy8xOTk5LzAyLzIyLXJkZi1zeW50YXgtbnMjIj4gPHJkZjpEZXNj
cmlwdGlvbiByZGY6YWJvdXQ9IiIgeG1sbnM6eG1wPSJodHRwOi8vbnMuYWRvYmUuY29tL3hhcC8xLjAvIiB4bWxuczp4bX
BNTTOiaHR0cDovL25zLmFkb2JlLmNvbS94YXAvMS4wL21tLyIgeG1sbnM6c3RSZWY9Imh0dHA6Ly9ucy5hZG9iZS5jb20
veGFwLzEuMC9zVHlwZS9SZXNvdXJjZVJlZiMiIHhtcDpDcmVhdG9yVG9vbDOiQWRvYmUgUGhvdG9zaG9wIENTNiAoTWF
jaW50b3NoKSIgeG1wTUO6SW5zdGFuY2VJRDOieG1wLmlpZDo5MORFQzE3RUJDRUUxMUUzQUQyNkYORUE1MjU3NzRBNCI
geG1wTUO6RG9jdW1lbnRJRDOieG1wLmRpZDo5MORFQzE3RkJDRUUxMUUzQUQyNkYORUE1MjU3NzRBNCI+IDx4bXBNTT
pEZXJpdmVkRnJvbSBzdFJlZjppbnN0YW5jZUlEPSJ4bXAuaWlkOjkzREVDMTdDQkNFRTExRTNBRDI2RjRFQTUyNTc
3NEEOIiBzdFJlZjpkb2N1bWVudElEPSJ4bXAuZGlkOjkzREVDMTdEQkNFRTExRTNBRDI2RjRFQTUyNTc3NEEOIi8+
IDwvcmRmOkRlc2NyaXB0aW9uPiA8L3JkZjpSREY+IDwveDp4bXBtZXRhPiA8P3hwYWNrZXQgZW5kPSJyIj8+
teXwJgAAAARpQTFRF//z5/4wv/3wS//37/34W/3sQ/3sR/+va/7qC/9i4/3oP/72I/6dg//z6/34V/4su/44y/6JW/+
nX/9Cq/38Y//v3/8CN/6xp/4os/+LL/9Ku//v4/8KR/40x//r2/+HJ/7+L//fx/+nY/+zc/6tn/7Jz/8KQ/9/F/
8ib/7Bx/8md/4Mf/3gK/6lj/6xo/5ZC//jy/5xM/3QE/9Gr/6df/9u+/5I5/5tL/5Q+/4Eb/3oO/+LK/9a1/
/nO/3UG/+vb/+3f/72H/6lk/30T/4AZ/8ic//38/3YH/5hF//jz/9q8/5Q9/7yF/4cm/38X/5M7//n1/6Vd/

```
8GP/9e3/+3e/40w/55Q/76J/+PM//Hl/8qf/5ZB/////3IAhKDRywAAARNJREFUeNpiiIEABk5xRqZY
JkY9TgaYCJhkdrWMhQEWMV6EjL1sLDIIVYLJSDrHogI2eYiMMl8sOmBSAskwCwCZHIocUEEORR8gycg
LlFED8RliPKEycjG2IEohhoFBBMTgDuCGyjjKhYNdKMogFYsdCDM44ZDhYWDEISPBwIZDhovBCIdM
LB49jLHmghjCdjpAe3Rj/SNDAv2Qxd15TAWBbgP6JxoYDfJaqmEeFt76hioyXtIx3CD/gMLAz
CAGBaiCwyAmCKjfSsYNIW7jCwk3SFjHcplEqbM7KEcYa2qDuPygsI5hx4wfViFonDKhR5w
1LB2wo6YDfiGktKPhgpR2GJBSFSS9scayMqoESONFAAIMACNkvRK6zkxYAAAAElFTkSuQmCC
```

You need to be aware that an image encoded using Base64 has a larger footprint than the image file itself. In the above example, the original image was 1.4KB, however, the Base64 encoded image is in fact 1.95KB, which is an increase in footprint of about 39 percent. So, although you have decreased the number of HTTP requests, you have also increased the file size.

Aside from the increase in file size of the image, you also need to consider that you are increasing the file size of the style sheet. This leads to an increase in the download time, which in turn can lead to a bigger delay in the rendering of the page. With this in mind, you need to think about where using this technique is appropriate and where it is not.

A prime example of where it would be appropriate to include your images as part of your style sheet would be for the icons used for navigation. This kind of image would be relatively small, so it wouldn't overbloat the style sheet, and because they are used across the site, preloading them as part of the style sheet makes sense to avoid an extra HTTP request. To minimize the size added to your style sheet, you could Base64 to encode a single sprite of your icons and then use the image as you would use a sprite.

Using the Correct Image Formats

When developing a web site, it is important to consider the file formats used for the different images across a site. There are four main file formats used on the Web today for images: JPEG, PNG, GIF, and SVG.

GIF

The GIF format is an 8-bit image format that supports a color palette of 256 colors.

When building your site, the GIF format is most suitable for images with relatively few colors such as logos, simple graphics, and diagrams.

Recently, use of the GIF format has seen a revival due to its support for animation, which has led to it being used for displaying video-like content on the Web.

JPEG

The JPEG format is a 24-bit, lossy format developed by the Joint Photographic Experts Group and is the most popular file format used for images on the Web. The reason for this popularity is that the compression achieved by JPEG is very good and the format allows you to choose the balance you want between file size and quality.

The compression levels achieved by using the JPEG format are a result of the way it discards data of the image deemed unnecessary. The person saving the image has the option to choose different levels of compression, however, the more compression you apply to the images, the more data are discarded by the format, leading to lower quality images. If you want to maintain a good quality-to-compression ratio, you would typically want to save your images with the compression level set to around 70 or 75 percent.

When building web sites, the most likely place where you will find the JPEG format used is for photographs, as they usually have a lot of detail, which in other formats could lead to a large file.

Due to the way it compresses the image, the JPEG format is not suitable for images with only a few colors (like a logo). This is because using the JPEG format will reduce the quality and potentially introduce some artifacts, which are noticeable on an image with only a few colors. In these circumstances, you should instead look at using one of the other image formats. In addition, the JPEG format does not support transparency, so if you require transparency you will need to use a different file format like PNG.

PNG

The PNG format is a loss-less format that comes in two different flavors: PNG-8 and PNG-24. PNG-8 supports 256 different colors, while the PNG-24 format has support for 16 million colors. The format also supports transparency.

When looking at where PNG is most suitable, it depends on the flavor of the PNG format. The PNG-8 flavor is suitable for images with relatively few colors, such as logos, simple graphics, and diagrams. In the majority of cases, a PNG-8 file will have a smaller file size than a GIF file.

The PNG-24 flavor, however, is very different and can be used for a wide range of purposes. It supports full alpha transparency so you can have transparency as part of a detailed image. Being a loss-less format means that PNG-24 files can be very large, so it is important to not overuse the format as it can have a negative effect on the file size of your site.

SVG

SVG, short for Scalable Vector Graphics, is an XML-based vector image format that can be used on web sites. It is best suited for images like icons and logos, where there are a limited amount of colors.

As a vector format, the images can be scaled without losing any image quality. For responsive design, this is ideal as it means the images will look crisp across a wide variety of different devices, including those with a high-pixel density.

Unfortunately, the SVG image format will not work in Internet Explorer 8 and lower. The easiest way to support SVG in these older browsers is to simply enable the image to fall back to a PNG, using some basic JavaScript. In Chapter 9 I discussed Modernizr.js, which allows you to detect browser features, and one of the features that can be detected is SVG.

Let's look at an example of handing this fallback to a PNG using Modernizr.js for feature detection, along with jQuery to handle some quick DOM manipulation. First, you need to write the HTML. Let's reference the URL to the PNG version of the image in a data attribute called `data-png`. You will also have to add a class called `svg` to highlight that this is an image you want to update with a PNG. Use the following code to accomplish this:

```
<img id="logo" src="logo.svg" data-png="logo.png" width="50" height="50" alt="Logo" />
```

With the HTML in place, you can now write the JavaScript to handle swapping out the SVG for a PNG. First use `Modernizr` to check if SVG is supported by the browser; if it isn't, you then use jQuery to loop through each of the elements you have added `.svg` to and then replace the current `src` attribute with the value stored in `data-png`:

```
if(!Modernizr.svg){
    $('.svg').each(function(){
        var $this = $(this);
        $this.attr('src', $this.attr('data-png'));
    });
}
```

Image Compression

Having considered what image formats you are going to use, it is important that you minimize the file size of your images. Often graphics packages like Adobe Photoshop and GIMP do not save images in the most optimized way, however, there are third-party tools that can maximize the compression so you can minimize your file sizes. The aim is to reduce the file size of the images without reducing the quality of the image.

There are a number of tools that enable image compression; let's explore a few of these different tools.

Smush.it

Smush.it is an image compression tool developed by Yahoo! that is able to perform compression on a variety of different image file types.

The tool can be used in several different ways, the first being by uploading your images to the web site (`http://www.smushit.com/ysmush.it/`). Upon uploading your images, the site will process them and then allow you to download the compressed versions.

Unfortunately, uploading all your images manually to the web site can be quite time-consuming, so an alternative option is to use the command-line tool. This command-line tool is a Node utility, so you will need to ensure you have Node installed (a tutorial for which can be found in Chapter 7). To install the tool, you should use the terminal command:

```
npm install node-smushit -g
```

Once installed, you can compress an individual image using the command:

```
smushit imagename.png
```

Although it is easy to compress a single image, often you may want to compress an entire folder of images rather than a single image. To do this, you can pass a folder rather than an image name to the smushit command:

```
smushit images/
```

If you are using Grunt, you can automate the compression of images using Smush.it by using the grunt-smushit task. This is installed the same way as other Grunt tasks, as discussed Chapter 7.

ImageOptim

Another tool for image optimization is ImageOptim, which can be downloaded from `http://imageoptim.com`. To use the tool, upon opening the app, you will see the window shown in Figure 10-4.

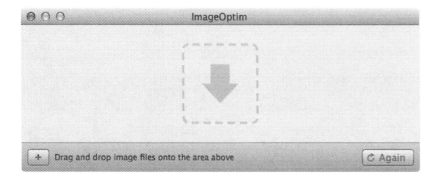

Figure 10-4. *The ImageOptim tool, drag your images onto the window to compress them*

To compress images, simply drag the images you want to compress onto the center of the window. After images have been dropped into the tool, it will then start to compress your images. When it is done with an image, a little tick will appear on the left of the row and information is provided about how much was saved by the compression. This is illustrated in Figure 10-5.

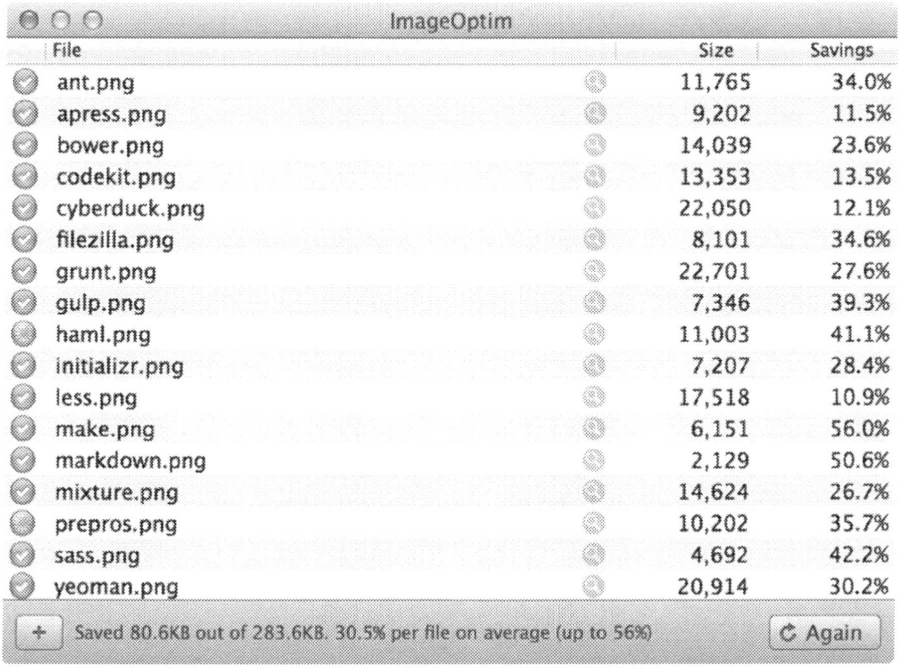

File	Size	Savings
ant.png	11,765	34.0%
apress.png	9,202	11.5%
bower.png	14,039	23.6%
codekit.png	13,353	13.5%
cyberduck.png	22,050	12.1%
filezilla.png	8,101	34.6%
grunt.png	22,701	27.6%
gulp.png	7,346	39.3%
haml.png	11,003	41.1%
initializr.png	7,207	28.4%
less.png	17,518	10.9%
make.png	6,151	56.0%
markdown.png	2,129	50.6%
mixture.png	14,624	26.7%
prepros.png	10,202	35.7%
sass.png	4,692	42.2%
yeoman.png	20,914	30.2%

Saved 80.6KB out of 283.6KB. 30.5% per file on average (up to 56%)   ↻ Again

Figure 10-5. ImageOptim showing a list of images along with the savings made by compressing

Target Images Responsively

Earlier when looking at the network, I discussed how the bandwidth available at any given moment affects the speed at which a web site downloads the site's assets. I also noted that the bandwidth available to smaller devices is typically lower than that available on larger devices due to the types of connections they use.

When working on a responsive site, it is likely that you are showing your images at different sizes, with the size dependent on the size of the device's viewport width. Although the browser could simply scale the images based on the size of the viewport, a better option is to load an image specific to that viewport size. As images account for a large percentage of the file size of a web site, it makes sense that for these smaller devices, which usually will be running on connections with increased latency and reduced bandwidth, you ensure that the images you deliver are as small as possible. Although using the correct file types and image compression can help, where you can make the most savings is through using smaller images on these smaller devices.

There are two ways in which you can implement responsive images, both of which are part of the specification for the "picture" element (The specification is part of the HTML living standard which can be found at `http://www.whatwg.org/specs/web-apps/current-work/multipage/embedded-content.html`).

img Element

One approach to implementing responsive images is through use of the new `srcset` attribute on the `img` HTML element, which allows you to define multiple images, along with hints for when each should be used.

The first use of `srcset` we are going to look at is targeting images based on the pixel density of the device, the main benefit here being that you can have higher-resolution images for devices with high pixel density screens, which will make them look crisper. To achieve this we need to use the attribute "srcset", setting the value to a comma separated list of images, each with the pixel density the image is targeted towards. I have shown this in Figure 10-6.

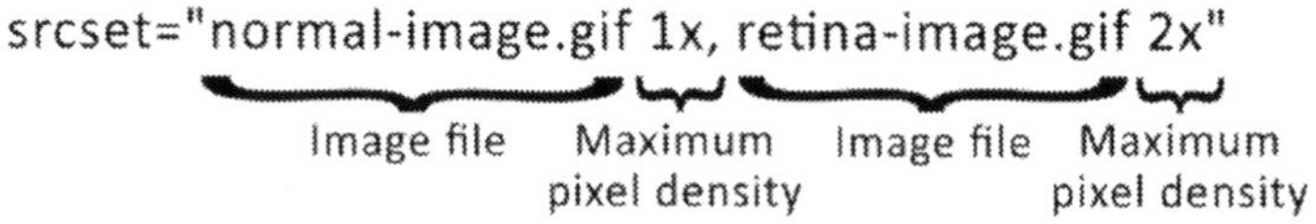

```
srcset="normal-image.gif 1x, retina-image.gif 2x"
```

Image file   Maximum   Image file   Maximum
             pixel density   pixel density

Figure 10-6. *The logic required for targeting images based on pixel density*

Having looked at the logic to use the srcset attribute, we will now look at an example of how this might look in our code:

```
<img srcset="low-res-image.png 1x, high-res-image.png 2x">
```

It is important to note that in this example I hav also included a `src` attribute, this allows legacy browsers that do not support `srcset` to fallback to the lower quality image rather than being unable to show an image. I have shown this here:

```
<img srcset="low-res-image.png 1x, high-res-image.png 2x" src="low-res-image.png">
```

A better way to use the `srcset` attribute is to target images based on the width of the viewport. The first step to achieve this is to set the value of the `srcset` attribute; for this you use comma-separated images, each with the width of the source image defined (see Figure 10-7).

```
srcset="mobile-image.gif 480w, tablet-image.gif 992w, desktop-image.gif 1200w"
```

Image file   Image   Image file   Image   Image file
             width   width

Figure 10-7. *"srcset" being used to define the widths of our images*

This is where it starts to get a bit more complicated, although you have told the browser how big each of the images is, what you haven't told the browser is how big the image is at any given point. This is where the `sizes` attribute comes in. Using the `sizes` attribute, you can tell the browser what size you expect the image to be at for any given viewport size. You can achieve this using the same media expressions that we used as part of our media queries in Chapter 3. For each media expression, we also specify the width that the image would be when the media expression is true/matched. If you specify a value for the width without including a media expression, this width will be taken as the default width of the image when no media queries match (see Figure 10-8).

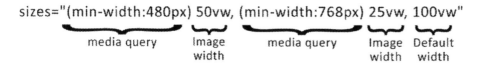

```
sizes="(min-width:480px) 50vw, (min-width:768px) 25vw, 100vw"
```

media query   Image   media query   Image   Default
              width   width   width

Figure 10-8. *"sizes" attribute being used to define the widths the image appears at each breakpoint*

You will notice in the above example I have specified the widths using the vw unit, which is expressed as a percentage of the viewport width. So when you specify 50vw, you are indicating 50 percent of the viewport width. If the image is always 100 percent of the browser width, you can just set the default value to 100vw and not specify any other rules. The `sizes` attribute does not limit you to using the vw unit for your widths, and you could choose to use other width units such as em or px instead.

With both the srcset and the sizes attributes set up, your browser is able to automatically determine the most appropriate image to load. In doing this, the browser can take into account a number of characteristics of the device, these include the pixel density of the display, the size of the image relative to the viewport width, user preferences (a user may choose to load lower quality images to reduce data consumption) and type of network the user is connected to. A finished img element implementing the srcset attribute with image widths would look like this:

```
<img srcset="low-res.png 500w, high-res.png 1000w" sizes="(min-width:480px) 50vw, 100vw" >
```

It is important to be aware that you cannot mix width-based srcset with the pixel density-based srcset, therefore while it is important to be aware of the pixel density based srcset it is better to use width-based srcset. This is because, as we have already covered, it gives the browser the control to be able choose the most appropriate image.

Being a new attribute, native support for srcset in browsers is limited, however, because it augments the existing src attribute, you can still use this to load a default image for the browser. If, however, you want to fully use srcset in all browsers, you can choose to use a polyfill. One such polyfill is PictureFill by Scott Jehl, which can be found at https://github.com/scottjehl/picturefill. PictureFill aims to polyfill the full specification for the picture element, which includes adding srcset to the img element.

Image Sources

Another way to define responsive images is by using the new picture element. The picture element is being developed as a way to allow developers to deliver device-appropriate images based on a number of characteristics, including format, resolution, and orientation. The aim is that the browser can then select the optimum version of an image to load based on the browser's current environment.

If we now look at each of the components that make up the picture element, the first part to look at is the picture tag. This wraps all the parts that make up our picture element.

```
<picture>
</picture>
```

Inside of the picture element we then have multiple "source" elements. Each of these "source" elements should have a "media" attribute used for a media expression. When determining which image should be shown, the browser will go through each of the "source" elements until it finds an image which has a media expression that is matched/true. Along side this, we also need to include a "srcset" attribute specifying the image to be used. Similar to the "srcset" we have already used on our img element, we can use it to specify multiple images. In the below example we have specified a single image for each of our "source" elements.

```
<picture>
    <source srcset="large.jpg" media="(min-width: 980px)">
    <source srcset="medium.jpg" media="(min-width: 768px)">
</picture>
```

After our source elements we also need to include an img element. When using the img element as part of our picture element we can use the srcset attribute to specify the default image. In addition we need to specify the alt text for our image on the img element. We should also include a default image using the src attribute for browsers that do not support the picture element.

```
<picture>
    <source srcset="large.jpg" media="(min-width: 980px)">
    <source srcset="medium.jpg" media="(min-width: 768px)">
    <img src="small.jpg" srcset="small.jpg" alt="A responsive image">
</picture>
```

Having looked at the different parts of the picture element we will now look at an example of how it can be used. In our example below we have defined three images, the first two as source elements and the third as our img element. For each of the source elements we have used the media attribute to apply a media expression.

```
<picture>
    <source srcset="large.jpg" media="(min-width: 1200px)">
    <source srcset="medium.jpg" media="(min-width: 600px)">
    <img src="small.jpg" srcset="small.jpg" alt="The church where I got married">
</picture>
```

If we then load our page within our browser with a small viewport (in this case less than 600px wide) and then we open up the developer tools we will see that the browser only downloads the smaller image, as shown in Figure 10-9.

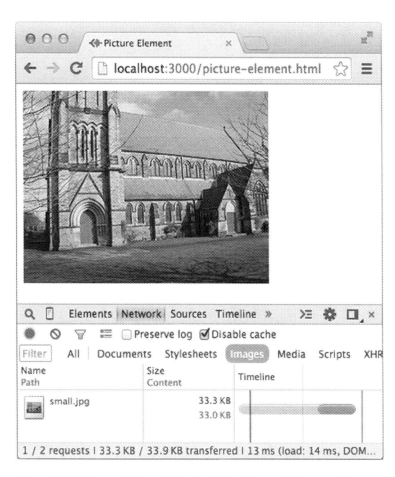

Figure 10-9. *Our small image being loaded on the small viewport size*

By only downloading a smaller image to devices with a smaller viewport we are reducing the file size of our page, which can help increase the performance of our site on smaller devices. While this could have been achieved using scrset, the added verbosity of the picture element allows us to choose which image to show on which device rather than give the browser the choice. This gives us the flexibility to change the art direction of the image shown dependent on the size of the device. Having looked at what happens when loading our site on smaller viewports, we will now load our page on a medium sized viewport as shown in Figure 10-10.

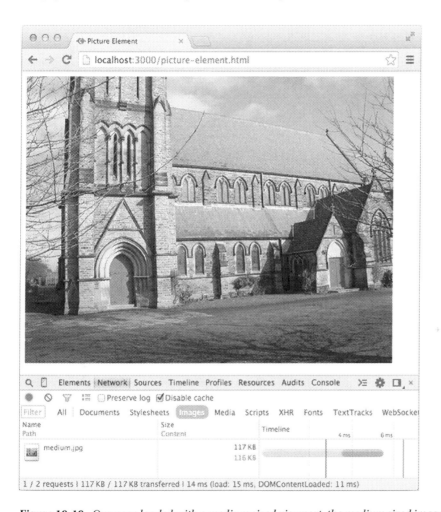

Figure 10-10. *Our page loaded with a medium sized viewport, the medium sized image is therefore loaded*

As expected, the browser instead chooses to download the medium sized image we specified as one of the source elements.

The browser support for the picture element is good, as the specification is designed to allow browsers that do not support it to simply fall back to using the contained image element. In addition, if we want to enable full support for the picture element rather than just this fallback we can use the PictureFill polyfill we have already mentioned.

The exception in this is Internet Explorer 9, which unfortunately has an issue with the source elements we have included inside our picture element, in that it will remove them from the page. To prevent this we can use a hack which involves wrapping the source elements in a video element. Targeting the functionality towards Internet Explorer 9 using conditional comments, we can then style the video element to not be visible. This prevents Internet Explorer 9 from removing the source elements so the polyfill will be able to utilize them. To illustrate how we do this, in the example below we have used conditional comments around an opening video element tag before our source elements and around the closing video element tag.

```
<picture>
    <!--[if IE 9]><video style="display: none;"><![endif]-->
    <source srcset="large.jpg" media="(min-width: 1200px)">
    <source srcset="medium.jpg" media="(min-width: 600px)">
    <!--[if IE 9]></video><![endif]-->
    <img srcset="small.jpg" alt="The church where I got married">
</picture>
```

As you can use both the srcset attribute and picture element together it is not a case of choosing whether you should use the picture element or use the srcset attribute. It is instead a case of choosing the level of verbosity you need for your specific situation.

If you are simply serving the same image at different resolutions so that your site is offering optimum images, allowing the browser to choose the image best suited for the browser environment then using the srcset and sizes attributes will do you well. If however you want to target different images towards specific viewport sizes, and have full control over at what viewport sizes an image is shown, then you should choose to use the picture element specifying the images as source elements.

We could also choose to use the srcset and sizes attributes to specify different images for each of the source elements. In doing this we can use the media expressions on our source elements to control the art direction, then specify multiple images as part of the srcset, along with defining the sizes to enable the browser to choose the optimum version of the image to show.

Conditionally Load Content

With a responsive site, typically you already have all your content preloaded into the page; however, sometimes you might want to conditionally load content based on the size of your viewport. When building a web site mobile first, you focus on the core content on the page. However, when the site is viewed on a larger device first, you have all this extra room that you could potentially put to good use. Rather than add the content into the HTML and hide it (which simply adds to the page weight), you can actually test whether the viewport is large enough and then load in the additional content dynamically using AJAX.

The benefit of loading content conditionally is that you reduce the initial page weight by taking content not seen on all devices out of the initial page load. Any assets included in this additional content would also not be downloaded.

The main disadvantage, however, is that you are using an extra HTTP request, which means that the user will have to wait for the additional content to load, so if the content is really important, you might not want to take this approach so that the user is able to see it immediately.

Domain Sharding

The current implementation of HTTP in browsers limits the number of HTTP requests that can be handled simultaneously, and this figure varies between two to eight connections from browser to browser. In contrast, on average the number of HTTP requests made to the site's main domain is 51 requests (March 2014, HTTP Archive). What this means is that a lot of the requests will be waiting for others to be completed, which can delay the loading of the web site.

To overcome this limitation, you can use a technique called Domain Sharding, which is where you deploy the assets for your pages across a series of domains or subdomains to enable more files to be simultaneously requested by the browser. This enables you to overcome the eight HTTP requests' limit imposed by the current implementation of HTTP.

By loading the assets across the series of domains, you can overcome the eight HTTP requests' limit and in theory load your assets faster. The problem here is that the mileage with this might vary, as Domain Sharding is in fact an antipattern for modern browsers. By this I mean that Domain Sharding is a common solution to overcome the limits imposed by the current browser's implementation of HTTP. However, although in some cases it might work, in others it might actually degrade performance. The reason for this degradation of performance is that the browser is required to do additional DNS requests for each of the domains used, so if the DNS is slow to respond, the content may in fact take longer to download.

Mobify (`http://www.mobify.com/blog/domain-sharding-bad-news-mobile-performance/`) did some research into whether Domain Sharding is in fact of benefit in this multidevice world we are now living in. Their research focused on testing in mobile browsers and found that across all the browsers tested, there was little benefit to Domain Sharding, and in fact in some tests it actually led to an increase in the time the page took to load the assets.

Server Configuration

The way in which your server is configured can make a noticeable difference to the way your web site performs for the end users, therefore, it makes sense to try to optimize this wherever possible.

Enable Server-Side Compression

The first thing you can do to improve the server performance is to enable server-side compression for text-based assets.

When the user's web browser requests a page from a web server, the browser will send a header to let the server know it supports compressed content. It also lets the server know what type of compression is supported, with the two most common compression types of GZIP and deflate.

Because the server knows that the user's browser supports compression, prior to sending each requested file, it will compress it and then send the compressed version to the user's browser. Upon receiving a file, the browser looks at the headers of the file, and in the case of a compressed file, it will indicate to the browser that the file is compressed, along with what sort of compression has been used. The browser can decompress and then process the file.

Enabling compression in Apache can be achieved through the `.htaccess` file and you can set up rules based on the file types your site is serving up. There are two ways you can enable compression using the `.htaccess` file, the first is to add output filters to the file type:

```
AddOutputFilterByType DEFLATE text/plain
AddOutputFilterByType DEFLATE text/html
AddOutputFilterByType DEFLATE text/css
AddOutputFilterByType DEFLATE application/javascript
```

The second way to enable compression is to add compression to all files with a particular extension:

```
<files *.html>
SetOutputFilter DEFLATE
</files>
```

Use Expires Headers

When the users of your site first visit, their browser needs to download all the assets for the page, including the HTML, images, CSS, and JavaScript. Without browser caching, the user's browser has to do this every time the user visits the web site.

Unfortunately, web browsers simply cannot know whether these files have changed, so that is why it needs to reload them every time the user visits the site. As developers, we need to inform the browser about which files are unlikely to change often so that the browser is able to cache them effectively, which can be achieved by using Expires Headers.

Expires Headers tells the browser that the file it is receiving will not change until after a certain amount of time. The benefit of this to the browser is that it is able to cache the file in the knowledge that it won't have to refetch the file again until the defined amount of time has passed. When your user visits the site again, rather than fetching the file, the browser simply loads it from the cache.

Before configuring your Expires Headers, it is important to consider what type of files you want the users' browser to be caching, some suggestions of what you might want to cache are:

1. CSS

2. JavaScript

3. Images

There are also some examples of where you will not want to use Expires Headers:

1. AJAX APIs

2. Dynamic pages

Setting up Expires Headers in Apache can be achieved by adding them to the sites .htaccess file. The first step is to enable Expires Headers and to set up a default rule, which will be added to all files served by the web site, in the example that follows, I have set up a default rule of 1 week:

```
<IfModule mod_expires.c>
ExpiresActive On

# Add a default rule
ExpiresDefault "access plus 1 week"
</IfModule>
```

After enabling Expires Headers, you can start defining custom rules for the CSS, JavaScript, and images. you would do this by using ExpiresByType, including both the file type and the length of time you want to keep the file in the user's cache.

```
<IfModule mod_expires.c>
ExpiresActive On

# Add a default rule
ExpiresDefault "access plus 1 week"

# CSS rules
ExpiresByType text/css "access 1 year"

# Javascript rules
ExpiresByType application/javascript "access plus 1 year"
```

```
# Images rules
ExpiresByType image/jpeg "access plus 1 month"
ExpiresByType image/jpg "access plus 1 month"
ExpiresByType image/gif "access plus 1 month"
ExpiresByType image/png "access plus 1 month"
</IfModule>
```

Host on a CDN

One option when deciding how to improve your network performance is to look at using a Content Delivery Network (CDN) to serve your sites assets. The reason this can improve performance is that the user's proximity to your web server can have an impact on the response times. A CDN is a distributed network of servers located across several geographic locations, meaning your users are able to view your site via servers that are located closest to them.

Aside from simply being closer to your users, using a CDN can also help you improve the availability of your site. By being distributed across several locations, if one location should experience connectivity issues, your users can continue to be served by the other locations.

There are a number of CDN providers available, some popular ones include:

1. Akamai

2. Amazon Web Services CloudFront

3. Cloudflare

SPDY/HTTP 2.0

Both SPDY and HTTP 2.0 are replacements for the aging HTTP protocol and offer benefits over their predecessor in both performance and features.

Of the mentioned areas of network performance, latency is the one area that the existing HTTP protocol falls down. This is because HTTP was designed for a very different type of web page than we build today, and the way in which the Web has evolved could not have been anticipated when the original HTTP protocol was developed.

The Chromium SPDY white paper[7] highlights some of the problems faced with the existing HTTP protocol:

1. Single request per connection

2. Only clients can initiate a request

3. HTTP headers are uncompressed

4. Redundant HTTP headers

To try to overcome these issues, Google developed the SPDY protocol. The goals that they laid out in their white paper were:

1. Allow concurrent requests across a single TCP connection

2. Reduce the bandwidth by compressing headers and eliminating unnecessary headers

3. Reduce complexity that we get when using HTTP

4. Enforce SSL as standard by using it as the underlying transport protocol

5. Allow the server to initiate connections to the user's browser

---

[7]http://www.chromium.org/spdy/spdy-whitepaper.

To get started with SPDY, you need to ensure that your server is set up to support the protocol. If you are using Apache, you will need to install the mod_spdy module, if you are using nginx you will need to install the http_spdy_module module. With this set up you will also need to purchase an SSL certificate and set it up on your domain. Finally, you will want to redirect all traffic to use the HTTPS version of your site so that all users see the same version of the site and share the same links, and those with a browser that supports SPDY will start to see the performance benefits.

SPDY offers the most benefit to sites that have a large number of assets to load. This is because it allows the site's files to be downloaded in parallel rather than in batches, and as this parallel download happens across a single TCP connection, it also results in reduced packet loss.

Aside from these benefits, SPDY also allows the server to push content to the user's browser without it being requested. The idea here is that before the page has even finished downloading, the server can send the related files such as images, style sheets, and JavaScript files.

SPDY is being implemented in all the major browsers, with Safari support recently being announced at the Worldwide Developers Conference in 2014. This means that it's likely that a large number of your users will be using, or will soon be using, a browser that supports SPDY. Therefore, it is up to you to ensure that the servers your site is hosted on is set up to support SPDY.

After looking at what SPDY is and the new performance benefits it offers, it provides a good grounding of what to expect when the HTTP 2.0 protocol is finalized. The HTTP 2.0 protocol is currently in development and is based on the SPDY protocol that Google have developed.

Critical Rendering Path

An important concept in the performance of loading a web page is the critical rendering path. Google defines the *critical rendering path* as "the code and resources required to render the initial view of a web page."[8]

To render the web page, the users' browsers must download the resources it uses from the web servers they are hosted on. The critical path is the files that must be downloaded and processed before anything can be shown to the user, therefore, improving the performance of the critical rendering path can help improve the perceived performance of the site by your users.

Let's look at a simple example of how the critical rendering path renders in a browser. Let's start with some typical HTML, featuring a single style sheet, a JavaScript file, and a couple of images:

```
<!doctype html>
<html lang="en">
<head>
    <title>Page Not Found</title>
    <link rel="stylesheet" href="css/screen.css">
    <script src="js/main.js"></script>
</head>
<body>
    <img src="images/photo1.jpg" width="500" height="500" alt="an image" />
    <img src="images/photo2.jpg" width="500" height="500" alt="an image" />
</body>
</html>
```

The first step the browser takes is to download the HTML file; upon completion of the download, the browser will then start to parse the HTML document.

In a modern browser, two separate parsers are used for HTML parsing: the first being the preparser (also known as the speculative parser) and the second being the main HTML parser.

---

[8]https://developers.google.com/speed/docs/best-practices/rtt.

As the preparser reads through the HTML, it will try to find any resources that will need to be downloaded in order to render the page. In the example given, the preparser will find the style sheet, then the JS file, followed by both of the images. Upon finding each of these resources, the preparser will request them from the network. It is important to note that the preparser will only parse the references to the resources and does not construct or modify the DOM tree.

While the preparser is going through the HTML document looking for resources it needs to get, the browser's main parser starts to parse the HTML, using it to build the DOM tree.

When the main HTML parser is parsing the HTML, it will not stop upon finding the style sheet because it is not blocked from continuing to parse the HTML document as the CSS is unable to make any changes to the DOM tree. Although the browser will not block the parsing of the HTML document while downloading the CSS document, it will block rendering of the page until the CSS document is fully downloaded. It is also important to be aware that in some browsers, scripts might be blocked while the browser waits for the CSS to be fully downloaded.

If the main HTML parser comes across a JavaScript file, things are slightly different. Although the browser's preparser would have already requested the file from the server and continued parsing the rest of the page, the main HTML parser will need to wait until it is fully downloaded. This is because the HTML parser has to account for the situation where the JavaScript author might be expecting the script to be executed when the HTML parser reaches the <script> tag. This means that the HTML parser will stop constructing the DOM until the JavaScript has been both downloaded and executed. This is where the term *JavaScript is blocking* comes from.

Improving the Critical Rendering Path

With an understanding about what the critical rendering path is, let's look at how to improve the critical rendering path of a web site. There are several key areas to focus on, and these are explained in the sections that follow.

Reduce Blocking

As mentioned previously, when the main browser parser finds a script tag, it will stop parsing the page so the JavaScript can be executed.

There are two ways to avoid this blocking behavior:

1. Move all the scripts to the bottom of the HTML document.

2. Add the defer attribute to the script tag so the browser will execute after the document is parsed.

This is really easy to implement when it's in your own scripts, however, often you are required to include third-party scripts in a web site, which simply provide the code that needs to be embed. Examples of third-party scripts that might need to be included are:

1. Social share buttons

2. Analytics

The social buttons that can be added to web sites are typically included through adding small snippets of code to the part of the site where you want to use them. The problem here is that they usually require the site to load some external script, which could potentially block parsing or block the page load event until it has finished loading. One solution to this is to defer the loading of the social buttons until after the page is fully loaded. This can be achieved using a JavaScript library called Socialite.js (http://socialitejs.com/), which gives you the flexibility over when you want to load your share buttons.

When it comes to Analytics packages, often they will suggest that you include the analytics code either inside your head element or at the top of your body. The primary reason for this is that they want to ensure that your user is tracked, even if they leave the page before it has fully loaded. While some Analytics packages do offer an asynchronous version of the code that prevents blocking while waiting for the package to be loaded, it could potentially still block other more important files due to the maximum number of simultaneous connections the browser can make.

Remove Unused CSS

CSS that is unused on your site can affect the performance of your site in a couple of different ways, the first being that it increases the size of your CSS file, which leads to a longer download time.

The second reason you need to ensure that you remove unused CSS is that when parsing the HTML, the browser constructs the DOM tree. Having built the DOM tree, the CSS engine of the browser will then go through each of the elements in the tree and match the element to any selectors that are targeted toward it. The more selectors the CSS engine needs to evaluate, the more it will have an effect on the rendering performance.

Specify Image Dimensions

When the browser starts to lay out your web page, some, if not all, of the images you have included in your page will not have finished downloading. If you have not specified the size of your images, the browser will be unable to layout the correct amount of space for your image, so when your image is finished downloading, the browser then needs to perform a reflow of the content and repaint that section of the page.

By specifying the size of your images, either through the CSS or through defining it on your `img` element, the browser knows the size of the image, which will prevent the issue of having to reflow the content when the image has finished downloading.

Defer Loading Images

I have already mentioned deferring loading the social buttons on a site until after the page has fully loaded, however, a site could also benefit from deferring loading images until after the page has loaded.

Making the choice to defer your images is slightly more complicated, because you then need to make several choices. You will need to determine which images should be deferred and which need to be in the page all the time, and you will also need to decide when the deferred images will be loaded.

A popular way in which you can defer your images is to only load them when they become visible to the user, the idea here being that if the user never scrolls down on the page, their browser doesn't have to download the image. To implement deferred image loading in this way, you can use a library called Echo.js (`https://github.com/toddmotto/echo`), which will allow you to define your image using a loader GIF as the `src` and a data attribute for the actual image. When the image comes into view, it will load the image and replace the loading image with the actual image.

Server-Side Optimization

One of the ways you can optimize your responsive site for the different devices your site supports is to use server-side device detection. This means that on your server, you do some detection of which device your user is using and perform actions based on this.

What Can the Server Optimize?

Any server-side optimization you choose to use should focus on optimizing the payload you deliver to your users' devices. With this in mind, let's focus the server-side optimization to look at images and content blocks.

Images

Rather than deliver generic images meant to be viewed across several device types, you can detect the device server side and then serve an optimized image to the device.

Content Blocks

Even on a responsive site, there are circumstances where you might want to serve up different content blocks to different devices, and there are several ways this can be achieved. The first would be to simply show and hide it using a media query, with the disadvantage here being that you are delivering both sets of content to the user.

The other option is to use server-side code to determine which content block should be shown on a particular device and only include that content within the HTML of the page. The advantage here being that you are only delivering the content the user's device requires.

Implementing Server-Side Optimization

To implement any kind of server-side optimization, you need to be able to determine what kind of device the users are using. You are limited by what information the browser provides, and the main source of information they do provide is the user-agent string.

For many years, as developers, we have been told "user-agent sniffing is bad," and for good reason; the user-agent string is easily spoofable and has a history of browsers pretending to be other browsers because they want their users to get the same experience as users in these other browsers.[9] There are edge cases where we have to use user-agent sniffing because there is nothing else available to use, and server-side optimization is one of those use cases.

Although it is very easy to do device detection through basic user-agent sniffing, there is an extremely large number of devices available and each has their own unique user-agent string (with a couple of exceptions). Therefore, keeping track yourself of the different user agents to sniff can be difficult. This is where you can use a Device Description Repository (DDR). A DDR is essentially a catalog of information about different devices, which includes a wide variety of information including the operating system it runs, the viewport size of the device, and the features it supports.

There are three prominent DDRs available: WURFL, OpenDDR, and Apache DeviceMap. Let's look at each of these in more detail so you can choose which option is right for your project.

WURFL

WURFL (Wireless Universal Resource FiLe) (`http://wurfl.sourceforge.net/`) is a DDR that was developed by a company called ScientaMobile, which develops and maintains both the DDR and a php library used to interface with it.

Each device that is detected by WURFL has a profile that indicates the capabilities of the device. This enables you to detect the device, and upon successfully determining the device, makes choices on what assets you should serve to the device.

The WURFL repository is maintained by ScientaMobile, which also offers a paid for, hosted solution, called WURFL Cloud. The benefit of using the hosted version of WURFL is that you do not need to take responsibility for ensuring the list of devices is kept up to date.

OpenDDR

OpenDDR (`http://www.openddr.org/`) was created with the aim to build an always up-to-date device description. It is an alternative to WURFL in that rather than being maintained by a single entity, the community as a whole develops and maintains it. The database for OpenDDR was originally based on an older WURFL database, which has been maintained by the OpenDDR team independently since the license was changed on the original WURFL project.

---

[9]If you're interested in reading the history of the browser user-agent string, you can find it at `http://webaim.org/blog/user-agent-string-history/`.

Apache DeviceMap

Apache DeviceMap (http://incubator.apache.org/devicemap/) is an incubating project that aims to create an open repository storing device information. It has similar aims to those of the OpenDDR team, which has led to the OpenDDR team agreeing to donate the OpenDDR code base to DeviceMap. What this means is that, although at this time the DeviceMap project is in its early infancy, in the future we should expect it to become a popular option if you are looking to do device detection on the server.

Benefits of Server-Side Optimization

There are many benefits of using server-side optimization techniques, the first being that you are able to target your image assets based on the size of the device being used to view them. This means that rather than simply scaling images for smaller devices, you can instead choose to send smaller images to the device in the first place, enabling your site to load faster on smaller devices.

In addition to simply targeting images for different devices, you can also target entire code blocks, meaning you can easily swap out modules dependent on the device. This approach allows you to mix responsive design approaches with adaptive design approaches, where they are best appropriate.

Disadvantages of Server-Side Optimization

The biggest disadvantage of using server-side optimization is that it often relies on user-agent sniffing, meaning that when new devices or new browsers are released, you would need to ensure you are regularly updating whichever library you have chosen. Although the libraries discussed here help alleviate this problem by being regularly updated with support for new devices, you would be relying on the continued maintenance of these libraries to allow you to continue to support new devices.

Similarly, we might find in the future that devices are released that share the same user agent as another device. This could potentially cause issues with how we are targeting code using server-side optimization as it could mistakenly identify a device and send incorrect content. There is precedence for this, not only in mobile devices, but also in the early days of the web browser where the browsers spoofed each other's user-agent strings to overcome cases of user-agent sniffing, which reflected badly on their web site.

Third-Party Server-Side Solutions

Aside from writing your own server-side solution, there is the option to look at using a third-party service that will handle these server-side optimizations for you.

One such service is ReSRC.it, which allows you to add responsive images to your site through a combination of JavaScript and server-side code. You first prefix the path to your image with a call to the ReSRC.it servers, then you simply include the ReSRC.it script, which will handle showing the correct image to the users:

```
<img src="//app.resrc.it/s=w280/o=60(80)/http://www.your-domain.com/image.jpg" class="resrc"
alt=""/>
<script src="//use.resrc.it"></script>
```

By using this kind of service, you can avoid having to build your own back-end solution, however, the limitation of this service is that it requires JavaScript to load the correct version of your images. If the JavaScript fails to load, the user will be left with the lower-quality version of your image.

Measuring Your Sites' Performance

To be able to successfully optimize your site, you need to be able to measure the performance of your site and the performance gains of any changes that you make.

There are a wide variety of tools available that allow you to test the performance of your site, so let's look at a few of these tools to see how they could benefit you when trying to optimize the performance of your site.

Pingdom Website Speed Test

One of the tools that can be used to test the performance of a web site is the Pingdom Website Speed Test (`http://tools.pingdom.com/fpt/`), which allows you to enter the URL of your site to test performance, as shown in Figure 10-11.

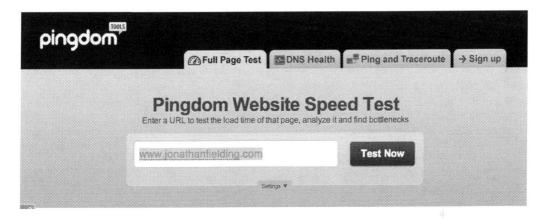

Figure 10-11. *The Pingdom Website Speed Test, just enter your URL and click Test Now*

Upon clicking the Test Now button, the tool will then analyze the site and find any potential performance issues. Initially after running the test you will be shown some basic performance information about your site (as shown in Figure 10-12), which includes the number of HTTP requests your site makes, the load time, and the size of your page.

Figure 10-12. *The basic performance grade for the site*

Waterfall

Below the summary, the Waterfall shows the HTTP requests the web page has made to the server. A sample of the Waterfall view is shown in Figure 10-13. Each request is color coded:

1. *Pink*: DNS

2. *Blue*: Connection to server

3. *Orange*: Browser sends request to the server

4. *Yellow*: Browser waits for response from server

5. *Green*: The browser is receiving data from the server

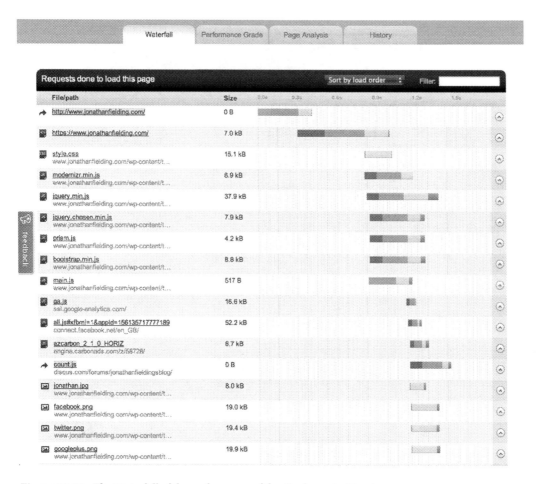

Figure 10-13. The Waterfall of the performance of the site shown in Pingdom

Performance Scoring

Pingdom also offers the ability to see individual performance scores covering different areas of performance. This allows you as the developer to quickly see any areas where your site is doing really badly so you can rectify them because these areas are likely to give you the highest gains in performance if you fix them. The performance scoring for my blog (www.jonathanfielding.com) is shown in Figure 10-14.

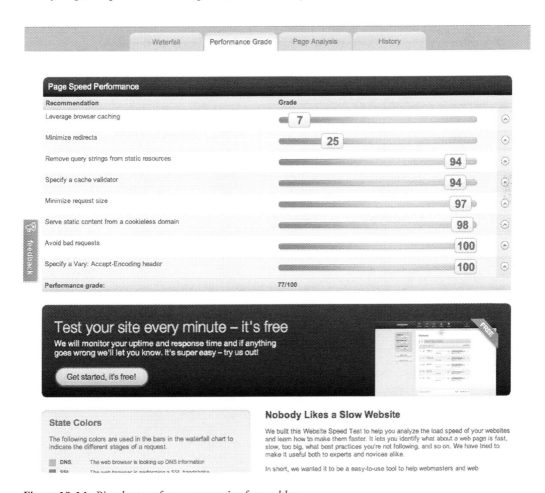

Figure 10-14. *Pingdom performance scoring for my blog*

Page Analysis

Pingdom also offers some further page analysis data that can be quite useful when looking at issues with performance on your site. The data it provides can be split into three categories: Load time analysis, Size analysis, and Request analysis. The full page analysis for my blog is shown in Figure 10-15.

Figure 10-15. Pingdom full page analysis

Load time analysis is data related to how long your page took to load; it includes information about how long the site took in each of the states shown in the Waterfall, how much time is spent with loading each of the content types, and the time spent loading from each domain. The latter can be especially useful as it allows you to easily see bottlenecks in your page loading caused by third-party services, such as ads that have been included on your site.

The size analysis data provide a detailed breakdown of where the weight of the page comes from. In particular, it shows the size per content type, which shows what type of content is the largest. It also shows the size of the content being served from other domains, which can be useful when you're trying to determine why your site appears to be bloated in size when you feel your own files are a comfortable size.

The request analysis information is related to the number of requests your site had to make. This is separated into two types of data: the number of requests per content type and the number of requests per domain. Again, this allows you to see if the third-party plug-ins are creating excessive numbers of HTTP requests you might not be aware of.

YSlow

YSlow (`https://developer.yahoo.com/yslow/`) is a tool developed by Yahoo! that allows you to test your web page's performance. It is available to install as a browser plug-in, which means you can measure your web page's performance directly in your own browser.

To get started with YSlow, visit `http://yslow.org/` where you are able to select your browser and install the relevant version of the YSlow plug-in. Once installed, visit your web site and click the YSlow icon that has been added to your browser. The icon is shown in Figure 10-16.

Figure 10-16. *Chrome toolbar, the YSlow icon is highlighted*

After clicking the YSlow icon, you will be presented with a pop-up window that gives you some information about YSlow. If your site prevents itself from being embedded in an iframe, then you need to ensure you check the check box on this page. To run the YSlow tests, you can simply click the Run Test button, as shown in Figure 10-17.

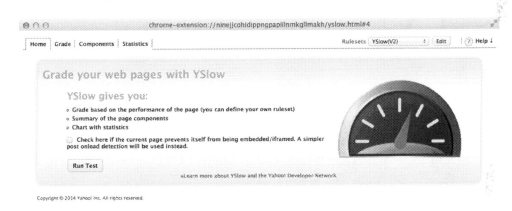

Figure 10-17. *The YSlow panel*

Once YSlow has run its tests, you will then be able to navigate through each of the tabs to determine how your site is performing.

Grade

Once YSlow has run its tests, you will be taken to the Grade tab where YSlow will have given your site a grade based on its performance. It also gives you a score in 23 different areas, and you can click these scores to get more information about why you got that score and what you can do to improve it. The Grade view after running the test on my blog is shown in Figure 10-18.

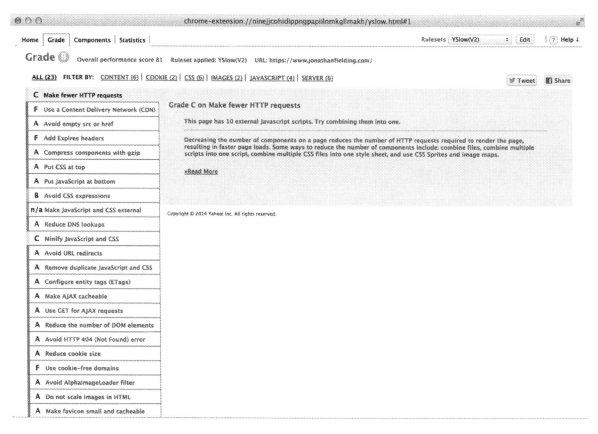

Figure 10-18. *The YSlow Grade panel for my blog*

Components

The Components tab of YSlow provides information about the individual resources that make up your site. They are sorted into type, and you can find out more information about each of the resources by expanding the type so you can see the individual files.

When looking at the individual files, you can see information about the size of the file, the file headers, and the cookies that have been sent and received with the file. This can be useful as it means you can easily see if you are sending large amount of cookie data with your files so you can address this while optimizing your site. The Components information for my blog is shown in Figure 10-19.

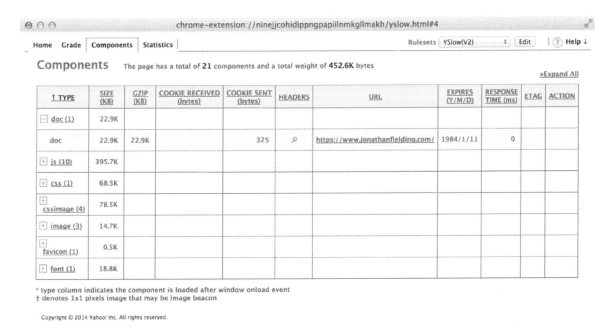

Figure 10-19. *The YSlow Components panel for my blog*

Statistics

The Statistics tab of YSlow provides you with graphs showing what percentage of the request comes with each content type and the number of HTTP requests made per content type. The Statistics panel for my blog is shown in Figure 10-20.

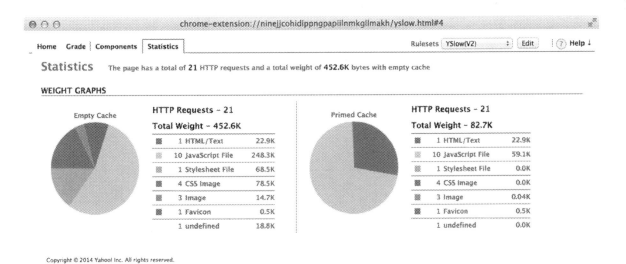

Figure 10-20. *The YSlow Statistics panel for my blog*

WebPageTest

WebPageTest (http://www.webpagetest.org) is a free tool for measuring page performance, which was originally developed by AOL for use internally but then was open sourced in 2008 under the BSD license. The hosted version of the tool is run by the WPO Foundation, which is a nonprofit business with the aim of improving web performance.

WebPageTest enables you to run web performance tests on your site from a number of different locations across the world in a number of different browsers. It also allows you to run some advanced tests by customizing the advanced settings.

To get started testing your site using WebPageTest, you need to visit their web site and enter the URL of your site. You have the option to select a test location, meaning you are able to select the location of your target market, enabling you to see the performance your real users might get when accessing your site. Additionally, you can select the browser used to run your performance tests. Some features of WebPageTest are not available across all browsers, so you might need to run the tests in multiple browsers to make use of all the features. The start page for running a test with WebPageTest is shown in Figure 10-21.

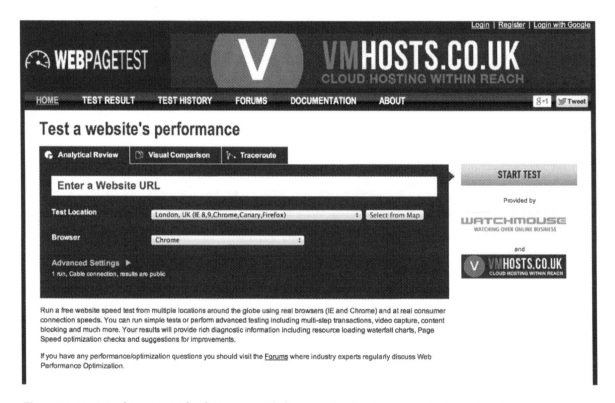

Figure 10-21. *Initial start page of WebPageTest, with the option to select browser and advanced options*

Because the WebPageTest site is a popular service, you might have to wait in a queue to use it. However, normally you won't have to wait more than a few minutes.

Once the results have loaded, similar to the other tests, WebPageTest gives your site a performance grade. In addition, the page also shows information about how long the site took to load both on the first view and the repeat view. The performance grade for my blog is shown in Figure 10-22.

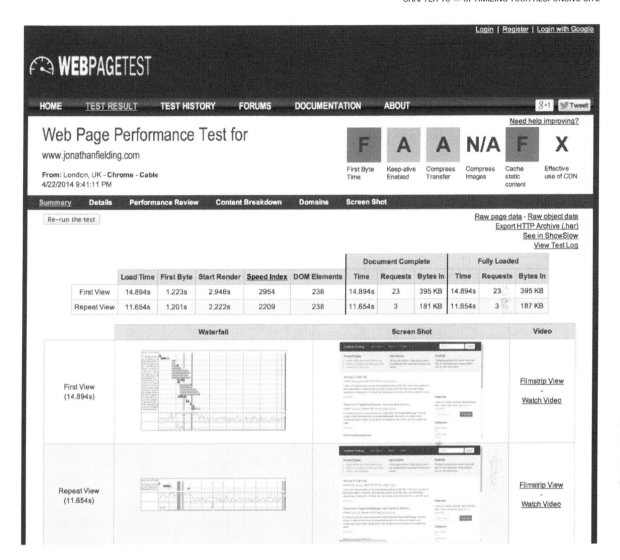

Figure 10-22. *The WebPageTest performance grade for my blog*

Waterfall View

Having run this test, you can click the waterfall image shown to take you to the Waterfall View. This view shows detailed information about how long it took to load each of the files, including the DNS Lookup, Initial Connection, SSL Negotiation, Time to First Byte, and the Content Download.

This view is very useful to allow you to see anywhere that the loading of the assets is blocked or any issues with the transferring of the assets. The Waterfall View results for my blog are shown in Figure 10-23.

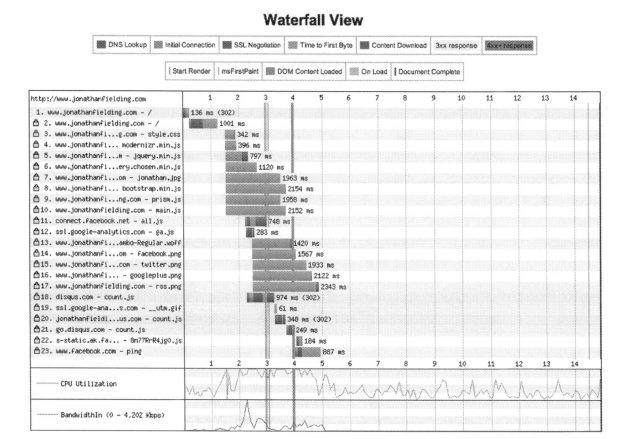

Figure 10-23. *The WebPageTest Waterfall View after testing my blog*

Advanced Tests

Where WebPageTest really stands out from the rest of the tools to measure the performance of a web site is in its configurability. By this I mean when setting up your performance test, there are a variety of options you can select from several advanced options.

To select these advanced options, you simply click the Advanced Settings link, which will expand this section of the site so you can select the advanced options you desire. The advanced options are split into the following tabs:

1. Test Settings

2. Advanced

3. Chrome

4. Auth

5. Script

6. Block

7. SPOF

Although I won't explain all of these options in great detail, one of the most important settings is the Connection setting shown on the first(Test Settings) tab. This setting enables you as the developer to test the web site in the kind of conditions your users might be facing by allowing you to select different connection speeds. The options available range from a fast cable connection to a 56K modem. When deciding which speeds to test, you need to be realistic about what your target audience might be using. The menu used to select these advanced options is shown in Figure 10-24.

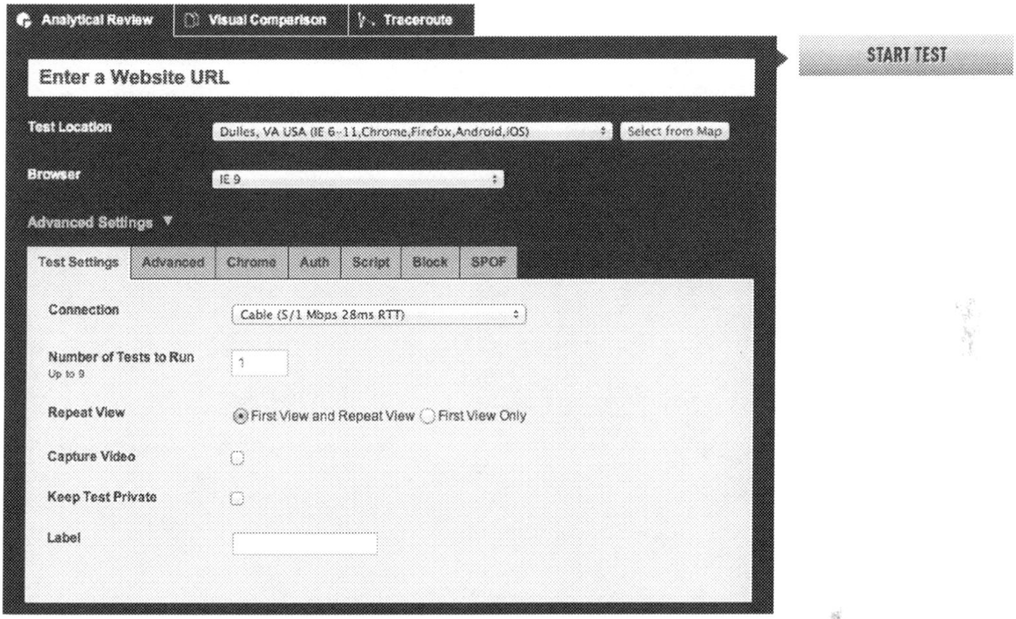

Figure 10-24. *The WebPageTest advanced testing menu*

Google Analytics Site Speed

Although ensuring that everything works okay in the test environments goes a long way toward ensuring a site will perform well for the end users, we are unable to test every use case as there are a variety of combinations of connections with devices.

In Chapter 9 you learned how you could use Google Analytics to enable you to measure the user's journey, another way in which Google Analytics can help you is by looking at how your site actually performs for your end users.

When using Google Analytics to look at how a site is performing for the end users, you can start by looking at the Site Speed Overview page. By default the page shows the following information:

1. Average page load time

2. Average redirection time

3. Average domain lookup time

4. Average server connection time

5. Average server response time

6. Average page download time

This information is displayed with averages for the past month along with a graph for each showing how the value has fluctuated over the selected period of time (defaults to month). The Site Speed Overview page is shown in Figure 10-25.

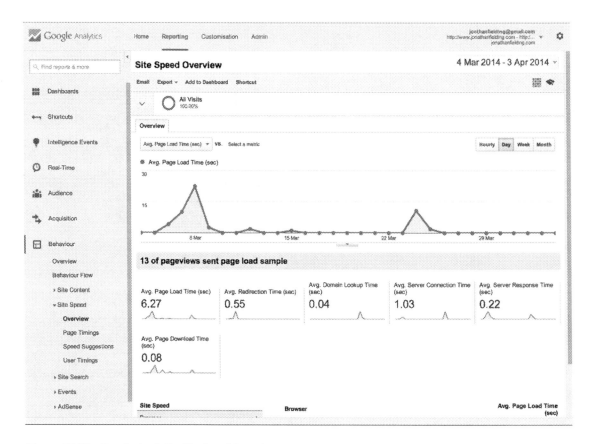

Figure 10-25. *Google Analytics Site Speed Overview*

Alongside the general overview, Google Analytics is also able to give some suggestions on how to improve your page's performance. This can be found on the Site Speed Suggestions page. The initial view includes a list of the pages with a column titled "Speed Suggestions" with each row having a link you can click to see suggestions for that page (as illustrated in Figure 10-26).

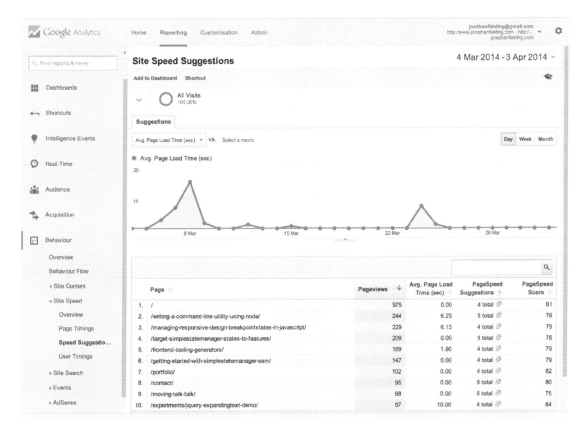

Figure 10-26. *Google Analytics site Speed Suggestions*

Summary

This chapter discussed the ways in which you can optimize the performance of your web site. Because performance is a huge subject, I focused on areas that would make the biggest difference to a responsive site.

One of the first areas discussed was the importance of network performance, and you should now have a good understanding of what both latency and bandwidth are and how they affect the network performance of your site. I then discussed how you could optimize your site to best work with these limitations by using techniques that allow you to reduce HTTP requests and optimize the server set up.

I then explained how you could optimize your site performance by using server-side technologies to determine what to serve to the users of your site. This involved looking at how you could use a Device Description Repository to determine the kinds of devices your users were using so you could provide them with optimized content.

Although understanding the way you can optimize performance enables you to build your sites using performance-responsive techniques, it is also important that you are able to measure the performance. To enable you to do this, I presented two types of tools you could use during the development of your site: the measurement tools WebPageTest, Pingdom, and YSlow, and the life tools, meaning tools that measure the performance of your site on the users' devices, specifically the Google Analytics Site Speed tool.

Hopefully this book has helped you in your endeavors to build responsive web pages. Through this book you will have learned about the steps you would take to either start a site from scratch or adapt an existing site. Through applying these skills to your work you will help improve the experience of your users when they are using our site.

I really hope you enjoyed reading this book as much as I have enjoyed writing it, and that you can return to it later as a reference when looking to try different techniques or improve your responsive sites.

Index

■ D

■ E

Get the eBook for only $10!

Now you can take the weightless companion with you anywhere, anytime. Your purchase of this book entitles you to 3 electronic versions for only $10.

This Apress title will prove so indispensible that you'll want to carry it with you everywhere, which is why we are offering the eBook in 3 formats for only $10 if you have already purchased the print book.

Convenient and fully searchable, the PDF version enables you to easily find and copy code—or perform examples by quickly toggling between instructions and applications. The MOBI format is ideal for your Kindle, while the ePUB can be utilized on a variety of mobile devices.

Go to www.apress.com/promo/tendollars to purchase your companion eBook.